LGBTQ
MENTAL HEALTH

PERSPECTIVES ON SEXUAL ORIENTATION AND DIVERSITY

Maria Lucia Miville, Series Editor

LGBTQ
MENTAL HEALTH

International Perspectives and Experiences

EDITED BY

Nadine Nakamura AND
Carmen H. Logie

AMERICAN PSYCHOLOGICAL ASSOCIATION
Washington, DC

Published by
American Psychological Association
750 First Street, NE
Washington, DC 20002
https://www.apa.org

Order Department
https://www.apa.org/pubs/books
order@apa.org

In the U.K., Europe, Africa, and the Middle East, copies may be ordered from Eurospan
https://www.eurospanbookstore.com/apa
info@eurospangroup.com

Typeset in Meridien and Ortodoxa by Circle Graphics, Inc., Reisterstown, MD

Printer: Sheridan Books, Chelsea, MI
Cover Designer: Anne C. Kerns, Anne Likes Red, Inc., Silver Spring, MD

Library of Congress Cataloging-in-Publication Data

Names: Nakamura, Nadine, editor. | Logie, Carmen H., editor.
Title: LGBTQ mental health : international perspectives and experiences /
  edited by Nadine Nakamura and Carmen H. Logie.
Description: Washington, DC : American Psychological Association, [2020] |
  Series: Perspectives on sexual orientation and diversity |
  Includes bibliographical references and index.
Identifiers: LCCN 2019023405 (print) | LCCN 2019023406 (ebook) |
  ISBN 9781433830914 (hardcover) | ISBN 9781433831638 (ebook)
Subjects: LCSH: Sexual minorities—Mental health.
Classification: LCC RC451.4.G39 L485 2020 (print) | LCC RC451.4.G39 (ebook) |
  DDC 362.2086/6—dc23
LC record available at https://lccn.loc.gov/2019023405
LC ebook record available at https://lccn.loc.gov/2019023406

http://dx.doi.org/10.1037/0000159-000

Printed in the United States of America

10 9 8 7 6 5 4 3 2 1

CONTENTS

CONTRIBUTORS

Peru

Amaya Perez-Brumer, MSc, is a doctoral candidate in the Department of Sociomedical Sciences at Columbia University Mailman School of Public Health and Columbia University Graduate School of Arts and Science Department of Sociology. Having worked in Peru for over a decade, she applies her research to broadly seek to integrate interdisciplinary research methods and theory to improve health disparities for people of diverse genders and sexualities.

Alfonso Silva-Santisteban, MD, MPH, is a Peruvian physician–researcher dedicated to improving health systems and health policy for traditionally underserved communities. He is affiliated with the Universidad Peruana Cayetano Heredia Centro de Investigación Interdisciplinaria en Sexualidad, Sida y Sociedad (Sexuality and Human Development Research Group) in Lima, Peru.

Ximena Salazar, PhD, is a Peruvian senior researcher at the Universidad Peruana Cayetano Heredia Centro de Investigación Interdisciplinaria en Sexualidad, Sida y Sociedad (Sexuality and Human Development Research Group) in Lima, Peru. Trained in anthropology, her work uses a participatory population perspective to explore the lived experience of marginalized populations in Peru.

Jesse Vilela is director of Sociedad Trans FTM Peru and Staff at the Universidad Peruana Cayetano Heredia Centro de Investigación Inter-disciplinaria en Sexualidad, Sida y Sociedad (Sexuality and Human Development Research Group) in Lima, Peru.

Sari L. Reisner, ScD, is an assistant professor of pediatrics at Harvard Medical School and Boston Children's Hospital and assistant professor in the Department of Epidemiology at Harvard T.H. Chan School of Public Health. He is trained as a social and psychiatric epidemiologist, and his research focuses on health disparities and inequities in lesbian, gay, bisexual, transgender, and queer/questioning populations globally. He has been working in Peru for more than 5 years.

Colombia

Karen Nieves-Lugo, PhD, is a research assistant professor at The George Washington University, Washington, DC. Her research interests include HIV prevention among Latino men who have sex with men. She is a member of the Latino Health Research Center at The George Washington University.

Andrew P. Barnett, MA, is a clinical psychology doctoral student at The George Washington University, Washington, DC. His research focuses on behavioral factors associated with HIV risk among gay and bisexual men. He is a member of the Latino Health Research Center at The George Washington University.

Veronica Pinho, MA, is a clinical psychology doctoral student at The George Washington University, Washington, DC. Her research focuses on HIV prevention and mental health among Latino populations, including Colombian men who have sex with men.

Miguel Rueda Sáenz, PhD, is a professor at Universidad de los Andes in Bogotá, Colombia. His research interests include gender identity development and the effects that prejudice has on well-being.

Maria Cecilia Zea, PhD, is a professor of psychology at The George Washington University, Washington, DC. Her research interests include HIV risk and promotion of HIV testing among gay and bisexual men and transgender women in the United States and in Colombia. She was born in Colombia.

Ecuador

Donatella Di Marco, PhD, is an assistant professor in work and organizational psychology at the University of Seville, Spain and researcher of the Business Research Unit (BRU-IUL) in Lisbon, Portugal. Her research interests include voice, modern discrimination, selective incivility, and the workplace experiences of LGBT people. She has led several international research projects with vulnerable groups (e.g., LGBT people, Indigenous people) in Ecuador.

Alicia Arenas, PhD, is an associate professor in work and organizational psychology at the University of Seville, Spain. Her research interests include the promotion of healthy and inclusive organizations. She is participating in an international research project on the experiences of Ecuadorean LGBT people.

Helge Hoel, PhD, is a professor in organizational behavior at the University of Manchester, England. His research interests include bullying, violence, and harassment. He is participating in an international research project on the experiences of Ecuadorean LGBT people.

Lourdes Munduate, PhD, is a professor of organizational psychology at the University of Seville, Spain. Her research interests include conflict management, negotiation and mediation strategies, power dynamics, and employment relations. She is participating in an international research project on the experiences of Ecuadorean LGBT people.

Jamaica

Natania L. Marcus is a PhD candidate in clinical and counseling psychology in the Department of Applied Psychology and Human Development at the University of Toronto. Her research focuses on sexuality and the mental health impact of minority stress among LGBTQ+ communities. Under the supervision of Dr. Carmen H. Logie, Ms. Marcus has been involved in researching the mental health and sexual health impacts of minority stress among LGBTQ communities in Jamaica for more than 2 years.

Nicolette Jones (Richardson), MA, has worked across the globe. She is currently working with a community health center in Manitoba to host Lived Experience Advisory workshops as well as to examine the intersecting vulnerabilities among newcomer and Indigenous populations. She led the team of peer researchers on the project of focus described in this chapter.

Nicolette Bryan is a social worker and executive director of WE-Change in Jamaica, an organization that champions the rights of LBT+ and ally women and their increased participation in social justice advocacy. Her research interests include women's issues in general, particularly those that interrogate queer women's lived experiences.

Kandasi Levermore is the executive director of Jamaica AIDS Support for Life, Jamaica's largest AIDS Service Organization that provides services, supportive programs, and advocacy for and with LGBT persons. Her work and research interests focus on people-centered inclusion and development and on helping persons to recognize their strengths and realize their potential.

Russia

Sharon G. Horne, PhD, is a professor of counseling psychology at the University of Massachusetts Boston, United States. Her research interests include sexual orientation and gender identity mental health concerns and transnational psychology. She has experience working in former postcommunist countries, including Russia, Hungary, Romania, Uzbekistan, and Kyrgyzstan. She is a Global Fulbright scholar researching the impact of psychology guidelines and practices on LGBT mental health in Colombia, South Africa, and the Philippines.

Lindsey White, MA, is a doctoral student in counseling psychology at the University of Massachusetts Boston, United States. Her research interests include social support networks for LGBT communities, particularly transgender and gender nonbinary communities.

Mongolia

Julie M. Koch, PhD, is an associate professor of counseling psychology and is the head of the School of Community Health Sciences, Counseling, and Counseling Psychology at Oklahoma State University, United States. Her research interests include microaffirmation, faculty multicultural competence, counselor development and training, issues related to diverse populations, and prevention in school settings. She was a Fulbright specialist in Mongolia in 2015 and collaborated with the LGBT Centre of Mongolia in Ulaanbaatar on programming and training.

Douglas Knutson, PhD, is an assistant professor in the Department of Psychology at Southern Illinois University–Carbondale, United States. His research focuses on transgender health.

Anaraa Nyamdorj, ML, is the cofounder of the LGBT Centre of Mongolia in Ulaanbaatar. He is passionate about improving the social conditions of LGBT people in Mongolia through policy and social change.

India

Venkatesan Chakrapani, MD, PhD, is the founder, director, and chairperson of the Centre for Sexuality and Health Research and Policy (C-SHaRP), Chennai, India, as well as a Wellcome Trust/DBT India Senior Fellow in PGIMER, Chandigarh, India. His research focus is on applied and policy-oriented health research among marginalized communities, especially sexual and gender minorities in India.

Peter A. Newman, **PhD,** is a professor at the Factor-Inwentash Faculty of Social Work, University of Toronto, and former Canada Research Chair in Health & Social Justice. His research focuses on global HIV prevention and human rights among marginalized populations, including community-based research projects with sexual and gender minorities in India for 20 years.

Murali Shunmugam, MSW, is a codirector of the Centre for Sexuality and Health Research and Policy (C-SHaRP), Chennai, India. His research focuses on national and international advocacy efforts to promote the health and rights of people living with HIV and sexual and gender minorities in India.

Malaysia

Hemla Singaravelu, PhD, LPC, is a professor in the Department of Professional Counseling at Webster University, United States. Her scholarly and counseling interests include cross-cultural adaptation, internationals, LGBT+ populations, and individuals with multiple identification. She serves on the editorial board of the *Journal of LGBT Issues in Counseling* and *Journal of Asia Pacific Counseling*. She is coeditor of *A Handbook for Counseling International Students in the United States*. She was born and raised in Malaysia.

Wai Hsien Cheah, PhD, is a professor of communication studies in the Department of Applied Communication Studies at Southern Illinois University Edwardsville, United States. His research interests include cross-cultural adaptations of refugees and examining the barriers and challenges faced by gays and lesbians in Islamic Malaysia. He was born and raised in Malaysia.

Thailand

Timo T. Ojanen works as a foreign expert at the Faculty of Learning Sciences and Education, Thammasat University, Thailand. He has been involved in research, counseling, and advocacy on LGBTIQ health and rights issues for over a decade in Thailand.

Peter A. Newman, PhD, is a professor at the Factor-Inwentash Faculty of Social Work, University of Toronto, Canada, and principal investigator of Mobilizing for a Research Revolution to Ensure LGBTIQ Inclusion in Asia (MFARR-Asia), funded by the Social Sciences and Humanities Research Council of Canada. His research focuses on global HIV prevention and human rights among marginalized populations and includes 15 years of community-based research with sexual and gender minority populations in Thailand.

Rattanakorn Ratanashevorn formerly worked as a counseling psychologist at Chula Student Wellness, Chulalongkorn University, Thailand. At the time of publication, he had been accepted as a student in the PhD program in counselor education at the University of Missouri, St. Louis. His research and practice focus on counseling interventions and their efficacy among LGBTIQ populations in his home country, Thailand.

Jan W. de Lind van Wijngaarden, **PhD,** is a foreign expert at the Faculty of Public Health, Burapha University, Thailand. His research and practice focus on HIV prevention programming, training, evaluation, and policy advocacy for young men who have sex with men and young transgender women in Thailand. He has lived and worked in Asia for 25 years.

Suchon Tepjan is vice president and research manager at VOICES-Thailand Foundation. He has successfully managed and conducted community-based research for 9 years with sexual and gender minority youth in Thailand, and vulnerable populations in Canada, India, and South Africa, focused on HIV prevention and human rights.

Sub-Saharan Africa

Carolyn Brown is a doctoral candidate in the Department of Epidemiology, Emory Rollins School of Public Health, United States. Her research interests include HIV and cancer-related research and implementation projects with key populations across sub-Saharan Africa. She has contributed to research projects on this topic in Botswana, Rwanda, South Africa, Swaziland, and Tanzania.

Keletso Makofane is a doctoral candidate in social epidemiology at Harvard University's T.H. Chan School of Public Health, United States. His research interests include community-based HIV programs for men who have sex with men in sub-Saharan Africa. He is a South African social epidemiologist and activist.

Contributors

Kevin Rebe is a specialist medical consultant at Health4Men at the Anova Health Institute, South Africa. His research interests include studying infectious diseases and HIV and increasing access to health care for South African key populations. He is also currently working on scaling up PrEP for key populations.

L. Leigh Ann van der Merwe is founder and director of Social, Health and Empowerment Feminist Collective of Transgender Women of Africa. Her work centers on feminism, HIV, human rights, and their intersections, for and with transgender women in Africa.

Bhekie Sithole is the program technical lead for FHI 360, Elizabeth Glaser Pediatric AIDS Foundation, Swaziland (Eswatini). He has been working with the LGBT population, as well as other marginalized groups, since 2010 and has been involved in community mobilization, capacity building, and research on HIV programs in Swaziland.

Daouda Diouf is executive director of ENDA Sante, Guinea-Bissau. He is committed to improving access to and quality of health care for the most vulnerable populations in West Africa.

Kevin Kapila, MD, is a physician and medical director of Behavioral Health at Fenway Health, United States. He has created and provided trainings for the medical and mental health care of sexual minorities in Malawi, South Africa, and Nigeria.

Carrie Lyons is a senior research program coordinator II in the Department of Epidemiology at Johns Hopkins Bloomberg School of Public Health, United States. Her research interests include program implementation across sub-Saharan Africa. She has contributed to research projects on this topic in Benin, Burkina Faso, Cameroon, Cote d'Ivoire, Eswatini, Ghana, Guinea Bissau, Lesotho, Nigeria, Rwanda, Senegal, South Africa, The Gambia, and Togo.

Tonia Poteat, PhD, is an assistant professor, Department of Social Medicine, University of North Carolina at Chapel Hill, United States. Her research interests include community-engaged research with LGBTQ local partners in sub-Saharan Africa.

Shauna Stahlman, PhD, is a postdoctoral researcher in the Department of Epidemiology at Johns Hopkins Bloomberg School of Public Health, United States. Her research interests include implementation science studies for HIV treatment uptake in South Africa and HIV-related stigma in multiple countries in sub-Saharan Africa.

Stefan Baral, PhD, is an associate professor in the Department of Epidemiology at Johns Hopkins Bloomberg School of Public Health (JHSPH) and the director of the Key Populations Program for the Center for Public Health and Human Rights at the JHSPH, United States. His research interests include characterizing the intersections of structural determinants of HIV including criminalization and stigma, network-level determinants, and individual-level outcomes in more than 20 countries across sub-Saharan Africa.

LGBTQ
MENTAL HEALTH

Introduction

Nadine Nakamura and Carmen H. Logie

What does it mean to be a healthy, functioning lesbian, gay, bisexual, transgender, or queer (LGBTQ) person? Is there a universal LGBTQ experience? If you consume U.S. popular media, which is exported around the globe, to inform your ideas of what it means to be LGBTQ, you might assume that "coming out" is a key part of being a healthy, well-functioning LGBTQ person. But coming out publicly, as a rite of passage, was not the norm 50 years ago in the United States. Just as time influences our norms, so does place. However, there is little in the psychological theoretical and practice literature to inform us of what it means to be LGBTQ outside of the United States, Canada, and Western Europe. Therefore, our understandings of what life is like for LGBTQ persons in the Majority World is quite limited, and we tend to apply the lens of the West as though one size fits all.

Several authors have noted how U.S.-centric psychological research is (Arnett, 2008; Cole, 2006; Sue, 1999). Sue (1999) pointed out that American psychologists and their American samples dominate psychological research, but then findings from these studies generate theories that are assumed to be universal. Arnett (2008) critiqued psychology for "neglecting" 95% of the world population in its research, which results in "an understanding of psychology that is incomplete and does not adequately represent humanity" (p. 602). He conducted a content analysis of American Psychological Association journals and found that 68% of samples were in the United States, with an additional 14% from other English-speaking countries and an additional 13% from

http://dx.doi.org/10.1037/0000159-001
LGBTQ Mental Health: International Perspectives and Experiences, N. Nakamura and
C. H. Logie (Editors)

other European countries. Thus, the vast majority of research is based on 5% of the world population (Americans), and adding other English-speaking countries and European countries takes us to only 12% of the world's population. In other words, what we consider normative likely applies only to a small segment of the world. For example, Reisner and colleagues (2016) conducted a review of peer-reviewed literature from 2008 to 2014 on transgender health, and of the 116 quantitative studies they identified, the majority were from the United States. The majority of the countries around the world had no studies or only a single study. This has real implications for people's lives: Without culturally and contextually relevant theories for understanding LGBTQ persons' lived experiences, we will not be able to design interventions and practice models that meet their needs and priorities and that reflect their realities.

Given the dominance of Western psychology broadly and U.S. psychology specifically, it is likely that mental health providers who want to help LGBTQ clients in the Majority World will turn to Western psychological literature to educate them about the types of challenges their clients might face. These mental health providers may live in places where same-sex sexual practices are criminalized. Criminalization of same-sex practices constrains funding and programs for LGBTQ persons; presents barriers for accessing social and health services; limits the ability to engage in relationships; and often results in discrimination across education, employment, housing, and health care services (Logie et al., 2017). Criminalization makes it challenging to conduct research on LGBTQ populations who may be distrustful of being discovered. In addition, research projects on LGBTQ populations may threaten the careers and safety of academics who live in countries that criminalize same-sex sexual behavior through "guilt by association." These systemic barriers make it difficult for LGBTQ people in the Majority World to receive relevant, culturally competent services. We hope that this book will generate understandings of how LGBTQ persons navigate life, identities, and relationships across the world. This understanding can inform research that further explores how to advance mental health among LGBTQ persons from intersectional, strengths-based, and contextually grounded approaches.

Another reason that it is imperative that we expand our understanding of what it means to be LGBTQ beyond our Western lens is that international migration is currently at an all-time high across many parts of the world (Banks, Suárez-Orozco, & Ben-Peretz, 2016). Among those migrants are LGBTQ people who cross borders to be reunited with family, to seek education or employment, or to live in a place where they can lead a more openly LGBTQ life. Mental health providers may encounter migrants as clients who need mental health services, including therapy and assessment. As a part of therapy, it would be useful for the therapist to have access to information about what it is like to be LGBTQ in the client's home country. Without this knowledge, it is likely that the therapist will solely rely on Western notions of what a healthy, functioning LGBTQ person looks like. Therapists may encounter parents of

LGBTQ children who believe their children's sexual orientation or gender identity to be influenced by their new culture. Having background information on what it is like to be LGBTQ in the parents' home country could help the therapist have a greater understanding about why parents might oppose their child's LGBTQ identity.

In addition, there are LGBTQ people who flee their home countries to seek asylum from persecution. Immigration Equality (n.d.), an LGBTQ immigrant rights organization that handles asylum cases, reported a record caseload due to the worldwide persecution of LGBTQ people. According to their website,

> Over the last 20 years, the largest percentage of our clients has come from the Caribbean and Latin America, but, as conditions deteriorate for LGBTQ and HIV-positive people around the world, the number of individuals reaching out to us from Russia, the Middle East, and Sub-Saharan Africa has increased. ("Record Caseload," para. 3)

Clinicians can play a role for asylum seekers by helping them prepare to give their testimony and helping them cope with both past traumas and retraumatization (Reading & Rubin, 2011). In addition, clinicians may be called to testify or write affidavits on behalf of LGBTQ asylum seekers. In such cases, it is useful for clinicians to have psychological literature to draw from that addresses the experiences of their clients. LGBTQ asylum seekers have likely concealed their sexual orientation for safety reasons in their country of origin (Heller, 2009). Now, to gain asylum, they must put their LGBTQ identity on display to convince decision makers they are in fact LGBTQ and would be persecuted in their home country (Heller, 2009; Piwowarczyk, Fernandez, & Sharma, 2017). Gay men who present as "masculine" often face discrimination in the asylum process (UN High Commissioner for Refugees, 2010). Lesbians often face persecution from private actors (e.g., family members); this asylum claim can be harder to make, and lesbian asylum claims are more likely to be denied (UN High Commissioner for Refugees, 2010). Bisexuals tend to be invisible in the asylum process (UN High Commissioner for Refugees, 2010). LGBTQ persons in humanitarian settings face barriers to health care and are overlooked in most emergency responses (Ghose, Boucicaut, King, Doyle, & Shubert, 2013; Singh et al., 2018). We hope that the intersectional, strengths-based, and contextually grounded approach to exploring LGBTQ mental health in this book can inform research and practice with LGBTQ migrants, refugees, asylum seekers, and displaced persons globally.

Through globalization and migration, we see the exchange of cultures as ideas and people move around the world. Of course, power and privilege must be considered when we think about which cultures have more influence over others. That is, typically Western notions are spread across the world through media, as well as through academia. Taken together, popular and academic understandings of LGBTQ mental health from the Majority World have less visibility, and Western perspectives cannot provide us with a global understanding of what it means to be to be LGBTQ.

PURPOSE OF THE BOOK

The purpose of this book is to expand the understanding of LGBTQ people's lives beyond the dominant narrative of the West to include the experiences of LGBTQ people from around the world. In the United States, Canada, and Western Europe, much has been written about LGBTQ health and mental health. There exists a popular discourse around the coming out experience that presumes that healthy, high-functioning LGBTQ people go through a similar experience of self-discovery and disclosure to friends, family, and society. Oftentimes this research gets disseminated to other parts of the world that may be experiencing very different realities and priorities, and self-discovery may take a different trajectory than Western notions of coming out. Chapters in this book cover LGBTQ populations that are largely invisible in the psychological literature by focusing on the Majority World to expand our understanding of what it means to be LGBTQ and how mental health needs and priorities contextually vary. Throughout the book, various chapters use varying terms, including *lesbian, gay, bisexual, transgender, intersex,* and *queer* (LGBTIQ) and corresponding acronyms, including LGBTQ, LGB, and so on, to indicate the specific populations on which these chapters focus. We endeavored to use accurate terminology rather than defaulting to the lengthier acronym if the chapter was not, in fact, inclusive of all of those identities.

When soliciting chapters for this book, we were especially interested in authors with firsthand experience living and/or working in the countries about which they were writing. This is one of the reasons we felt strongly that this needed to be an edited volume rather than one written by one or two authors. However, we also recognized the reality that countries with well-financed high education systems are those most likely to produce and support scholars and their research (Cole, 2006). As Arnett (2008) pointed out, "The rich get researched" (p. 609), which explains some of our lack of knowledge of LGBTQ issues globally. Those who have material wealth as well as freedom of expression have the ability to share their experiences in academic forums. Another barrier is that political and social climates that are hostile toward LGBTQ populations generally do not provide a supportive environment for research on these populations. Researchers who are living and working in such places might be fearful that research on LGBTQ populations could put their careers and even their lives in jeopardy. In fact, some of our chapter authors noted this difficulty when attempting to include colleagues from the countries that their chapters covered. Therefore, we bring you this collection of chapters appreciative of the voices and perspectives that we are able to include but mindful of those voices and perspectives that continue to be left out. Oftentimes these are the voices of those who experience the greatest amount of oppression, and therefore this book is only the tip of the iceberg of perspectives on international LGBTQ mental health.

This book provides an overview of LGBTQ mental health from an international perspective using intersectionality as the theoretical framework (Crenshaw, 1991). Bowleg (2012) defined *intersectionality* as

> a theoretical framework for understanding how multiple social identities such as race, gender, sexual orientation, SES, and disability intersect at the micro level of individual experience to reflect interlocking systems of privilege and oppression (i.e., racism, sexism, heterosexism, classism) at the macro social-structural level. (p. 1267)

That is, we attempt to look beyond sexual orientation or gender identity alone as we consider the experiences of LGBTQ people in various countries to consider other positionalities important in shaping lived experiences and access to support and other resources. The book chapters address the concerns of LGBTQ people of various regions of the world, including South Asia, Southeast Asia, Northern Asia, Eastern Europe, Latin America, the Caribbean, and sub-Saharan Africa.

These chapters provide some historical perspective, as well as cultural factors and values, conceptualizations of gender and sexuality, perspectives and concerns of LGBTQ people, and relevant clinical issues and recommendations for mental health practitioners to consider. Authors address how being a sexual and/or gender diverse person may impact mental health and highlight challenges faced by LGBTQ populations as they relate to laws, policies, and cultural beliefs. Chapters include one or more vignettes based either on one or more authors' experiences or on a fictionalized or deidentified case in order to give readers a sense of what concerns are relevant to the LGBTQ population from that particular country or region. Some chapters focus on LGBTQ populations within a specific country or region broadly, whereas others focus specifically on a subsection of the LGBTQ population. Book chapters are organized to allow readers to compare and contrast LGBTQ experiences within and between regions. Each chapter is briefly introduced, and major themes are highlighted.

OVERVIEW OF CHAPTERS

We begin with Peru, where Perez-Brumer, Silva-Santisteban, Salazar, Vilela, and Reisner (Chapter 1) explore mental health among transmasculine persons. They highlight the dearth of knowledge about transmasculine persons outside of the global North, and their qualitative study presents findings regarding gender identity formation, challenges in negotiating gender in daily life and public spaces, and ways in which persons engage in self-love and resilience. Educational, familial, religious, and legal identification systems were key sites of marginalization for gender-nonconforming persons, with harmful impacts on mental health resulting in depression, anxiety, self-harm, and in some cases suicidal ideation and attempts. Participants described tensions and a balancing act to negotiate familial acceptance. To navigate self-love and resilience, transmasculine persons described processes of self-acceptance, social media support, and online spaces of connection. The authors call for multi-level strategies that include accessible transgender-specific mental health care that acknowledges the diversity of needs within transgender communities, as well as structural changes in health care, education, and legal systems to protect transgender persons from stigma and discrimination.

Nieves-Lugo, Barnett, Pinho, Rueda Sáenz, and Zea (Chapter 2) examine mental health of LGBT people in Colombia. The authors address LGBT civil rights from a historical perspective. They present information on experiences of discrimination and violence experienced by LGBT people in Colombia despite many progressive laws designed to provide them with equality. Discrimination also gets in the way of LGBT Colombians' access to health and mental health services, and there is need for greater cultural competency in treating this population. They also address internal displacement and international migration by LGBT Colombians. Recommendations are made to mental health providers and researchers.

Di Marco, Arenas, Hoel, and Munduate (Chapter 3) address how Ecuadorean LGB workers manage their sexual orientation disclosure by examining the role of cultural factors and the consequences for their health and well-being. The authors conducted two qualitative studies to examine these issues. The first was based on 15 interviews with Ecuadorean LGB workers, and the second was with six focus groups of Ecuadorean heterosexual workers. These studies brought to light how LGB people manage their sexual orientation in the workplace and the negative attitudes they face. The consequences on the mental health of Ecuadorean LGB workers is addressed, and recommendations to organizations are made.

Marcus, Logie, Jones, Bryan, and Levermore (Chapter 4) examine gender norms and coping with sexual stigma among LBQ women in Jamaica through a qualitative study. Themes that emerged included hegemonic gender norms and stereotypes where physical appearance, housework, and child-rearing were prized in broader society and stereotypes also existed within the lesbian community. The theme of stigma, discrimination, and minority stress comprised enacted stigma and sources of discrimination (e.g., familial, hegemonic masculinity, structural, religious). Emotional and behavioral impacts of discrimination included a range of negative emotions and restriction of behavior, and navigating outness encompassed staying in the closet as a form of self-protection. Coping included self-acceptance and community support. Narratives also illuminated the need for counselling services.

Horne and White (Chapter 5) describe the anti-LGBTQ climate that exists in Russia today, which includes laws that make it illegal to treat LGBTQ people and relationships as equal to heterosexual people and relationships in the presence of minors and ban Pride parades. With the increase in anti-LGBTQ laws and rhetoric, there has been an upsurge in hate crimes based on sexual orientation and gender identity, including state-sponsored violence as seen in the Chechen Republic. Russia also has the largest HIV epidemic in Europe. Another ongoing issue addressed in this chapter is the attitudes of mental health providers toward LGBTQ clients and ongoing sexual orientation and gender identity change efforts to which many clients are subjected. Recommendations for mental health providers are made.

Koch, Knutson, and Nyamdorj (Chapter 6) provide a brief history of Mongolia to demonstrate the role of the former Soviet Union in shaping attitudes toward sexual orientation and gender diversity. They present information on traditional cultural values of Mongolians as well. They address the rise of anti-LGBT sentiments and the lack of legal protections for LGBT Mongolians. The authors examine the role of various intersecting identities (e.g., gender, location, socioeconomic status) and the roles they play in the lived experiences of LGBT people in Mongolia. Recommendations are made for culturally relevant interventions and prevention work in the areas of for health, education, law enforcement, and legislation and policy.

Chakrapani, Newman, and Shunmugam (Chapter 7) describe India's rich history of sexual and gender diversity and the subsequent changes in acceptance toward LGBTQ persons following the British introduction of criminalization of consensual same-sex practices during colonization. The authors also discuss evolving culturally specific conceptualizations of sexual and gender diversity in India. Stigma and discrimination, patriarchal norms, and familial rejection and disapproval are associated with the high prevalence of depression among gay, bisexual, and other men who have sex with men, and among transgender women, in India. Yet persons do negotiate family approval, access community support from other sexually and gender diverse persons, and mobilize in Pride and other events. The authors call for affirmative mental health services competent in meeting sexually and gender diverse persons' needs as well as social and structural changes to advance human rights protections.

Next, we consider what it means to be gay and lesbian in Malaysia. Singaravelu and Cheah (Chapter 8) provide an overview of the historical, sociopolitical, and cultural context of Malaysia and discuss attitudes toward LGBT and gender-nonconforming Malaysians. They present qualitative research that they conducted on 10 gay and seven lesbian Malaysians of Chinese and Indian descent to address their coming out experience. Although many participants describe having come out to friends and siblings, fewer have come out to their parents, and if they have, it is often in an indirect manner. The chapter concludes with recommendations for mental health practitioners in Malaysia, as well as those working with gay and lesbian Malaysians in other countries.

Ojanen, Newman, Ratanashevorn, de Lind van Wijngaarden, and Tepjan (Chapter 9) present the paradox between Thailand as a vacation destination for LGBTIQ tourists and the realities of LGBTIQ Thai people. They present the cultural and historical context of Thailand and the evolution of Thai LGBTIQ identities. They address conceptualizations of mental health in Thailand, as well as both indigenous and modern medical options for treatment. They also examine stigma associated with mental health and LGBTIQ identities, as well as specific challenges faced by the LGBTIQ community such as substance use. They conclude with initiatives for improving LGBTIQ mental health in Thailand through community empowerment and advocacy and through LGBTIQ-affirmative mental health care.

Chapter 10, by Brown and colleagues, addresses the region of sub-Saharan Africa. This final chapter focuses on the perspectives of activists and leaders of LGBT community-based organizations from Botswana, Kenya, Liberia, Tanzania, Zambia, and Zimbabwe. Themes that emerged from the interviews included social isolation among LGBT populations, access to mental health services, stigma toward mental health services, stigmatizing mental health care practices, and community-delivered mental health services. Participants also provided recommendations for advancing mental health services through integration with other health systems, as well as engagement with religious leaders and traditional healers. The authors give additional recommendations for mental health practitioners.

Taken together, these chapters provide a glimpse into the richness of LGBTQ persons' lives and experiences across international contexts. They highlight some shared LGBTQ experiences, such as stigma and discrimination, which have negative impacts on mental health. The authors also draw attention to the ways that people navigate their lives with social, cultural, familial, and at times legally constraining environments in ways that underscore resilience and the power of community support. Yet the stories shared in each chapter bring to light important differences in the ways that people can be "out" publicly or within families; the ways that persons navigate same-sex relationships; and the ways that people negotiate the interaction between their sexual and gender identities and their social, familial, and cultural identities.

REFERENCES

Arnett, J. J. (2008). The neglected 95%: Why American psychology needs to become less American. *American Psychologist, 63*, 602–614. http://dx.doi.org/10.1037/0003-066X.63.7.602

Banks, J. A., Suárez-Orozco, M. M., & Ben-Peretz, M. (Eds.). (2016). *Global migration, diversity, and civic education: Improving policy and practice*. New York, NY: Teachers College Press.

Bowleg, L. (2012). The problem with the phrase *women and minorities*: Intersectionality—An important theoretical framework for public health. *American Journal of Public Health, 102*, 1267–1273. http://dx.doi.org/10.2105/AJPH.2012.300750

Cole, M. (2006). Internationalism in psychology: We need it now more than ever. *American Psychologist, 61*, 904–917. http://dx.doi.org/10.1037/0003-066X.61.8.904

Crenshaw, K. (1991). Mapping the margins: Intersectionality, identity politics, and violence against women of color. *Stanford Law Review, 43*, 1241–1299. http://dx.doi.org/10.2307/1229039

Ghose, T., Boucicaut, E., King, C., Doyle, A., & Shubert, V. (2013). Surviving the aftershock: Postearthquake access and adherence to HIV treatment among Haiti's tent residents. *Qualitative Health Research, 23*, 495–506. http://dx.doi.org/10.1177/1049732312469463

Heller, P. (2009). Challenges facing LGBT asylum-seekers: The role of social work in correcting oppressive immigration processes. *Journal of Gay & Lesbian Social Services, 21*, 294–308. http://dx.doi.org/10.1080/10538720902772246

Immigration Equality. (n.d.). *Our clients*. Retrieved from https://www.immigration equality.org/about-us/our-clients/

Logie, C. H., Lacombe-Duncan, A., Kenny, K. S., Levermore, K., Jones, N., Marshall, A., & Newman, P. A. (2017). Associations between police harassment and HIV vulnerabilities among men who have sex with men and transgender women in Jamaica. *Health and Human Rights Journal, 19*, 147–154.

Piwowarczyk, L., Fernandez, P., & Sharma, A. (2017). Seeking asylum: Challenges faced by the LGB community. *Journal of Immigrant and Minority Health, 19*, 723–732. http://dx.doi.org/10.1007/s10903-016-0363-9

Reading, R., & Rubin, L. R. (2011). Advocacy and empowerment: Group therapy for LGBT asylum seekers. *Traumatology, 17*, 86–98. http://dx.doi.org/10.1177/1534765610395622

Reisner, S. L., Poteat, T., Keatley, J., Cabral, M., Mothopeng, T., Dunham, E., . . . Baral, S. D. (2016). Global health burden and needs of transgender populations: A review. *The Lancet, 388*, 412–436. http://dx.doi.org/10.1016/S0140-6736(16)00684-X

Singh, N. S., Aryasinghe, S., Smith, J., Khosla, R., Say, L., & Blanchet, K. (2018). A long way to go: A systematic review to assess the utilisation of sexual and reproductive health services during humanitarian crises. *BMJ Global Health, 3*, e000682. http://dx.doi.org/10.1136/bmjgh-2017-000682

Sue, S. (1999). Science, ethnicity, and bias: Where have we gone wrong? *American Psychologist, 54*, 1070–1077. http://dx.doi.org/10.1037/0003-066X.54.12.1070

UN High Commissioner for Refugees. (2010, September 22). *The protection of lesbian, gay, bisexual, transgender and intersex asylum-seekers and refugees*. Retrieved from http://www.refworld.org/docid/4cff9a8f2.html

1

In Search of "My True Self"

Transmasculine Gender Identity Processes, Stigma, and Mental Health in Peru

Amaya Perez-Brumer, Alfonso Silva-Santisteban, Ximena Salazar, Jesse Vilela, and Sari L. Reisner

The following is a fictional story comprising interwoven themes that emerged from the narratives of transgender men who shared stories of their lives with us. We mark for the reader that this is meant to be a snapshot combining diverse experiences that frequently overlap, not a summary of a homogenous reality of what it means to be a transgender man in Peru. It is important to note that we have chosen to write this narrative in the third person to respectfully acknowledge the distance between an academic retelling and the unique life experiences that are intertwined here to represent a united narrative.

"I am a man, but being recognized as one takes work every single day," Javier reflected as he recounted his experience being transgender. Javier, assigned female sex at birth, remembers always rejecting items and behaviors that symbolize femininity, such as dolls, dresses, and playing house. For him, his internal sense of self was masculine; however, what the world saw was a girl; a butch woman; and later, at times, a man.

When Javier was around age 10, his rejection of feminine dress and behaviors started to cause problems for him in his home and at school. He was labeled "unruly" and "problematic," and his parents became ashamed to take Javier into public spaces such as church on Sunday mornings or on strolls around the community plaza on weekend evenings. Concerned that he was spending too much time with his older brothers and that Javier could be a corrupting influence on his younger sister, his parents made the decision to send Javier to live with his grandmother, aunt, and two older cousins on the outskirts of Lima (a 2-hour bus ride from his home).

http://dx.doi.org/10.1037/0000159-002

LGBTQ Mental Health: International Perspectives and Experiences, N. Nakamura and C. H. Logie (Editors)

To rebel against the forced move, Javier described cutting off his hair and wearing the same outfit every day, the one outfit that did not have pink in it: soccer shorts and one of his brother's old shirts. Missing his family and friends was compounded with a sense of difference as a newcomer and the questioning looks he received when introduced into a new community. Throughout adolescence, he struck a balance with his grandmother. At home, he could dress in gender-neutral clothing and keep his hair short, but he was referred to with feminine pronouns and by his legal name, Jazmin. At school, the dress code was not up for debate, and Javier was forced to wear a skirt. However, Javier described that while his aunt and grandmother continued to buy him pink and flower-printed underwear and training bras, they turned a blind eye to the boxers he would steal from his cousins. Unfortunately, this delicate balance was upset during puberty.

As his body started to change and his slim athletic build slowly began to show signs of hips and breasts that could not be hidden under shorts and baggy T-shirts, Javier recounted the growing sense of despair and isolation. Feelings of being caught in between two genders led Javier to pull away from his family and friends and even think about suicide. His daily routine now included wearing two sport bras, wrapping a medical bandage around his chest, and using duct tape to compress his growing breasts. He described that his personality was changing, and he was always irritable because of being physically constricted and battling with his fluctuating hormones.

Adolescence also introduced the complexity of sexuality. Javier described this time as marked by the constant bodily explorations that his friends and classmates engaged in through flirtations and initial heterosexual couplings. For Javier, the tensions between internal sense of self and external expressions were magnified by his fear and desire to explore his own sexuality. Around age 16, he was tired of being the odd one out and of the continual energy that he exerted to be masculine. He stopped cutting his hair, wore the bras bought for him, and started mimicking his friends by engaging in heterosexual flirtations. Javier said that during this stage, he felt like an actor and not himself but continued in the role because of the positive attention he received. At school, bullying slowed and he made more friends, he was receiving attention from boys, and his parents invited him to visit on the weekends to see his siblings.

This stage was short-lived, and he quickly realized the he felt like a stranger in his own body. Through the exploration of his sexuality, he described enjoying erotic encounters but often being more attracted to girls than boys. His denunciation of a feminine gender presentation and return to more masculine expression was rejected by friends and family. This resulted in a magnification of his sense of isolation. To cope, Javier turned to alcohol. Unable to continue to wear a female uniform, Javier dropped out of school. The growing social loneliness pushed Javier to spend the daytime hours asleep and nighttime hours awake, alone in his bedroom.

His cousins started to refer to him as a lesbian. Unsure what that meant, he went online to figure it out. In the privacy of the night, Javier discovered the Internet as an oasis of information. He described the sensation of no longer being alone because of a connection with the YouTube, blog, and Facebook communities that he found. In fact, he stated that some of his closest friends are virtual friends who supported him in his exploration of gender identity. Today, at the age of 18, Javier has returned to school and is still living with his grandmother—though she still refers to him with feminine pronouns; his aunt and cousins at times call him Javier and use masculine pronouns. For Javier, online resources and virtual communities enabled him to access needed information and education about gender identity. Although he is more comfortable in his own sense of self, he described that this process is ongoing, and he recognizes that because of the daily challenges he faces, he needs to have a strong support network to help him navigate the daily prejudices in his life.

TRANSMASCULINE HEALTH AND TERMINOLOGY

Globally, transgender health as a field has grown remarkably in the past 5 years (Olson-Kennedy, 2016; Reisner et al., 2016). Yet the majority of available transgender health research tends to focus on assessments of HIV risk, prevention, and treatment among adult male-to-female transgender women populations (Baral et al., 2013; Herbst ct al., 2008; IIwahng & Nuttbrock, 2014). Although some epidemiologic studies have included transmasculine communities, they are often conflated with male-to-female transfeminine populations to improve statistical power (Clements-Nolle, Marx, & Katz, 2006; Conron, Scott, Stowell, & Landers, 2012). As a result, the health needs of transmasculine individuals—those assigned a female sex at birth who identify as men, male, transgender men, or another diverse gender different from their assigned birth sex—remain largely unknown.

Evidence from available literature suggests that transmasculine people are at risk for multiple mental health challenges, including depression, anxiety, suicidal ideation, and self-harm (James et al., 2016; Olson, Schrager, Belzer, Simons, & Clark, 2015; Reisner et al., 2015, 2016; Rood, Puckett, Pantalone, & Bradford, 2015). To better understand the pathways that lead to these negative mental health outcomes, stigma needs to be recognized as a powerful social determinant of health and a fundamental cause of health disparities (Hatzenbuehler, Phelan, & Link, 2013). Assessing multilevel stigma and its impact on transgender health is crucial given the systematic discrimination and devaluation as a result of social stigma attached to gender nonconformity (Bockting, Miner, Swinburne Romine, Hamilton, & Coleman, 2013; Perez-Brumer, Hatzenbuehler, Oldenburg, & Bockting, 2015; Poteat, German, & Kerrigan, 2013; White Hughto, Reisner, & Pachankis, 2015).

Within the field of transgender health research, it is important to recognize the dominance of scientific knowledge that is being created from the Global North. Notably, the majority of the literature on transgender health originates from the Global North (viz., the United States) and is published in English

(Reisner et al., 2016). This dominance flags the ways in which sociocultural understandings of gender variance are primarily understood from a Global North framework (Dutta, 2013; Reicherzer, 2008; Stryker, 2008). Although there is recognition that not everyone whose behavior, appearance, or expression is gender fluid and/or nonconforming will identify as transgender, *transgender* is still considered the governing umbrella term used to describe people whose gender expression and/or identity does not align with the socially prescribed gender norms associated with their sex assigned at birth (American Psychological Association, 2015). However, it is important to note that the complexity of how gender is understood is grounded in local cultures. Thus, caution needs to be taken when categorizing which bodies and identities are legible within the transgender category across cultures and to recognize the specificity of gender norms across social contexts.

As the field recognizes that current omission of data on transmasculine health needs, more studies have begun to emerge (Peitzmeier, Reisner, Harigopal, & Potter, 2014; Rachlin, Green, & Lombardi, 2008; Reisner, Gamarel, Dunham, Hopwood, & Hwahng, 2013). However, this research includes primarily samples from the Global North. To the best of our knowledge, no publications have reported on the health needs of transgender men in Peru. To address these limitations, this chapter aims to gain a more in-depth understanding of culturally situated meanings and understandings of Peruvian transmasculine identity.

INTERSECTIONAL UNDERSTANDINGS OF GENDER IDENTITY

We use theories of structural gender identity formation and intersectionality as guiding frameworks. To underscore the knitted relationship between power and gender, we are guided by R. W. Connell's (1987, 2010) interactional conceptualization of gender as shaped by and shaping society. Connell's formulation of gender—in particular, gender regimes—is useful here, as it allows for an analysis of gender as a dynamic process enacted within and through institutions rather than solely on gender roles or status.

Another grounding theory to the present analysis is intersectionality. Kimberlé Crenshaw (1991), building on collective theorizations by Black cisgender women feminists, introduced the theory of intersectionality to reframe and complicate the discussion of marginalization beyond a single axis concept. Crenshaw argued for multiple marginalizations by highlighting cases of overlapping systems of oppression in the realities experienced by women of color. Counter to unitary approaches, such as identity politics that posit one master category, intersectionality theory brings to light the various axes that depend on a person's age, race, gender identity, sexual orientation, economic status, ability, and education and that intersect to constitute vulnerability and inequality. Crenshaw's work has been extremely influential across academic fields, including transgender studies (de Vries, 2012; Dutta, 2012; Irving, 2013), marking the need to understand the lived realities of transgender people as a dynamic, interactional phenomenon.

In Peru, the importance of intersectional identity statuses (e.g., religious affiliation, positionality on a gender spectrum, age, race) among transgender women in understanding how they access social services has been documented (Perez-Brumer et al., 2017; Reisner et al., 2017; Salazar, 2015). Yet, further theoretical depth is necessary to highlight how Peruvian institutions and social spaces are key sites of power within which understandings of gender are shaped and to analyze how cultural norms and expectations regarding femininity and masculinity are enforced and disrupted among the lives of transmasculine people. As with the dominance of the Global North in the understandings of terminology and of which bodies and identities are counted within transgender health as a field, it is important to recognize the primary use of these theories in English-speaking Global North settings. As such, these theories are employed as a framework, not a rubric to guide our analyses to look at individual-, community-, and structural-level processes that influence the lives of transmasculine people in Peru.

METHOD AND CONTEXT

Between August 2016 and January 2017, we conducted a mixed methods study exploring holistic health care needs of transmasculine individuals in Lima, Peru. A sample of 36 transmasculine adults participated in four qualitative focus group discussions; subsequently, 10 in-depth interviews were conducted to further explore themes elicited from focus groups. Institutional Review Boards at the Universidad Peruana Cayetano Heredia in Lima, Peru, and The Fenway Institute in Boston, Massachusetts, approved study procedures. Participants received PEN 30 (approximately USD$10) as financial compensation for their time.

All research methods were conducted in Spanish by native Spanish speakers, and qualitative data from audio files were transcribed verbatim. Analysis involved both inductive and deductive approaches to identify salient themes across in-depth interviews and focus groups and was guided by the immersion–crystallization approach (Borkan, 1999). To organize our findings, we applied conceptual frameworks of structural gender identity formation and intersectionality to identify consistencies and discordances between selected themes.

This study was conducted in Lima, the capital of Peru and the second largest city in South America (after São Paolo), with close to 10 million inhabitants (Instituto Nacional de Estadística e Informática, 2017). Most adults in Lima receive at least a secondary education; nonetheless, the quality of education varies greatly depending on the districts in which the person resides (Brent Hall & Peters, 2003). Research within Peruvian schools has highlighted the ways in which gender and sexuality are approached and taught based on normative perspectives (Motta, Keogh, Prada, Núnez-Curto, & Konda, 2017). The majority of Peruvians are adherent to Christian religions (81% Roman Catholic, 15% Evangelical), which is reflected in social tensions, conservative policy agendas, and educational policies that marginalize lesbian, gay, bisexual, and transgender persons (Cáceres, Cueto, & Palomino, 2008). Specifically, although the 2016 Peruvian Department of Education curriculum included education about gender such as "construct your identity," "gender identity," and even "what is masculine or feminine is constructed day by day," extreme lobbying by the Catholic Church and affiliated organizations put pressure to excluded these changes on the grounds of "gender ideology" and reimplement the 2009 version of the curriculum (Motta et al., 2017).

Within the health sector, the high concentration of HIV infection among transgender women has been documented (Silva-Santisteban et al., 2012). Differential access to social services has also been associated with health disparities among transgender women through exposure to high levels of stigma, discrimination, poor specialized knowledge among medical providers, and structural barriers stemming from enforced binary gender identity (e.g., legal documentation, sex-segregated hospital wards, gender-based school uniforms; Perez-Brumer et al., 2017; Reisner et al., 2017; Salazar, 2015).

RESULTS

Results are presented in three thematic groupings across social contexts and their intersections with mental health: (a) formation of gender identity, (b) challenges negotiating gender in daily life and public spaces, and (c) engaging in self-love and resiliency practices. Next we discuss each of these themes in greater detail and explore how transmasculine narratives elicited distinct understandings of mental health at the intersection of social space, cultural norms, and beliefs related to gender identity.

Formation of Gender Identity

Narratives highlighted that early in childhood (preadolescence), most participants started to question—and, in some cases, reject—their feminine gender identity. Participants recounted common questions of "Who am I?" and "What am I?" when searching for "[their] true self" (Interview 6) and a general sentiment of discomfort with games and dress that reified normative gender expression and performance. As described, "I felt like Pinocchio, I could never truly be myself, I felt as though I was always going to stay this way [in between two genders]" (Interview 1).

School emerged as an important social space for identity development, where participants described frictions between who they were and who they were expected to be, discrimination and bullying victimization based on masculine gender identity, and other forms of gender policing. For example, one participant described the following:

> I knew I was different in elementary school. I must have been around six years old and I felt like I wasn't a girl but I also wasn't a boy. I just didn't know. . . . I wanted to be like the boys, play soccer and to be part of their games, but the teachers they would always push me towards the girls. (Interview 4)

Notably, this quote shows the ways in which gender identity formation occurs within social structures (e.g., schools) and is policed by people in power within those institutions (e.g., teachers and adults in schools). Other narratives highlighted how play as a form of socialization teaches children the "ways" that girls play (e.g., swings, talking, dolls) and the "ways" that boys play (e.g., football, tag). Policies, such as sex-segregated dress code, enforced within schools further support socially constructed understandings of normative gender. As described,

> I would hate to leave my house to go to school with my skirt on. I remember purposefully staining and ruining my school uniform skirts so that I could wear my sweatpants. I always felt more comfortable in sweatpants and an oversized shirt. (Interview 1)

Long hair and uniforms were described as constant reminders of being forced to be feminine and of the discomfort when one's internal sense of self did not match a gender identity ascribed on the basis of natal sex. However, as just stated, participants shared examples of bounded agency and resistance to push back against gender norms. Regarding hair, one participant shared the following strategy:

> I remember that my family wanted me to have long hair and wouldn't let me cut it short. I didn't want this, so I told a friend who I knew had lice to infect me so that they would cut my hair off. (Focus Group 4)

Gender nonconformity within school was described as generally not accepted among peers and school faculty, resulting in discrimination and bullying victimization for people who did not fit or chose to push against binary understandings of gender. Terms such as *bicho raro* (literal translated as "strange animal," but in slang it has pejorative connotations and is more colloquially understood as "weirdo"; Focus Group 4) and *la rara* (translated as "the strange one"; Interview 8) were frequently used by participants to highlight labels placed on them as part of gender-identity-based discrimination. Beyond labels, one participant described experiences with bullying: "They [peers] would take photos of me on their cell phones while I was in the bathroom. They would mock me and talk about me as though I wasn't there. I was isolated, never included in group activities" (Interview 10). Another participant explained that the concept of transgender identity is not well understood, and thus most discrimination was due to being perceived as a lesbian. For example, "I suffered from discrimination in school mainly because people thought I was a lesbian since I was always in sweatpants and liked to play football. Even teachers would discriminate against me" (Focus Group 2).

Many of our participants either attended a religious school or were raised in religious families. Religion was described as heightening the level of rejection by family, peers, and oneself due to teachings on the sin of homosexuality:

> I went to an evangelical school and in those years, I didn't know what I was [regarding gender identity] but I knew I was different. . . . We were taught that homosexuality was a sin and that homosexuals would go to hell, and at that age I believed it. Psychologically, I couldn't accept myself because I thought I would go to hell. . . . I tried to remind myself that I wanted God to love me and forced myself to dress like a woman and to try and forget how I felt. (Interview 1)

Assessments of mental health were retrospective, and most participants recounted that in those moments, particularly during school, stressors primarily manifested into feelings of isolation and confusion. Continual harassment and routinized practices to enforce normative understandings of gender (e.g., uniforms, child play) were described as cumulative stressors. Exposure to these stressors were described as negatively impacting mental health and well-being, resulting in outcomes including depression, anxiety, self-harm, and in some cases suicidal ideation and even suicide attempts. For example, one participant shared this experience: "In my head I thought that I would kill myself. My grandfather was a cop and had a gun in the house. One day I grabbed it, looked at it, and felt no, no I can't do this" (Interview 7). Another participant stated, "I was isolated and ridiculed. . . . I only went between school and my room. I was super depressed and trying to kill myself two times" (Interview 1).

Challenges Negotiating Gender in Daily Life and Public Spaces

The second emergent theme highlights how standards of gender are maintained, managed, and deciphered in everyday practices. Intersections of gender identity formation processes and multilevel stigma show the continual work and energy required to be recognized as masculine in Peruvian society. Intrapersonally, participants described exhaustion in constantly asserting their gender identity to the outside world, often not having it reflected back to them, which resulted in self-blame or internalized stigma. Interpersonal barriers in relationships, particularly with family, were challenging, as names and pronouns were constant sites of gender negotiation. Structural barriers, namely, legal forms of identification, were described as delegitimizing and violently invalidating one's felt gender identity because of the contradiction presented between presentation of self as masculine and legal documentation. This theme emerged across multiple domains including school, work, public life, and health.

Although initial questioning of nonbinary gender identity was described across narratives as a slow process, starting in early childhood and continuing through formative years of adolescence, the act of "coming out" was recounted as abrupt and a turning point for one's felt and expressed gender identity. For most, the first time they disclosed their transmasculine gender identity was to their family members—in particular, their mothers. One participant recounted, "I felt that I just couldn't do it anymore and I told my mother everything" (Focus Group 1). Familial acceptance was mixed among participants. Whereas some maintained relationships with their family, others were no longer able to continue a relationship postdisclosure of a transmasculine identity. However, across all narratives the way in which participants expressed their gender identity within familial spaces was described as a delicate balance: "They [family members] know and accept it but still call me by female pronouns" (Interview 6).

Gender affirmation as described by participants primarily included behavioral practices for social gender affirmation such as binding (using constrictive materials to flatten the breast tissue and create a male-appearing chest) and packing (using a nonflesh penis to give the appearance of having a male bulge in one's pants). Although most participants were interested in accessing masculinizing hormone therapy (testosterone), only about 30% reported currently using hormones. Furthermore, only one participant reported being able to obtain "top" surgery (a mastectomy for male chest contouring). Gender-affirming procedures were described as important for the individual, as well, as increasing ease of navigating social spaces:

> If you physically look like a man, people will think you are a man, and they will treat [you] as such. The problem if you still have feminine characteristics people will see you and think "here something is weird." For example, I always have issues entering a bathroom. Honestly, I am scared to enter a public bathroom. Because in the women's bathroom I am not enough of a woman to enter and for the men's bathroom I am not masculine enough. (Focus Group 4)

This quote also highlights embedded natal sex-segregated structures (e.g., bathrooms) within society that function to police normative gender practices. As described, this is particularly problematic for transgender, gender-nonconforming, and other people whose gender expression does not conform with their sex assigned at birth.

Another structural barrier cited across narratives was difficulty with natal sex gender markers on legal forms of identification. Specifically, although changing gender markers on *Document Nacional de Identidad* (DNI)—the national identity document required of all adult Peruvian citizens—is possible, none of the participants interviewed reported being able to successfully do so or have knowledge of other individuals who had successes. Instead, the DNI was described as the main barrier for accessing employment, health services, and other resources (e.g., banking). For example, "I have never liked going to the hospital or a doctor because of my DNI . . . the contradiction between my name and my appearance" (Focus Group 1). Within the employment domain, participants described that they were offered jobs until they presented their identity documents, and then employment offers were withdrawn. To explain the crucial role that legal documents play in everyday life, one participant stated the following:

> My physical appearance is an important factor. I undergo hormone therapy but if I want to change my name and gender on my DNI what can I do? I can't,

at least in this country I can't. So physically I will be a man, with a deep voice, beard, but my DNI? Whenever I show my DNI they will look at me and say "no this isn't you." (Focus Group 4)

The structural barrier of not being able to change one's name and gender marker on the DNI in Peru was described as a source of chronic stress and strain. Constantly negotiating a masculine presentation not supported by a legal identity document meant that gender, specifically nonconformity to societal gender standards, was at the forefront of everyday living.

Engaging in Self-Love and Resiliency Practices

The third emergent theme showcases the enacted practices that participants engaged in to promote self-love and seek support. Recognition of and identification with a transmasculine identity was described as a key step to self-acceptance and, for some, happiness. One participant shared, "When I began my transition socially I began to feel better. This was my true self and through acceptance and expression I felt better" (Focus Group 1). Another stated,

> One needs to be true to themselves, it shouldn't matter what people think. . . . One needs to be strong, move forward, and always look ahead. I won't bow my head anymore; I won't feel shame for who I am because I am a human. (Focus Group 2)

Furthermore, self-acceptance of a transmasculine identity was often described as increasing self-confidence.

Participants reported that virtual networks facilitated through online social media platforms (e.g., Facebook, YouTube, Instagram) were an important source of educational resources and support from peers. Of interest, one participant describes the importance of being able to create three Facebook profiles while investigating and learning about their felt sense of gender identity: "Yes, I had about three Facebook accounts, one for my family, another for my friends, and a third for my friends who knew [about my transmasculine gender identity]. . . . [Facebook] was the only place I felt free expressing myself" (Interview 4). This quote highlights the multiple intersecting identities (child, friend, transgender, etc.) that jointly reflect this person's identity status.

The importance of WhatsApp to create a virtual support network and community was also described:

> On Tumblr I saw an advertisement about an LGBT group and to leave your WhatsApp information to join. So, I left my information and they added me right away. It's been about two or three years since I began to speak with them. I began to speak to everyone, they were from Chile and other places, not one person from Peru, I was the only one. So I began to talk to them about everything and we became super friends. There was even a girl in the group that I began to like, she was from Panama. (Interview 1)

Online spaces were voiced as a respite from daily oppression, social marginalization, and exclusion experienced. In addition, they are resources that can be accessed any time of day and in the privacy of one's room, which participants explained as key attributes as to why a virtual platform became a key foundation of information and support. Interfacing with other transmasculine people and finding supportive people and communities were also described as lessening feelings of isolation and alienation and increasing a feeling of belongingness.

CONCLUSION

Our findings highlight the extent to which intersectional stigma management processes dominate Peruvian transmasculine people's lives and directly influence mental health and well-being, both negatively and positively. Although meanings and expressions of gender identity are profoundly personal, emergent themes across these narratives showcase the ways wherein personal self-understanding intersects and implicates intrapersonal, community, and structural domains. These qualitative data provide key insights concerning how cultural dynamics and active policing of gender identity and gender norms oppress, marginalize, and stigmatize gender fluid individuals. While not taking away or distracting from the barriers and challenges faced by the transmasculine people we interviewed, our results also underscore the collective strategies evoked to disrupt the gender binary; build community; and, very important, prompt self-love. Given the dearth of literature on transmasculine identity and health care needs in Latin America, and no current evidence from Peru, this chapter provides preliminary information to raise awareness on the health needs of transgender men in Peru and to advocate for the incorporation of culturally appropriate mental health strategies within existing Peruvian health care systems.

Paralleling existing global literature, analysis emphasizes the role of multilevel stigma in negatively influencing transmasculine health (Reisner, Gamarel, et al., 2013; Reisner, Poteat, et al., 2016; Schilt & Westbrook, 2009; White Hughto et al., 2015). *Stigma* refers to a socially devalued identity (e.g., transmasculinity) or an unwanted characteristic (e.g., gender nonconformity) ascribed to a particular group (Goffman, 1963). As described, visible stigmas (e.g., those that are legible and readily read by others, passing) shaped personal safety in public spaces, including in schools and health care settings, and discrimination experienced. Visible stigmas were voiced as marking a social devalued identity or characteristic that was constantly present. Furthermore, participants recounted how being in-between gender categories or presenting social markers (e.g., identity documents) that disclose gender fluidity was frequently met with an onslaught of discrimination and stigma because of making gender transgressions societally visible.

Although more research is needed, these findings have implications for clinical practice. Namely, being visibly legible as transmasculine necessitates deploying strategies for stigma management that are intersectional and occur across multiple domains (e.g., home, school, work). Strategies are learned and can include self-monitoring (adjusting self-presentation to match the expectations of others) and presenting different gender expressions and performances based on social context. Such impression management approaches to navigating stigma can be detrimental to mental health and well-being, particularly when personal control over whether and how identity is visible is constrained by economic resources. Internalized stigma, whereby stigmatized communities cognitively or emotionally internalize or absorb negative attitudes or stereotypes from others, appears particularly salient for transmasculine people in Peru. Literature from the United States has found that internalized stigma among transgender individuals is associated with increased probability of lifetime suicide attempts, reduced help-seeking behaviors for mental health problems, and may negatively impact one's ability to cope with external stressors (Hendricks & Testa, 2012; Mizock & Mueser, 2014; Perez-Brumer et al., 2015). Our results support the need to provide accessible transgender-specific mental health services, including awareness as to the heterogeneous needs within transgender communities (e.g., for transmasculine *and* transfeminine individuals), to mitigate the impact of continued stigma management processes.

These results are a first step to understanding health needs and gender identity formation processes among Peruvian transmasculine communities and are limited because of the small sample size and scoping focus of this research. Other co-occurring psychosocial risk factors (e.g., anxiety, suicidality, posttraumatic stress) were not directly asked during qualitative interviews. Evaluating risk factors specific to mental health outcomes is a needed next step for this line of research. In addition, our sample represents people from the middle socioeconomic stratum in Peruvian society, and emergent themes are therefore not generalizable.

Despite these limitations, our data underscore the importance of assessing culturally situated meanings of gender identity and understanding stigma management processes among Peruvian transmasculine people. Intersections of gender identity formation processes and multilevel stigma suggest that depression, isolation, and experiences of discrimination could represent critical targets for intervention in clinical practice and care. To fully support individual-level mental health care and enhance the well-being of Peruvian transmasculine communities, results highlight the urgent need for structural interventions including, but not limited to, capacity building of educators and health care providers on transgender identity, legal systems that allow for natal sex and/or gender markers on governmental documents to reflect an individual's gender identity, and recognition that transmasculine people exist and deserve to not just survive but thrive.

REFERENCES

American Psychological Association. (2015). Guidelines for psychological practice with transgender and gender nonconforming people. *American Psychologist, 70*, 832–864. http://dx.doi.org/10.1037/a0039906

Baral, S. D., Poteat, T., Strömdahl, S., Wirtz, A. L., Guadamuz, T. E., & Beyrer, C. (2013). Worldwide burden of HIV in transgender women: A systematic review and meta-analysis. *The Lancet Infectious Diseases*, *13*, 214–222. http://dx.doi.org/10.1016/S1473-3099(12)70315-8

Bockting, W. O., Miner, M. H., Swinburne Romine, R. E., Hamilton, A., & Coleman, E. (2013). Stigma, mental health, and resilience in an online sample of the US transgender population. *American Journal of Public Health*, *103*, 943–951. http://dx.doi.org/10.2105/AJPH.2013.301241

Borkan, J. (1999). Immersion/crystallization. In B. F. Crabtree & W. L. Miller (Eds.), *Doing qualitative research* (2nd ed., pp. 179–194). Thousand Oaks, CA: Sage.

Brent Hall, G., & Peters, P. A. (2003). Global ideals and local practicalities in education policies and planning in Lima, Peru. *Habitat International*, *27*, 629–651. http://dx.doi.org/10.1016/S0197-3975(03)00009-2

Cáceres, C., Cueto, M., & Palomino, N. (2008). Sexual and reproductive rights policies in Peru: Unveiling false paradoxes. In R. Parker, R. Petchesky, & R. Sember (Eds.), *SexPolitics: Report from the front lines* (pp. 127–166). Rio de Janeiro, Brazil: Sexuality Policy Watch.

Clements-Nolle, K., Marx, R., & Katz, M. (2006). Attempted suicide among transgender persons: The influence of gender-based discrimination and victimization. *Journal of Homosexuality*, *51*(3), 53–69. http://dx.doi.org/10.1300/J082v51n03_04

Connell, R. W. (1987). *Gender and power: Society, the person and sexual politics*. Stanford, CA: Stanford University Press.

Connell, R. W. (2010). *Gender: Short introductions*. Malden, MA: Blackwell.

Conron, K. J., Scott, G., Stowell, G. S., & Landers, S. J. (2012). Transgender health in Massachusetts: Results from a household probability sample of adults. *American Journal of Public Health*, *102*, 118–122. http://dx.doi.org/10.2105/AJPH.2011.300315

Crenshaw, K. (1991). Mapping the margins: Intersectionality, identity politics, and violence against women of color. *Stanford Law Review*, *43*, 1241–1299. http://dx.doi.org/10.2307/1229039

De Vries, K. M. (2012). Intersectional identities and conceptions of the self: The experience of transgender people. *Symbolic Interaction*, *35*, 49–67. http://dx.doi.org/10.1002/symb.2

Dutta, A. (2012). An epistemology of collusion: *Hijras, Kothis* and the historical (dis)continuity of gender/sexual identities in Eastern India. *Gender & History*, *24*, 825–849. http://dx.doi.org/10.1111/j.1468-0424.2012.01712.x

Dutta, A. (2013). Legible identities and legitimate citizens. *International Feminist Journal of Politics*, *15*, 494–514. http://dx.doi.org/10.1080/14616742.2013.818279

Goffman, E. (1963). *Stigma: Notes on the management of spoiled identity*. New York, NY: Simon & Schuster.

Hatzenbuehler, M. L., Phelan, J. C., & Link, B. G. (2013). Stigma as a fundamental cause of population health inequalities. *American Journal of Public Health*, *103*, 813–821. http://dx.doi.org/10.2105/AJPH.2012.301069

Hendricks, M. L., & Testa, R. J. (2012). A conceptual framework for clinical work with transgender and gender nonconforming clients: An adaptation of the Minority Stress Model. *Professional Psychology: Research and Practice*, *43*, 460–467. http://dx.doi.org/10.1037/a0029597

Herbst, J. H., Jacobs, E. D., Finlayson, T. J., McKleroy, V. S., Neumann, M. S., & Crepaz, N. (2008). Estimating HIV prevalence and risk behaviors of transgender persons in the United States: A systematic review. *AIDS and Behavior*, *12*, 1–17. http://dx.doi.org/10.1007/s10461-007-9299-3

Hwahng, S. J., & Nuttbrock, L. (2014). Adolescent gender-related abuse, androphilia, and HIV risk among transfeminine people of color in New York City. *Journal of Homosexuality*, *61*, 691–713. http://dx.doi.org/10.1080/00918369.2014.870439

Instituto Nacional de Estadística e Informática. (2017). *Perfil Sociodemográfico Del Perú* [Sociodemographic profile of Peru]. Retrieved from https://www.inei.gob.pe/estadisticas/indice-tematico/population/

Irving, D. (2013). Against the grain: Teaching transgender human rights. *Sexualities, 16,* 319–335. http://dx.doi.org/10.1177/1363460713479746

James, S. E., Herman, J. L., Rankin, S., Keisling, M., Mottet, L., & Anafi, M. (2016). *The Report of the 2015 U.S. Transgender Survey.* Washington, DC: National Center for Transgender Equality. Retrieved from http://www.transequality.org/sites/default/files/docs/usts/USTS%20Full%20Report%20-%20FINAL%201.6.17.pdf

Mizock, L., & Mueser, K. T. (2014). Employment, mental health, internalized stigma, and coping with transphobia among transgender individuals. *Psychology of Sexual Orientation and Gender Diversity, 1,* 146–158. http://dx.doi.org/10.1037/sgd0000029

Motta, A., Keogh, S. C., Prada, E., Núñez-Curto, A., & Konda, K. (2017). *De la normativa a la práctica: La política de educación sexual y su implementación en el Perú* [From standards to practice: The politics and implementation of sexual education in Peru]. New York, NY: Guttmacher Institute. Retrieved from https://www.guttmacher.org/es/report/politica-de-educacion-sexual-peru

Olson, J., Schrager, S. M., Belzer, M., Simons, L. K., & Clark, L. F. (2015). Baseline physiologic and psychosocial characteristics of transgender youth seeking care for gender dysphoria. *Journal of Adolescent Health, 57,* 374–380. http://dx.doi.org/10.1016/j.jadohealth.2015.04.027

Olson-Kennedy, J. (2016). Mental health disparities among transgender youth: Rethinking the role of professionals. *JAMA Pediatrics, 170,* 423–424. http://dx.doi.org/10.1001/jamapediatrics.2016.0155

Peitzmeier, S. M., Reisner, S. L., Harigopal, P., & Potter, J. (2014). Female-to-male patients have high prevalence of unsatisfactory paps compared to non-transgender females: Implications for cervical cancer screening. *Journal of General Internal Medicine, 29,* 778–784. http://dx.doi.org/10.1007/s11606-013-2753-1

Perez-Brumer, A., Hatzenbuehler, M. L., Oldenburg, C. E., & Bockting, W. (2015). Individual- and structural-level risk factors for suicide attempts among transgender adults. *Behavioral Medicine, 41,* 164–171. http://dx.doi.org/10.1080/08964289.2015.1028322

Perez-Brumer, A. G., Reisner, S. L., McLean, S. A., Silva-Santisteban, A., Huerta, L., Mayer, K. H., . . . Lama, J. R. (2017). Leveraging social capital: Multilevel stigma, associated HIV vulnerabilities, and social resilience strategies among transgender women in Lima, Peru. *Journal of the International AIDS Society, 20,* 21462. http://dx.doi.org/10.7448/IAS.20.1.21462

Poteat, T., German, D., & Kerrigan, D. (2013). Managing uncertainty: A grounded theory of stigma in transgender health care encounters. *Social Science & Medicine, 84,* 22–29. http://dx.doi.org/10.1016/j.socscimed.2013.02.019

Rachlin, K., Green, J., & Lombardi, E. (2008). Utilization of health care among female-to-male transgender individuals in the United States. *Journal of Homosexuality, 54,* 243–258. http://dx.doi.org/10.1080/00918360801982124

Reicherzer, S. (2008). Evolving language and understanding in the historical development of the gender identity disorder diagnosis. *Journal of LGBT Issues in Counseling, 2,* 326–347. http://dx.doi.org/10.1080/15538600802502035

Reisner, S. L., Gamarel, K. E., Dunham, E., Hopwood, R., & Hwahng, S. (2013). Female-to-male transmasculine adult health: A mixed-methods community-based needs assessment. *Journal of the American Psychiatric Nurses Association, 19,* 293–303. http://dx.doi.org/10.1177/1078390313500693

Reisner, S. L., Perez-Brumer, A. G., McLean, S. A., Lama, J. R., Silva-Santisteban, A., Huerta, L., . . . Mayer, K. H. (2017). Perceived barriers and facilitators to integrating HIV prevention and treatment with cross-sex hormone therapy for transgender women in Lima, Peru. *AIDS and Behavior*, *21*(Suppl. 3), 3299–3311. http://dx.doi.org/10.1007/s10461-017-1768-8

Reisner, S. L., Poteat, T., Keatley, J., Cabral, M., Mothopeng, T., Dunham, E., . . . Baral, S. D. (2016). Global health burden and needs of transgender populations: A review. *The Lancet*, *388*, 412–436. http://dx.doi.org/10.1016/S0140-6736(16)00684-X

Reisner, S. L., Vetters, R., Leclerc, M., Zaslow, S., Wolfrum, S., Shumer, D., & Mimiaga, M. J. (2015). Mental health of transgender youth in care at an adolescent urban community health center: A matched retrospective cohort study. *Journal of Adolescent Health*, *56*, 274–279. http://dx.doi.org/10.1016/j.jadohealth.2014.10.264

Rood, B. A., Puckett, J. A., Pantalone, D. W., & Bradford, J. B. (2015). Predictors of suicidal ideation in a statewide sample of transgender individuals. *LGBT Health*, *2*, 270–275. http://dx.doi.org/10.1089/lgbt.2013.0048.

Salazar, X. (2015). *Vine al mundo porque dios quiere que yo esté aqui* [I came to the world because God wants me to be here] (N. Fuller, Ed.). Lima: Pontificia Universidad Católica del Perú.

Schilt, K., & Westbrook, L. (2009). Doing gender, doing heteronormativity. *Gender & Society*, *23*, 440–464. http://dx.doi.org/10.1177/0891243209340034

Silva-Santisteban, A., Raymond, H. F., Salazar, X., Villayzan, J., Leon, S., McFarland, W., & Cáceres, C. F. (2012). Understanding the HIV/AIDS epidemic in transgender women of Lima, Peru: Results from a sero-epidemiologic study using respondent driven sampling. *AIDS and Behavior*, *16*, 872–881.

Stryker, S. (2008). *Transgender history*. Berkeley, CA: Seal Press.

White Hughto, J. M., Reisner, S. L., & Pachankis, J. E. (2015). Transgender stigma and health: A critical review of stigma determinants, mechanisms, and interventions. *Social Science & Medicine*, *147*, 222–231. http://dx.doi.org/10.1016/j.socscimed.2015.11.010

2

Mental Health of Lesbian, Gay, Bisexual, and Transgender People in Colombia

Karen Nieves-Lugo, Andrew P. Barnett, Veronica Pinho, Miguel Rueda Sáenz, and Maria Cecilia Zea

> Why did I come to Bogotá? Because in my town everyone discriminated against me. I would go into a store, and it was like they were seeing the devil, seeing Satan in person. People looked at me in a way that made me feel really bad. I felt worse than garbage. People at least pick up garbage, pick up garbage and lift it up, tie it, pick it up, and take it out. No, to me, they didn't even do that. . . . I had to run away and run, run, for my own protection. . . . Men threw rocks at me and then raped me. On one occasion they cracked my head open. Someone threw a big stone at me and yelled, "Fag, son of a bitch." I arrived in town all bloody, with my back full of blood. Here in Bogotá, I am filled with a lot of energy. There are a lot of gays here; there is less discrimination here. Here everyone minds his own business. And what one learns from that is that one has to learn to live one's own life. Nobody cares about you. In a town everyone cares about their neighbor . . . while here, no. Everyone is on his own. (Zea et al., 2013, p. 797)

José's narrative (pseudonym used to protect his identity) is an example of the discrimination and other forms of oppression that lesbian, gay, bisexual, and transgender (LGBT) people face in Colombia at the institutional and individual levels. The experiences of LGBT individuals living in small towns or rural places are different from those living in metropolitan áreas, as described by José. Although Colombia is one of the leading countries in Latin America promoting equality, rights, and constitutional protections for LGBT

This chapter was prepared while Karen Nieves-Lugo, PhD, MPH, was employed at The George Washington University. The opinions expressed in this chapter are the authors' own and do not reflect the view of the National Institutes of Health, the Department of Health and Human Services, or the U.S. government.

http://dx.doi.org/10.1037/0000159-003
LGBTQ Mental Health: International Perspectives and Experiences, N. Nakamura and C. H. Logie (Editors)

people, negative social attitudes toward this population persist. Furthermore, although all Colombians experience challenges related to the 50-year-long civil war in their country, the intersection of political upheaval and sexual minority status creates unique stressors for LGBT Colombians.

This chapter reviews the research on the mental health of LGBT individuals living in Colombia and the social, cultural, and political factors that influence mental health. We discuss the relationship between structural and social factors and sexual minority identities in Colombia, such as the effects of legal protections, discrimination, stigma, displacement, and migration on mental health. Finally, we explain how LGBT individuals access mental health services, highlight the protective factors and recent changes that could positively impact the mental health of LGBT communities in Colombia, and make recommendations on how to improve mental health care for LGBT communities.

CIVIL RIGHTS HISTORY AND THE SOCIOPOLITICAL CLIMATE FOR LGBT INDIVIDUALS IN COLOMBIA

Understanding the current context of mental health concerns among LGBT individuals in Colombia requires a brief overview of the history of LGBT communities in the country. Although we found no records on same-sex love during pre-Columbian times in Colombia, there is reason to believe that LGBT people existed, as has been found in many other cultures. In an excellent review of historical archives and scholarly papers on same-sex sexual practices and identities in colonial Latin America, Tortorici (2012) pointed out that only relatively recent scholarship has explored this topic, such as works by Carolina Giraldo Botero (2002) on same-sex desire and repression in Colombia in colonial times and by Rodríguez (1995) on lesbian love between two women from Popayán.

One of the first written references to LGBT individuals in postcolonial Colombia appears to be the criminalization of same-sex relationships in Article 419 of the Colombian Penal Code of 1890 (Nagle, 2012). In 1936, there was a movement to change the penal code with Article 323 to allow freedom of conduct; however, same-sex sexual activity was illegal for men and, at that time, being gay in Colombia was considered a mental illness. Nagle (2012) concluded that Article 323 reaffirmed fear against homosexuality and helped institutionalize homophobia in Colombia.

The history of the modern LGBT rights movement in Colombia begins in this context and shows that, like their counterparts in other countries around the world, LGBT communities in Colombia have a long history of advocating for equal legal recognition and the basic human right to express their sexual and/or gender identities without fear of persecution, discrimination, or violence. The earliest recorded modern LGBT advocacy began in Bogotá in 1940 with a clandestine group called *Los Felipitos* (Little Phillips), the purpose of which was to create a space in which gay men could socialize (Aparicio Erazo,

2009). From its early beginning, this movement continued to grow in aspirations and influence. In 1970, encouraged by the visibility of advocacy efforts in Europe and North America (e.g., the Stonewall uprising, feminism), gay activist León Zuleta founded the *Movimiento por la Liberación Homosexual* (Homosexual Liberation Movement) in Medellín (Aparicio Erazo, 2009; Mejía Turizo & Almanza Iglesia, 2010). Manuel Velandia founded a similar group in Bogotá, which was responsible for the first gay march in 1982 and the first gay-focused publication in Colombia.

The rise of these movements precipitated a pivotal amendment of the criminal code. Decree 100 of 1980 of the Colombian Penal Code decriminalized consensual same-sex activity throughout the country in 1981, a "crime" that once carried a penalty of imprisonment for 6 months to 2 years (Arenas, 1981; Bello, Miller, & Schneeweis, 2015). Moreover, LGBT political and social movements (e.g., *Marcha de la Ciudadanía LGBT* [LGBT Pride]) with support from the city of Bogotá's government, nongovernmental agencies (e.g., *Colombia Diversa, Círculo LGBT Uniandino, Stonewall Javeriano*), and academia (e.g., Ciclo Rosa Académico) contributed to increased social acceptance of LGBT communities and changes in laws (Brigeiro, Castillo, & Murad, 2009; Millán De Benavides, 2010; Sánchez Avella, 2014; Torres Molina, 2015). By creating laws that affirm and protect LGBT rights, Colombia established itself as a leader in the promotion of LGBT equality in Latin America (Mejía Turizo & Almanza Iglesia, 2010). Many pro-LGBT policies have been enacted, including the ability for gay men to serve openly in the military, bodily autonomy for intersex minors, equality in inmate conjugal visits, equality in patrimonial rights, testimonial privileges and protections for domestic violence victims, adoption rights, the ability for transgender individuals to change their legal name and gender marker on government identification cards, and in 2016 the ability for same-sex couples to marry (Bello et al., 2015; Colombia Diversa, 2010; Franco, 2015). Most recently, in 2017, Colombia legally recognized the marriage of three gay men as a first polyamorous family (Kale, 2017).

Despite these important victories, LGBT communities continue to face opposition in seeking expanded legal protections at both the institutional level (e.g., religious) and the individual level (e.g., attitudes). In 2015, the Senate threatened LGBT rights when it proposed a referendum to restrict adoption rights to different-sex couples ("La Batalla del Referendo," 2016). Conservative institutions such as churches and private agencies continue to propagate anti-LGBT messages, which in turn instigate crimes, aggression, and discrimination against LGBT people (Sánchez Avella, 2012). In 2016, the Minister of Education ordered a revision of school handbooks to include protections for students based on sexual orientation and gender identity. This revision was ordered after Sergio Urrego, a 16-year-old student, committed suicide due to discrimination for being gay ("Colegio de Joven," 2014). The proposed revision that would have expanded protections for LGBT students was met with large-scale demonstrations throughout Colombia (Cullinan Hoffman, 2016).

Discrimination and Violence

Although LGBT communities in Colombia have secured many important rights and legal protections, they still encounter homonegativity and other forms of anti-LGBT discrimination, such as name-calling, assault, sexual violence, and refusal of services (Zea et al., 2013). In a survey conducted at a 2007 gay Pride march in Bogotá, 77% of LGBT participants reported experiencing some form of discrimination, and 68% reported experiencing verbal or physical aggression (Brigeiro et al., 2009). Younger LGBT individuals and those with lower educational levels and socioeconomic status were at greater risk for experiencing discrimination or aggression. Furthermore, transgender participants reported higher levels of discrimination than lesbian, gay, and bisexual participants. Participants reported discrimination experiences in a variety of spaces of daily living, such as the workplace, schools, and universities; perpetrators included authorities (e.g., police, security guards), institutions (e.g., churches), neighbors, friends, or family. Similarly, a study of 1,213 LGBT individuals (358 lesbian, 351 gay, 194 bisexual, and 310 transgender) found that 54% of LGBT participants reported discrimination due to their sexual orientation or gender identity (Alcaldía Mayor de Bogotá, Secretaría Distrital de Planeación y Econometría S.A., 2010).

Research on the incidence of violence committed against LGBT people in Colombia is scant. However, reports of individual cases suggest that LGBT people are targeted on the basis of their sexual orientation and/or gender identity, particularly in rural areas or places controlled by paramilitary forces (Bello et al., 2015; Colombia Diversa, 2012; Ripoll, 2009; Zea et al., 2013). This experience is aggravated by "social cleansing," the practice of eliminating people considered undesirable (Schwartz, 1996; Zea et al., 2013). Documented violent incidents in recent years include soldiers being raped for being gay, a 14-year-old girl identified as a lesbian being raped and then killed, and transgender individuals being harassed and assaulted by the police (Ripoll, 2009). The Santa Maria Foundation, an LGBT rights organization, documented several cases of police abuse against transgender women (e.g., arbitrary detention, torture, physical and verbal violence) between 2005 and 2011 in Bogotá and Cali. Moreover, LGBT groups have argued that authorities do not investigate or protect LGBT victims from sexual abuse, hate crimes, or other human rights violations (Colombia Diversa, 2012; Serrano, 2009).

The internal armed conflict and political violence in Colombia have placed LGBT individuals at a higher risk of being killed (Nagle, 2012; Schwartz, 1996; Zea et al., 2013). Several recognized LGBT leaders and activists have been assassinated, such as Leon Zuleta in 1993, Fredy Pineda in 2008, Alvaro Miguel Rivera in 2009, and Guillermo Garzón Andrade in 2014 (Out Right Action International, 2009). In 2002, illegal armed groups attacked Manuel Velandia, founder of the LGBT movement in Colombia, for his LGBT advocacy and his denunciation of paramilitary groups' sexual exploitation of adolescents (Velandia, 2014). Velandia subsequently went into exile in Spain in 2007. Data from the national district attorney's office reported that, in 2014, 87 LGBT or intersex individuals were killed by armed forces ("LGBTI," 2014). This report also revealed that the national district attorney's office was investigating the homicides of 30 LGBT individuals, half of which were reported in Medellín ("LGBTI," 2014). These homicides occurred at the same time that the Colombian Supreme Court was deliberating on adoption rights for same-sex couples, exemplifying how LGBT civil rights victories are met with backlash and violence.

The violence and discrimination against LGBT communities and hetero-normative attitudes that persist at the institutional level might influence discriminatory behaviors at the interpersonal level (Estefan Vargas, 2013). Again, empirical research in Colombia in this area is sparse. One study revealed the prevalence of negative attitudes toward LGBT and queer individuals in health care professions through a qualitative analysis of Internet reactions to a news story about a transgender nurse (Campo Arias, Oviedo, & Herazo, 2014). The majority of the comments on the blog story constituted negative beliefs, including that LGBT identities were mental disorders; that LGBT and queer health care professionals were carriers of multiple infections (e.g., HIV, gonorrhea) and were child sex predators; and that LGBT health care professionals were underprepared, unprofessional, and unethical in their workplace. Research has also shown that interpersonal discrimination occurs in prisons, where LGBT inmates experience bullying, physical violence, isolation, prohibition of conjugal or general visits, and food deprivation (Parra Pérez, 2015).

Despite the existing legal protections, LGBT individuals are invisible in the majority of social contexts in Colombia. Fear of being rejected or even murdered often forces LGBT individuals to hide their sexual orientation and gender identity (López López, Pérez Durán, & Pineda Marín, 2016). Invisibility pervades even in settings that are generally more open and accepting, such as universities. A study of LGBT university students showed that the majority of participants perceived that the curriculum privileged heterosexuality and that the schools did not offer space and freedom for self-expression for LGBT students (Rodón Cárdenas, 2012). In response to this pervasive problem, LGBT organizations push forward the visibility and rights of sexual minorities in Colombia (Bello et al., 2015). These groups encourage LGBT individuals to improve their quality of life and fight against the dominant structures that privilege heterosexuality (Nieves-Lugo, Rohrbeck, Nakamura, & Zea, 2016).

Internal Displacement

Colombia has a long history of internal displacements. For LGBT Colombians, research has shown that unique factors contribute to the circumstances surrounding their displacement and their subsequent experiences. Internal displacements are associated with particular risks for LGBT individuals, including being the targets of killings, sexual violence, discrimination, and harassment (Barrett, 2018; Zea et al., 2013).

Migration to a major city can also grant protection for LGBT populations. Internal displacement from rural to urban areas in Colombia offers the opportunity to escape the poverty, food insecurity, violence, homelessness, and homophobia that LGBT individuals experience in their hometowns (Alcaldía Mayor de Bogotá, Secretaría Distrital de Planeación y Econometría S.A., 2010; Valenzuela Díaz, 2009; Zea et al., 2013). A government survey in Bogotá found that lesbian, gay, and bisexual individuals reported economic reasons, whereas transgender individuals reported gender identity, as the main motivation to migrate to Bogotá (Brigeiro et al., 2009).

Migration, however, also brings new challenges, such as the loss of family and social support, housing insecurity, decreased ability to access medical care and well-paid jobs, and increased risk of poverty (Zea et al., 2013). Significant barriers to economic well-being outside of urban centers are closely tied to internal displacement for LGBT individuals. A study of 1,275 internally displaced Colombians, of whom 1,139 were LGBT, revealed that they have experienced discrimination in the workplace, limited political participation, and lack of access to education and employment in rural and urban areas outside of Colombia's major cities (Bello et al., 2015; Brigeiro et al., 2009).

International Migration

LGBT Colombians often migrate to other countries because they offer the opportunity to live an "out" life without the fear of being discriminated or persecuted due to their sexual orientation or gender identity (Adam & Rangel, 2015; Bianchi et al., 2007; Nagle, 2012; Restrepo Pineda, 2013). According to a qualitative study, migration to New York City influenced sexual practices, as well as the physical and mental health, of gay and bisexual Colombian men (Bianchi et al., 2007). In a cross-sectional quantitative study of Latinos in New York City, Colombian men who have sex with men (MSM) reported that their main motivations to migrate from Colombia to the United States were familial, financial, and political but also were to affirm their sexual orientation and to escape violence or persecution for being gay (Nieves-Lugo et al., 2019). Similarly, a qualitative study of Spanish-speaking gay men who migrated to Canada (of which one third were Colombian) reported that the main factors associated with migration were financial, armed conflict, and/or being gay (Adam & Rangel, 2015). Restrepo Pineda (2013) found that most gay and bisexual men who migrated to Spain were also looking for better opportunities and quality of life due to the discrimination and sociopolitical conditions in Colombia. In sum, LGBT Colombians migrate to live a better life when they feel constrained or discriminated in their towns or cities; they may also be motivated to move to join a partner or friends.

MENTAL HEALTH AMONG LGBT INDIVIDUALS LIVING IN COLOMBIA

Advancements in mental health policies and laws have been taking place in Colombia since 2000. The Colombian Congress enacted Law 1616 of 2013, which guarantees mental health promotion and the prevention and treatment of mental health disorders for all Colombian citizens (Congreso de Colombia, 2013). At the same time, similar to other countries, stigma related to mental health, as well as negative attitudes and misperceptions about people living with mental disorders, is present in Colombia (Alvarez Ramírez & Almeida Salinas, 2008; Uribe Restrepo, Mora, & Cortés Rodríguez, 2007). For example, one study found that Colombians living with mental health issues had experienced stigma, rejection, discrimination (e.g., people used pejorative words when referring to them), poor social support, and lack of awareness about mental health issues (Uribe Restrepo et al., 2007).

Although research about LGBT mental health issues in Colombia is scarce, extant studies suggest that mental health problems and related health risk behaviors are a significant concern for this population. The homophobia, discrimination, harassment, and oppression that LGBT Colombians often experience make them more prone to developing negative mental health outcomes. As described by the minority stress model (Meyer, 2013), conflict with dominant social values and the environment can result in high levels of stress, which may increase the likelihood of negative mental health outcomes (Dentato, 2012). In a study conducted in Bogotá, 87% of LGBT participants ($n = 1,055$) reported mental health issues such as anxiety, depression, stress, suicidal ideation, and drug abuse or had suffered discrimination, sexual violence, and/or family problems (e.g., aggression; Alcaldía Mayor de Bogotá Secretaría Distrital de Planeación y Econometría S.A., 2010).

Assessing the extent of suicide among LGBT populations in Colombia is difficult because there is no official information about death by suicide for this community (Pineda Roa, 2013). Furthermore, suicide statistics among the general Colombian population are underreported due to stigma, political, social, or insurance policies (Pineda Roa, 2013). Research suggests that suicide risk behavior in the general population may be increasing: Epidemiological data in Bogotá found that suicide attempts were 3 times more prevalent in 2008 (27.3%) than in 2004 (9.3%; Forero & Cardona, 2011). Furthermore, violence, sexism, and homophobia are associated with sexual violence and self-harm, which in turn increase the risk of suicide in LGBT populations (Pineda Roa, 2013; Rocha Buelvas, 2015).

HIV Status

LGBT individuals in Colombia are more likely to experience sexual assault because of negative attitudes toward sexual minorities; this form of victimization also places them at risk for HIV infection (Zea et al., 2013). Moreover, being identified as HIV positive by their health care provider or family exacerbates the risk of violence for Colombians due to HIV-related stigma (Zea et al., 2013). As a whole, MSM and other vulnerable groups are disproportionally affected by HIV infection in Colombia. Taken together, these findings suggest that stigmas experienced by LGBT individuals and individuals living with HIV are closely connected with experiences of violence in Colombia.

Sex work places LGBT individuals at increased risk for discrimination and harassment, as well as HIV infection. Many MSM and transgender women engage in commercial sex work to survive due to marginalization of their sexual orientation and gender. In addition, transgender women and MSM expressed that because they have limited employment options due to discrimination and lack of education, sex work, which is legal in Colombia, is an acceptable alternative for them and their peers (Bianchi et al., 2014; Zea et al., 2013). Multiple social and contextual factors influence transgender individuals' engagement in sex work, including lack of social capital, limited employment opportunities, workplace discrimination, being stereotyped as a sex worker, and the perception that sex work is acceptable and normative for their community (Peñafiel & Waldo, 2016).

At the same time, knowledge of HIV serostatus is related to lower sexual risk and improved health behaviors among gay and bisexual men and transgender women. Zea et al. (2015) found that Colombian MSM and transgender women living with HIV who were aware of their status were less likely than those who were HIV-negative or HIV-positive unaware to report binge drinking (9% vs. 15% and 28%, respectively), drug use (23% vs. 26% and 41%), and condomless anal sex (38% vs. 62% and 66%) in the previous 3 months. However, insufficient access to HIV testing precludes gay, bisexual, and transgender individuals living with HIV and unaware of their status from engaging in healthier behaviors (Reisen et al., 2014). Increased efforts should be devoted to research on HIV among lesbian and bisexual women (Palma & Orcasita, 2017). In a qualitative study, Palma, Munévar Cabal, and Orcasita (2017) reported fairly low knowledge about HIV among lesbian and bisexual women in Cali. Moreover, when these women requested HIV testing, service providers deemed them at low risk and did not approve their tests. Thus, knowledge of their own HIV status is low.

Access to Mental Health Care

In addition to the evidence that LGBT individuals are at increased risk for negative mental health outcomes, research has also suggested that they face unique barriers in accessing services. Zea et al. (2015) found that, among a sample of 1,000 MSM and transwomen in Colombia, 13% reported receiving poor health services due to discrimination. Moreover, 37% of participants indicated not having health insurance, being partly covered by public health insurance, or not knowing their insurance status. Similarly, Brigeiro et al. (2009) found that 23% of lesbian, 22% of transgender, 12% of gay, and 8% of bisexual participants in Bogotá did not have health insurance. Transgender individuals were the most likely to report not receiving Colombian national health insurance, because they are often unemployed or excluded from educational and job opportunities. Transgender individuals (18%) reported the highest overall levels of discrimination in health care, followed by gay (14%), bisexual (10%), and lesbian respondents (9%).

Overall, few providers offer psychological services to LGBT individuals in Colombia. To our knowledge, most of those psychologists offer their services in larger cities like Bogotá. However, with the advancement of telecommunications technology, some mental health providers are now offering their services through video calls to LGBT individuals who do not feel comfortable visiting a psychologist's office and to those living outside major cities. Liberarte and Pink Consultores are examples of private practices providing psychotherapy to LGBT individuals in person in Bogotá and through video calls. Colombia Diversa has a partnership with the Department of Psychology at Universidad Santo Tomas, which offers psychological consultation to LGBT individuals in their office in Bogotá or via Skype. During these consultations, clinical psychology students and their supervisors have conversations with their clients to refer them to the appropriate organization for services. The government of Bogotá funded a project created by psychologists Sandra Monte Alegre, Angélica Badillo, and Laura Sofía Céspedes called Casa Refugio para Población LGBTI, an organization that offers protection and a place to live to LGBT individuals who have been victims of interpersonal violence or internal displacement.

Furthermore, there is evidence of homonegativity among mental health professionals, affecting the services offered to these populations. The Sexual Diversity Department of the Mayor's Office in Bogotá found that nearly one out of five participants reported experiencing discrimination from mental health care providers or staff. Transgender individuals reflect the highest prevalence of discrimination (26%), followed by lesbians (16%), gay persons (14%), and bisexual men and women (9%). Two thirds of lesbian, gay, and bisexual individuals reported having received professional mental health care, whereas only 15% of transgender individuals reported receiving the same care (Alcaldía Mayor de Bogotá, Secretaría Distrital de Planeación y Econometría S.A.).

Although Colombian laws guarantee mental health care for all Colombians, there is a need to train psychologists to understand the unique needs of LGBT populations. Chaparro-Clavijo (2015) found that psychologists and psychology students held negative attitudes toward lesbian, gay, and bisexual individuals engaging in public expression of affection and endorsed other forms of heterosexism. After LGBT cultural competency workshops, participants reported increased positive attitudes toward lesbian, gay, and bisexual parenting and family structures.

In addition, more research is needed to increase and improve mental health services for these populations. For instance, findings from research carried out by Vargas Trujillo, Ripoll Núñez, Carrillo Ávila, Rueda Sáenz, and Castro Muñoz (2013) can be used to understand the lived experiences of LGBT Colombians (e.g., the process of coming out). In addition, the adoption or replication of

LGBT-affirming policies and programs implemented by the Department of Sexual Diversity, Bogotá Mayor's Office (e.g., surveys and places that offer protection to LGBT individuals) in other cities or towns would benefit LGBT populations living there.

CONCLUSION

The sociopolitical context of LGBT individuals living in Colombia is one of contrasts. Colombia was one of the first South American countries to recognize civil rights for LGBT individuals in the 1980s. In the past 2 decades, there have been efforts from national and local governments to change the laws to increase legal protections for LGBT communities. Although they are not affirmed by all segments of society, many LGBT individuals in Colombia no longer feel like second-class citizens.

However, acceptance of LGBT individuals varies depending on region, most notably in terms of differences between major cities and other parts of the country. Public policies created in the last 2 decades are in effect only in larger cities like Bogotá and Medellín. Other cities have little or no public policies to protect LGBT people. Furthermore, even where laws and public policies protect them, LGBT people continue to be persecuted and discriminated against—or even murdered.

There are few studies focused on mental health issues among LGBT communities in Colombia despite the persistent discrimination they experience. The majority of the studies have focused on construction of political subject, rights, laws, heterosexism, and homophobia (e.g., discrimination, violence, prejudice and attitudes toward homosexuality; Ardila, 2002). Given the limited research in this area, the development of this chapter was challenging, and some information was gathered from newspapers or the authors' personal or research experiences.

LGBT communities in Colombia have demonstrated great resilience. However, there is a dearth of research examining protective factors among LGBT communities in Colombia. Resistance to discrimination takes place in two ways: First, each LGBT person develops their own way of responding to oppression; second, the LGBT community in Colombia has developed cohesion and advocated on behalf of their rights. Through social movements, the LGBT community in Colombia has changed the constitution and increased their visibility. Other important protective factors that help LGBT communities cope with a hostile environment include families and other social supports.

Psychologists and researchers have several important roles to play in the fight to increase the acceptance of LGBT people in all cities and towns throughout Colombia. Psychology students and mental health professionals should be trained in LGBT affirmative care to promote structural and institutional changes. Antidiscrimination campaigns and interventions to destigmatize LGBT identities are needed. Further research on mental health disparities among these communities is necessary to identify programs and policies to promote improved outcomes. Research can also guide LGBT-affirming clinicians in addressing mental health issues on individual and community levels (Nieves-Lugo et al., 2016). Finally, psychologists can contribute to positive social change through advocating for the needs of LGBT Colombians and providing training to governmental agencies, educational institutions, health care professionals, and the general public about the issues these communities face. We hope this chapter serves as an invitation for psychologists to further study LGBTQ communities in Colombia.

REFERENCES

Adam, B. D., & Rangel, J. C. (2015). The post-migration sexual citizenship of Latino gay men in Canada. *Citizenship Studies, 19*, 682–695. http://dx.doi.org/10.1080/13621025.2015.1053797

Alcaldía Mayor de Bogotá, Secretaría Distrital de Planeación y Econometría S.A. (2010). *Lesbianas, gays, bisexuales y transgeneristas en cifras* [Lesbians, gays, bisexuals and transgender people in numbers] (Bogotá, Ciudad Estadística, Boletín No. 25). Retrieved from http://www.sdp.gov.co/sites/default/files/dice108-cartillaestadisticaslgbt-2011.pdf

Alvarez Ramírez, L. Y., & Almeida Salinas, O. (2008). Adults' perception about mental illness and its psychological treatment in Bucaramanga city, Colombia. *Revista de la Facultad de Medicina, 56*, 91–100.

Aparicio Erazo, J. L. (2009). Ciudadanías y homosexualidades en Colombia [Homosexualities and citizenships in Colombia]. *Revista de Ciencias Sociales, 35*, 43–54. Retrieved from http://www.bdigital.unal.edu.co/48096/1/ciudadan%C3%ADasyhomosexualidadesencolombia.pdf

Ardila, R. (2002). *Homosexualidad y psicología* [Homosexuality and psychology]. Bogotá, Colombia: Manual Moderno.

Arenas, A. V. (1981). *Comentarios al nuevo Código Penal Decreto 100 de 1980, tomo II: Parte especial* [Comments to the new Penal Code Decree 100 of 1980, Volume II: Special part]. Bogotá, Colombia: Temis.

Barrett, S. (2018, February 26). *Colombia's LGBT community may not be benefiting fully from reparations system*. Retrieved from https://www.marketplace.org/2018/02/26/world/colombias-lgbt-community-may-not-be-benefiting-fully-reparations-system

Bello, C., Miller, K., & Schneeweis, I. (2015). *Colombia LGBTI: Landscape analysis of political, economic and social conditions*. New York, NY: Astraea Lesbian Foundation for Justice.

Bianchi, F. T., Reisen, C. A., Zea, M. C., Poppen, P. J., Shedlin, M. G., & Penha, M. M. (2007). The sexual experiences of Latino men who have sex with men who migrated to a gay epicentre in the USA. *Culture, Health & Sexuality, 9*, 505–518. http://dx.doi.org/10.1080/13691050701243547

Bianchi, F. T., Reisen, C. A., Zea, M. C., Vidal-Ortiz, S., Gonzales, F. A., Betancourt, F., . . . Poppen, P. J. (2014). Sex work among men who have sex with men and transgender women in Bogotá. *Archives of Sexual Behavior, 43*, 1637–1650. http://dx.doi.org/10.1007/s10508-014-0260-z

Brigeiro, M., Castillo, E., & Murad, R. (2009). *Encuesta LGBT: Sexualidad y derechos* [LGBT survey: Sexuality and rights]. Bogotá, Colombia: Universidad Nacional de Colombia/Profamilia/Centro Latinoamericano de Sexualidad y Derechos Humanos/IMS-UERJ.

Campo Arias, A., Oviedo, H. C., & Herazo, E. (2014). Estigma y discriminación a profesional de la salud transgénero [Stigma and discrimination against professionals of transgender health]. *Revista de la Facultad de Medicina, 62*, 41–45. http://dx.doi.org/10.15446/revfacmed.v62n1.43693

Chaparro Clavijo, R. A. (2015) *Efecto del entrenamiento para intervención psicológica con población de gays, lesbianas y bisexuales* [Impact of training on psychological interventions with gay, lesbian and bisexual populations] (Unpublished doctoral dissertation). Universidad Nacional de Colombia, Bogotá.

Colegio de joven que se suicidó en Bogotá, en la mira del Mineducación [High school of youth who died by suicide is under the scrutiny of the Ministry of Education]. (2014, September 9). *El Tiempo.* Retrieved from http://www.eltiempo.com/Bogotá/suicidio-de-estudiante-sergio-urrego-gobierno-investiga/14501101

Colombia Diversa. (2010). *Provisión de servicios afirmativos de salud para personas LGBT* [Provision of health affirmative services for LGBT people]. Bogotá, Colombia: Author.

Colombia Diversa. (2012). *Homicides, police abuse and impunity: Human Rights Report of LGBT people in Colombia 2010–2011.* Retrieved from http://colombiadiversa.org/colombiadiversa/documentos/informes-dh/colombia-diversa-informe-dh-2010-2011-summary.pdf

Congreso de Colombia. (2013). Por medio del cual se expide la ley de salud mental y se dictan otras disposiciones [Through which the law of the Galeon de San Jose is issued and other provisions are dictated]. *Ley, 1616* (Enero), 21. Bogotá, Colombia: Author.

Cullinan Hoffman, M. (2016, August 11). Thousands of Colombians join nationwide protest of gender ideology in public schools. *Lifesite News.* Retrieved from https://www.lifesitenews.com/news/thousands-of-colombians-join-nationwide-protest-of-gender-ideology-in-publi

Dentato, M. P. (2012, April). The minority stress perspective. *Psychology and AIDS Exchange Newsletter.* Retrieved from http://www.apa.org/pi/aids/resources/exchange/2012/04/minority-stress.aspx

Estefan Vargas, S. (2013). Discriminación estatal de la población LGBT: Casos de transgresiones a los Derechos Humanos en Latinoamérica [State discrimination against LGBT people: Violation of human rights cases in Latin America]. *Society and Economy, 25,* 183–204.

Forero, L. J., & Cardona, G. (2011). Epidemiologia de la conducta suicida en Bogotá [Epidemiology of suicidal behavior in Bogotá]. In L. C. Barbosa (Ed.), *Suicidio: Un reto para las comunidades educativas* (pp. 2–15). Bogotá, Colombia: Pontificia Universidad Javeriana.

Franco, D. (2015, June). *Colombia, the surprising global leader in transgender rights.* Retrieved from http://www.takepart.com/article/2015/06/10/colombia-surprising-global-leader-transgender-rights

Giraldo Botero, C. (2002). *Deseo y represión: Homoeroticidad en la Nueva Granada (1559–1822)* [Desire and repression: Homoerotism in Nueva Granada]. Bogotá, Colombia: CESO, 2002.

Kale, S. (2017, June 14). *Three men become first "polyamorous family" legally recognized in Colombia.* Retrieved from https://broadly.vice.com/en_us/article/vbgpka/gay-men-polyamorous-marriage-colombia

La batalla del referendo de Viviane Morales [The battle for the referendum proposed by Viviane Morales]. (2016, September 19). *Semana.* Retrieved from http://www.semana.com/nacion/articulo/polemica-por-referendo-de-viviane-morales-sobre-adopcion-gay/494035

LGBTI: Van 30 asesinados en el 2014 [LGBTI: 30 murdered in 2014]. (2014, August 21). *Semana.* Retrieved from http://www.semana.com/nacion/articulo/lgbti-van-30-asesinados-en-el-2014/399925-3

López López, W. L., Pérez Durán, C., & Pineda Marín, C. (2016). Relación entre el perdón, la reconciliación y la salud mental de las víctimas de la violencia socio-política [Relationship between forgiveness, reconciliation and mental health of socio-political violence victims]. *Revista de Victimología/Journal of Victimology, 3,* 141–159. http://dx.doi.org/10.12827/RVJV.3.06

Mejía Turizo, J., & Almanza Iglesia, M. (2010). Comunidad LGBT: Historia y recono-cimientos jurídicos [LGBT community: History and legal recognitions]. *Revista Justicia, 15*(17), 78–110.

Meyer, I. H. (2013). Prejudice, social stress, and mental health in lesbian, gay, and bisexual populations: Conceptual issues and research evidence. *Psychology of Sexual Orientation and Gender Diversity, 1*(S), 3–26. http://dx.doi.org/10.1037/2329-0382.1.S.3

Millán de Benavides, C. (2010). Rosa Von Praunheim y las políticas de inclusión ciudadana [Rosa Von Praunheim and the politics for citizen inclusion]. *Revista Via Iuris, 9,* 161–165.

Nagle, L. E. (2012). Giving shelter from the storm: Colombians fleeing persecution based on sexual orientation. *Tulsa Law Review, 48,* 1–26.

Nieves-Lugo, K., Barnett, A. P., Pinho, V., Reisen, C. A., Poppen, P. J., & Zea, M. C. (2019). Sexual migration and HIV risk in a sample of Brazilian, Colombian and Dominican immigrant MSM living in New York City. *Journal of Immigrant and Minority Health, 21,* 115–122.

Nieves-Lugo, K., Rohrbeck, C. A., Nakamura, N., & Zea, M. C. (2016). Interventions with lesbian, gay, bisexual, transgender, and questioning communities. In M. A. Bond, C. B. Keys, & I. Serrano-Garcia (Eds.), *Handbook of community psychology* (pp. 555–569). Washington, DC: American Psychological Association.

Out Right Action International. (2009). *The issues we face today.* Retrieved from https://www.outrightinternational.org/issues

Palma, D. M., Munévar Cabal, J., & Orcasita, L. T. (2017). HIV risk perception in young homosexual women from Cali, Colombia. *Arquivos Brasilerios de Psicologia, 69*(3), 83–99. Retrieved from http://pepsic.bvsalud.org/scielo.php?script=sci_arttext&pid=S1809-52672017000300007&lng=pt&tlng=en

Palma, D. M., & Orcasita, L. T. (2017). Considerations for the design of Human Immunodeficiency Virus (HIV) prevention programs for lesbian and bisexual women. *Interface: Comunicacao, Saude, Educacao, 21,* 1031–1038. http://dx.doi.org/10.1590/1807-57622016.0790

Parra Pérez, L. C. (2015). *La verdad de la comunidad LGTBI en las cárceles colombianas* [The reality of the LGTBI community in Colombian prisons]. Retrieved from http://repository.unimilitar.edu.co/bitstream/10654/14030/2/

Peñafiel, S., & Waldo, M. (2016). *Acercamiento sociocultural a un grupo de la comunidad LGBT de la ciudad de Cali: Identidad, sociedad y vocabulario* [Sociocultural approach to a group of the LGBT community in the city of Cali: Identity, society and vocabulary] (Unpublished doctoral dissertation). Retrieved from http://bibliotecadigital.univalle.edu.co/xmlui/bitstream/handle/10893/9794/CB0541289.pdf?sequence=1

Pineda Roa, C. A. (2013). Etiología social del riesgo de suicidio en adolescentes y jóvenes lesbianas, gay y bisexuales: Una revision [Social etiology of suicide risk in lesbian, gay and bisexual adolescents and youth: A review]. *Psicogente, 16*(29), 218–234.

Reisen, C. A., Zea, M. C., Bianchi, F. T., Poppen, P. J., del Río González, A. M., Romero, R. A., & Pérez, C. (2014). HIV testing among MSM in Bogotá, Colombia: The role of structural and individual characteristics. *AIDS Education and Prevention, 26,* 328–344. http://dx.doi.org/10.1521/aeap.2014.26.4.328

Restrepo Pineda, J. E. (2013). La experiencia migratoria de los hombres homosexuales y bisexuales colombianos en España. [Migratory experiences of homosexual and bisexual Colombian men]. In J. M. Valcuende Del Río, M. J. Marco Macarro, & D. Alarcón Rubio (Eds.), *Diversidad sexual en Iberoamérica* (pp. 89–104). Seville, Spain: Aconcagua Libros.

Ripoll, J. L. (2009). Love in the time of cholera: LGBT rights in Colombia. *SUR Journal, 11,* 72–89.

Rocha Buelvas, A. (2015). El riesgo suicida y los significados de las minorías sexuales: Un nuevo reto para la salud pública [Suicide risk and its meaning among sexual minorities: A new challenge for Public Health]. *Revista de la Facultad de Medicina, 63*, 537–544. http://dx.doi.org/10.15446/revfacmed.v63n3.43219

Rodón Cárdenas, F. (2012). LGBT students' short-range narratives and gender performance in the EFL classroom. *Colombian Applied Linguistics Journal, 14*, 77–91. http://dx.doi.org/10.14483/22487085.3814

Rodríguez, P. (1995). Historia de un amor lesbiano en la Colonia [History of a lesbian love in the Colony]. In M. V. Toro (Ed.), *Las mujeres en la historia de Colombia* (Vol. 3, pp. 169—174). Bogotá, Colombia: Grupo Editorial Norma.

Sánchez Avella, C. A. (2012). Sin la Corte no existiríamos: Discursos en torno a los núcleos familiares no heterosexuales en Colombia [Without the Court we would not exist: Discourses around nonheterosexual family units in Colombia]. *Revista Via Iuris, 13*, 23–41.

Sánchez Avella, C. A. (2014). øMarchar o no marchar? Esa es la cuestión: Movilización legal en tiempos de agitación para los sectores LGBT en Colombia [To march or not to march? That is the question: Legal mobilization in times of turmoil for the LGBT sectors in Colombia]. *Revista Via Iuris, 10*, 157–165.

Schwartz, E. F. (1996). Getting away with murder: Social cleansing in Colombia and the role of the United States. *The University of Miami Inter-American Law Review, 27*, 381–420.

Serrano, F. (2009). Colombia. In C. Stewart (Ed.), *The Greenwood encyclopedia of LGBT issues worldwide* (Vol. 1, p. 101). Santa Barbara, CA: Greenwood Press.

Torres Molina, L. E. (2015). Derechos en el procedimiento de la captura de personas integrantes de la población LGTBI [LGBTI population rights during in the arrest and detention procedures]. *Justicia, 28*, 56–70.

Tortorici, Z. (2012). Against nature: Sodomy and homosexuality in colonial Latin America. *History Compass, 10*, 161–178. http://dx.doi.org/10.1111/j.1478-0542.2011.00823.x

Uribe Restrepo, M., Mora, O. L., & Cortés Rodríguez, A. C. (2007). Voces del estigma: Percepción de estigma en pacientes y familias con enfermedad mental [Voices of stigma: Perception of stigma in patients and families with mental illness]. *Universitas Médica, 48*, 207–220.

Valenzuela Díaz, J. E. (2009). *Género y homofobia: Una revisión desde la psicología social contemporánea* [Gender and homophobia: A review from contemporary social psychology]. Retrieved from http://www.bdigital.unal.edu.co/10245/1/G%C3%A9nero%20y%20Homofobia%20(PDF)%202009.pdf

Vargas Trujillo, E., Ripoll Núñez, K., Carrillo Ávila, S., Rueda Sáenz, M., & Castro Muñoz, J. A. (2013). *Experiencias familiares de madres y padres con orientaciones sexuales diversas* [Family experiences of mothers and fathers with diverse sexual orientations]. Bogotá, Colombia: Ediciones Uniandes. http://dx.doi.org/10.7440/2013.49

Velandia, M. (2014, July 25). *Un homosexual es reconocido como víctima del conflicto armado en Colombia* [A homosexual is recognized as a victim of the armed conflict in Colombia] [Blog post]. Retrieved from http://asilolgbt.blogspot.com/2014/07/primer-caso-de-un-homosexual-reconocido.html

Zea, M. C., Reisen, C. A., Bianchi, F. T., Gonzales, F. A., Betancourt, F., Aguilar, M., & Poppen, P. J. (2013). Armed conflict, homonegativity and forced internal displacement: Implications for HIV among Colombian gay, bisexual and transgender individuals. *Culture, Health & Sexuality, 15*, 788–803. http://dx.doi.org/10.1080/13691058.2013.779028

Zea, M. C., Reisen, C. A., del Río-González, A. M., Bianchi, F. T., Ramírez-Valles, J., & Poppen, P. J. (2015). HIV prevalence and awareness of positive serostatus among men who have sex with men and transgender women in Bogotá, Colombia. *American Journal of Public Health, 105*, 1588–1595. http://dx.doi.org/10.2105/AJPH.2014.302307

3

Living a Double Life and Experiencing Modern Sexual Prejudice

The Effect on Ecuadorean Lesbian, Gay, and Bisexual Workers' Well-Being

Donatella Di Marco, Alicia Arenas, Helge Hoel, and Lourdes Munduate

You don't need to reveal [your sexual orientation] to the others, because people realize it. Firstly, because of your behavior, because they see that you go alone to social events, while they go with their wives or girlfriends. The most uncomfortable situation [is when they ask questions] . . .: you are always making up a new pretext to justify that you don't have a partner. . . . For example, during the last Christmas reunion everybody brought his wife and girlfriend. . . . At that moment, my colleagues said: "Lucio, why are you alone? You should have brought your mother, at least."

You try to avoid the conversation, not only at the workplace, also with your family, with your friends. Because apart from having LGBT friends, you also have a heterosexual group of friends and . . . it's always the same, they go out with their partners. I think these are the most uncomfortable moments I experience, when they ask after my girlfriend. . . . [When they ask about my weekend] I always tell the same story. When I go out with a partner, I say that I spent time with my family. . . . But it's a lie, and the truth always comes out, doesn't it? Other times you say something and then you say: "I believe that I said something else two weeks ago." . . . It's like having a double life. . . . The social pressure finally exhausts you. At work, in your personal life, with your family. Always being another person is very hard. . . . You spend 8 hours at work, therefore, you

This work was supported by the Spanish Ministry of Economy and Competitiveness (MINECO/FEDER, Grant No. PSI2015-64894-P) and by Fundação para a Ciência e a Tecnologia (FCT, Grant No. UID/GES/00315/2019).

http://dx.doi.org/10.1037/0000159-004
LGBTQ Mental Health: International Perspectives and Experiences, N. Nakamura and C. H. Logie (Editors)

spend your entire life here. . . . Pretending to be somebody else is very difficult, very difficult. (Lucio, gay, 23 years old)[1]

Lucio's double life is just one example of the daily stressors experienced by lesbian, gay, and bisexual (LGB) workers in Ecuador. For many years, Ecuadorean LGB people have been stigmatized and persecuted by law; it was only in 1997 that Ecuadorean Criminal Law eliminated the article that considered homosexuality a crime. Since that time, some progress has been made, following the rejection of discrimination on the basis of sexual orientation (Article 11, Ecuadorean Constitution, 2008) and the recognition of same-sex civil unions in 2008 (Article 68, Ecuadorean Constitution, 2008). Moreover, in 2015 the Ecuadorean Labor Code was modified, and firing an employee because of sexual orientation is now forbidden by law (Article 195, Labor Code, 2015). However, a recent study of the experiences of Ecuadorean lesbian, gay, bisexual, and transgender (LGBT) people showed that they perceive discrimination in many spheres of life, including the workplace, at school, in the health system, and in other public spaces (44%, 40%, 34%, and 56%, respectively; Instituto Nacional De Estadísticas Y Censos, 2013). Such data demonstrate that the shift in the legislative framework has not been followed by the elimination of prejudice and stereotypes that are deeply rooted in society, as illustrated in Lucio's story. Ecuadorean LGB people are still stigmatized and experience discrimination (Instituto Nacional De Estadísticas Y Censos, 2013), and "rehabilitation" clinics to "correct" LGB people's sexual orientation still exist (Deschamps, 2017). As a consequence, many may decide to hide their sexual orientation at work to avoid negative consequences (e.g., insults, being fired). However, as Lucio said, having to pretend about your personal life and continuously fielding questions about it are "uncomfortable situations" that expose Ecuadorean LGB people to excess stress that might adversely affect their well-being.

Prejudice and stereotypes against LGB people are reinforced by several cultural factors. Although studies about being LGB during the pre-Columbian era demonstrated that some Indigenous cultures tolerated it (Cromptone, 2003), the arrival of Spaniards was accompanied with the imposition of Catholic morality and the repression of (homo)sexuality. Today, Protestantism and Catholicism coexist (Kurian, 2011) and still play an important normative role. Nonheterosexuality is considered a sin or a deviance that should be corrected. In addition, the "culture of honor" (Dietrich & Schuett, 2013; Rodriguez Mosquera, Manstead, & Fischer, 2002), which entails a continuous search for social approval by showing the integrity of one's reputation through daily behaviors, characterizes Latino societies. In honor cultures, reputation threats might produce strong emotional reactions, such as anger and shame. Although

---

[1] The name and identity of the individual in this example have been altered to preserve this person's confidentiality.

anger may be felt toward the offender, shame may be internalized with fears that one's reputation is endangered (Rodriguez Mosquera et al., 2002). Religion fosters shame and guilt about behaving outside of the established social moral code (Luyten, Corveleyn, & Fontaine, 1998).

Traditional gender roles, still present in Ecuador (Mealy, Stephan, & Abalakina-Paap, 2006), are reinforced by religious beliefs (Dietrich & Schuett, 2013). According to the expectations of society (McGivern, 2012), men will demonstrate strength, virility, and power, whereas women are expected to be docile and show respect for authority even if they hold a key role in the family (Dietrich & Schuett, 2013; Rodriguez Mosquera et al., 2002). Ecuador is a country in which masculinity plays a salient role, having one of the highest scores in this cultural dimension in comparison with other Latin American countries (Hofstede, Hofstede, & Minkov, 2010). Thus, people grow up in a system that privileges competition and success and emphasizes the distinction between genders. Such cultural factors reinforce heteronormativity and might help us to understand why Ecuadorean LGB people face oppression (Day, 2005).

The aim of this chapter is to understand how Ecuadorean LGB workers manage their sexual orientation, stressing both cultural factors that might be affecting this process and the consequences for LGB people's well-being and health. In this sense, focusing on LGB workers is important because people spend a greater part of their adult time at the workplace, which represents one of the most important contexts for people's health and satisfaction. Although sexual identity management has been a widely studied issue in the United States and Europe (e.g., Griffith & Hebl, 2002), little is known about this process in Latin America, and we are not aware of any studies in Ecuador. This chapter does not focus on transgender and intersex people, as previous studies have reported that they might be perceived by heterosexuals in a different way and might experience unique forms of discrimination (e.g., Worthen, 2013). To understand in depth the experience of Ecuadorean LGB people, this chapter also explores heterosexual people's attitudes toward LGB workers. Therefore, this chapter also attempts to identify whether heterosexual people still hold sexual prejudices against LGB colleagues in Ecuador.

SEXUAL IDENTITY MANAGEMENT AT WORK, MODERN SEXUAL PREJUDICE, AND MINORITY STRESS

Managing sexual identity at work is a complex process that is affected by individual and situational factors. Disclosing sexual orientation might be harder in those contexts that are characterized by the presence of negative attitudes toward LGB people. Both perceiving discrimination and covering sexual orientation might be stressors with adverse effects for LGB people's well-being, as we analyze in the following sections.

Sexual Identity Management

Stigma can be visible or invisible (Goffman, 1963). Although the former is recognizable immediately, the latter can be hidden (and easily ignored by the other party) during social interactions. Although much progress has been made in terms of destigmatization of LGB people in some countries, being part of the LGB community is still associated with overt and covert discrimination in many areas of the world (Di Marco, Hoel, Arenas, & Munduate, 2018). Consequently, revealing one's sexual orientation to others (*disclosure process*) might be a hard decision. Disclosing sexual orientation in an intolerant work environment might produce adverse results, such as increasing discriminatory behaviors (Ragins, 2004). These, in turn, negatively affect individuals (e.g., harm LGB workers' well-being) and organizations (e.g., lower productivity; Ragins, 2004).

Previous studies have identified individual and environmental factors (e.g., identity centrality, zero-tolerance policies) that facilitate or prevent disclosure processes, recognizing strategies (and the consequences of these strategies) that people use to manage their sexual orientation at work (e.g., Clair, Beatty, & MacLean, 2005; Ragins, 2008). Such studies see disclosure as a complex decision for LGB workers (e.g., Clair et al., 2005; Ragins, 2008). Recent research has tried to understand the role played by third parties (colleagues, supervisors) during such a process and how these processes are shaped by interpersonal dynamics (Di Marco, Munduate, Arenas, & Hoel, 2017; Einarsdóttir, Hoel, & Lewis, 2016).

Research on disclosure in the workplace (e.g., Griffin, 1992) has identified strategies that LGB workers applied to manage disclosure processes. Strategies may be placed in two main groups: strategies for hiding and strategies for disclosing sexual orientation. For example, according to Griffin's (1992) study, LGB people might decide to hide their sexual orientation, *passing* as heterosexual (e.g., inventing a heterosexual partner) or *covering* all those aspects that can provide salient information about their sexual orientation (e.g., avoiding conversation about personal life, escaping from social events with colleagues). However, people can also decide to disclose their sexual orientation, being *explicitly out*, thus talking directly about it, or being *implicitly out*, thus sending information useful to deduce their sexual orientation (e.g., Griffin, 1992).

Research on disclosure strategies and sexual identity management models has been carried out mainly in Europe and the United States (e.g., Clair et al., 2005; Di Marco et al., 2017; Einarsdóttir et al., 2016). For this reason, one of the goals of this chapter is to identify how Ecuadorean LGB people manage their sexual orientation in the workplace, taking into account specific cultural features that might affect such processes.

Modern Sexual Prejudice

Sexual prejudice, which refers to negative attitudes against LGB people, still might be present even in societies where discrimination based on sexual orientation is illegal (Herek & McLemore, 2013). Such negative attitudes might be transmitted through behaviors that occur in the continuum of subtle to overt discrimination (Jones, Arena, Nittrouer, Alonso, & Lindsey, 2017). Discrimination might be expressed in more subtle ways in countries in which discrimination can produce negative responses at legal (e.g., a formal complaint to the authorities) or social (e.g., being rejected by one's ingroup) levels. When negative attitudes against a vulnerable group are not socially desirable, people might be less conscious of their behaviors and act in more subtle ways (e.g., avoiding contact; Jones et al., 2017). Therefore, people who want to maintain a progressive image might fall into *modern discrimination*, which refers to discriminatory acts characterized by ambiguity (Cortina, 2008). An example is *selective incivility*, which refers to rude behaviors for which the intention to harm is not clear (Cortina, 2008). When ambiguous and discriminatory attitudes are aimed at LGB people, this is conceptualized as *modern sexual prejudice* (Di Marco et al., 2018). Although modern and subtle discrimination might be harder to recognize, LGB people perceive subtle negative attitudes that could affect how they manage their sexual orientation at work. To our knowledge, there are no studies analyzing Ecuadorean heterosexual people's attitudes toward LGB coworkers.

LGB Workers and Minority Stress

People who identify with a minority group and hold a stigmatized identity might experience modern discrimination. Minority stress theory posits that minority status might expose those with this status to an excess of stress, producing negative effects on their health and well-being (Meyer, 1995, 2003). According to Meyer's (2003) minority stress theory, LGB people's stressors are on a continuum ranging from distal to proximal. Therefore, LGB people might experience objective (distal) stressors, such as discrimination, including violent and aggressive behaviors targeting LGB persons, or subjective (proximal) stressors, which refer to the individual perceptions and cognitive evaluation of stressors (Meyer, 2003). Examples of proximal stressors are expectations of discrimination, which lead LGB people to stay alert and monitor others' behaviors, internalization of negative attitudes against LGB people (internalized homophobia), and hiding one's sexual orientation (Chakrapani et al., 2017; Meyer, 2003). Counteracting minority stress is important due to its negative consequences on LGB people's health (Chakrapani et al., 2017; Meyer, 2003), including contributing to higher levels of depression and anxiety, lower levels of psychological well-being, and negative work-related outcomes.

In line with minority stress theory (Meyer, 2003), perceiving discrimination and hiding sexual orientation might be stressors with consequences for LGB people's well-being and health. This chapter examines the consequences both of hiding sexual orientation and of modern sexual prejudice on Ecuadorean LGB workers' well-being.

METHOD

Two qualitative studies were conducted to identify how Ecuadorean LGB workers manage their sexual orientation and to explore if modern sexual prejudice is present in the Ecuadorean workplaces, with a focus on the consequences for LGB individuals' well-being. Both studies were conducted in Loja, a city of almost 205,000 inhabitants in the south of Ecuador, between July 2015 and March 2016.

Study 1

The first study involved 15 in-depth semistructured interviews with Ecuadorean LGB workers recruited using a snowball sampling approach (Miles & Huberman, 1994). According to self-reports, seven lesbians, seven gay men, and one bisexual participated. Participants' mean age was 24.60 years (ages ranged from 20 to 37 years); all participants had a job at the time of the interview or had been working during the previous 6 months. Several work sectors were represented to obtain a wide range of experiences (e.g., education, banking, public sector). The interviews lasted between 40 and 90 minutes. The data collection continued until saturation was reached, that is, when new interviews did not generate any additional information (Morse, 2000).

Study 2

Six focus groups were conducted with 43 self-identified heterosexual workers (38 women and five men). Participants were recruited through collaboration with an Ecuadorean public institution that works on social and economic inclusion. The mean age was 34.70 years (ages ranged from 21 to 54 years). Discussions were stimulated through providing participants with three scenarios (Hoel, Lewis, & Einarsdóttir, 2014) that told the story of a lesbian, a gay man, and a bisexual woman, respectively. Scenarios were contextualized at work and represented several examples of modern sexual prejudice (e.g., jokes about LGB people, comments about style of dress, isolation, lack of promotion).

DATA ANALYSIS

Data from both studies were transcribed verbatim and analyzed using the software Atlas.ti 7. Template analysis (King, 2004), an approach that allows identifying codes a priori (before the analysis) and a posteriori (during and after the analysis), was implemented. Past research represents the beginning point for a priori codes. However, the flexibility of such a technique allows for elimination, modification, and addition of codes during and after the analysis. We adopted a social constructivist position (Madill, Jordan, & Shirley, 2000) that considers the role of both the researcher and the specific social context in determining the interpretation of the reality. The position adopted also invites reflection on the role of the researchers during the whole process. For instance, the researcher who carried out the interviews was a young woman from a European country. On one hand, this might have helped LGB participants to tell their story because Europe is perceived as advanced in terms of the acquisition of LGBT people's rights. Moreover, talking with a foreign interviewer might have encouraged participants to talk frankly. On the other hand, not sharing a common cultural background might have reduced the ability to understand and explore in depth those elements connected with the Ecuadorean culture.

All authors identified the a priori codes together based on the literature. For example, identity strategies identified by Griffin (1992) were included in the a priori template of interviews. Following this, each researcher analyzed the first interview independently to compare the results, and new codes emerged (e.g., culture, religion, negative acts). In most cases, authors agreed on the meaning of the codes identified, even if they had labeled them differently. The first author analyzed the remainder of the interviews; the research team maintained an open debate during the whole process. The same process was repeated for analyzing focus groups.

RESULTS AND DISCUSSION

During the interviews and the focus groups, several important themes were uncovered. Although interviews were useful in clarifying how people manage their sexual orientation at work and highlighted fears and general perceptions, the focus groups were useful for shedding light on subtle and overt negative attitudes still present in Ecuadorean society. In the following sections, preliminary results of both studies are presented, stressing cultural factors that might have influenced the results.

Sexual Identity Management

Our findings suggest that Ecuadorean LGB workers apply fewer disclosure strategies to manage their sexual orientation at the workplace in comparison with reports from U.S. and European research. A small number of LGB people said they were implicitly out at work. Therefore, they revealed their sexual orientation gradually or did so by existing outside of the heteronormative masculine image of men or feminine image of women. As observed in the following quotation, cultural expectations about masculine behaviors also play a role in the disclosure process: "I guess [they know] due to my behavior, because you know, gay people behave in a slightly different way to 'ordinary' people" (Santiago, gay, 28 years old).[2]

---

[2]The names and identities of the individuals represented as participants have been altered to preserve their confidentiality.

However, despite the legislative shift in favor of LGB people, most of the LGB workers reported that they do not feel safe when revealing their sexual orientation at work. For this reason, the covering strategy was most commonly applied, as articulated by the following participant: "I am ashamed that they [coworkers] might know or that they might think badly or that something very negative happened" (Gabriela, lesbian, 26 years old). Being afraid about potential negative consequences and having a sense of shame for losing her reputation in front of coworkers motivated this participant to not talk about her sexual orientation at work.

To avoid such negative consequences, LGB people attempt to escape from situations that necessitate talking about their personal life, partners, or activities in their leisure time. At the same time, LGB people avoid participating in social events in which colleagues' partners are also involved. As Lucio's story exemplified, people who apply this strategy feel that they are living a double life. Nevertheless, not disclosing sexual orientation does not prevent one from being asked uncomfortable questions, especially when not fulfilling expectations related to gender roles. As an example, one participant stated, "Sometimes I went to clients' houses to paint their nails. They stayed there with their sons and their husbands and they asked me 'Are you married?' 'I'm not.' 'So young and you are not married?'" (Ángeles, lesbian, 27 years old). In this way, traditional gender roles influence the disclosure process in Ecuador. Even if Ángeles had concealed her sexual orientation, she would still have had intrusive questions about her personal life due to gender roles (she should already be married), the presumption of heterosexuality, and the image she conveys (which is in line with the standards of femininity).

Although this finding is not different from the results of research carried out in European contexts (e.g., Losert, 2008), many Ecuadorean LGB people consider that covering their sexual orientation at work (and sometimes passing as heterosexual) is "normal." It is interesting to observe that even those people who think that their colleagues know about their sexual orientation do not talk about it openly. LGB people perceive that a strong boundary between their personal and work life exists that shapes the interactions with heterosexual coworkers. This information is confirmed in the focus group analysis, in which the idea that it is not appropriate to talk about sexual orientation at work is very common. As Debora, a 30-year-old heterosexual woman, explained, "It's not important for me to tell about my sexual orientation. . . . I came here to work. My sexual orientation is something I consider very private." According to Debora's narrative, (nonhetero)sexual orientation enters a private domain, as it is associated with a sexual sphere. Therefore, being LGB becomes a taboo issue that is not appropriate to talk about in a work context.

For people who wish to cover their sexual orientation at work, conveying an image that is not in line with the widespread expectations of masculinity or femininity is a potential "problem," as they may be recognized as LGB people. Some of the gay men who were interviewed talked about the need to modify and control their behavior to not be identified as gay. This feeling is shared by Carlos, a 24-year-old gay man who is aware of the stereotypical image that a man has to transmit to be considered masculine: "The rule of the game is that men shouldn't be very talkative or . . . dancers. It is due to prejudices, but since you know it, it is better to try to control yourself." During the interview, Carlos pointed out the role played by the size of the city where he lives. As stated previously, Loja is a small city, and social networks are very dense. Revealing sexual orientation in a specific context might entail a fast dissemination of rumors within the city. Many participants idealize the biggest cities in Ecuador, especially Quito and Guayaquil, where they believe they would experience greater invisibility and freedom. Ecuadorean gay men and lesbians experience the issue of visibility differently. In fact, being in line with normative feminine standards helps lesbians who want to cover their sexual orientation. Given the presumption of heterosexuality and cultural norms that tolerates closeness between women, lesbian couples may be seen as friends. This allows lesbians to pass if they do not want to disclose their sexual orientation, but at the same time, it reproduces the invisibility of lesbians at work and in society.

LGB participants perceive that lesbian and gay people are not afforded equal social acceptance. To some extent this depends on the degree of visibility that gay men and lesbians present in Ecuador. As a 20-year-old lesbian participant described, lesbians are accepted if they "dress as women" and conform to the established femininity rules. In line with LGB participants' perceptions, coworkers and society show more acceptance of lesbians than gay men. Lesbians are less recognizable, thus ignored. Moreover, even when lesbians are visible, the degree of "acceptance" is higher because they are seen as "sexual objects" by heterosexual men. However, heterosexual participants provided a contradictory perspective and reported that gay men are more accepted than lesbians because "people got used to them." During both studies, bisexuality was not discussed without prompting. The woman who defined as bisexual also did not focus on bisexuality, recognizing she does not identify herself with a specific LGBT group. In the focus groups, comments about bisexuality were stimulated by a scenario in which the protagonist was a bisexual woman. In general, for many heterosexual people, bisexuality does not exist. According to their comments, the protagonist "was confused" about being heterosexual or lesbian, demonstrating a lack of understanding of bisexuality. This, in turn, might present an obstacle toward the disclosure process of bisexual people at work.

Modern Sexual Prejudice

As previously discussed, most Ecuadorean LGB workers hide their sexual orientation at work. Although some described that it is not a necessity to integrate their sexual orientation at work, in many of the stories fear and the expectation of isolation, rejection, or losing their job emerged. Being uncertain about heterosexual coworkers' reactions was a topic often raised. To some extent, such doubts demonstrate that LGB workers perceive less direct discrimination than some years ago. However, they still feel that prejudice and stereotypes are present, as reported by Andrés, a 27-year-old gay man: "Before, people could aggressively attack [an LGB] person. Now people see [LGB people] and [if] they . . . say some negative comments, it is lighter." LGB participants recognize that discrimination has changed, possibly due to recent political and legislative shifts. However, jokes and negative comments are still present, and heterosexual people are not often able to recognize the discriminatory aspect of such acts. Thus, they still hold prejudices and negative stereotypes, as reflected in the following quote: "I'm not homophobic. I know LGBT people, but I have never maintained any type of friendly relationship with them, nor do I wish to do so" (Julián, heterosexual man, 39 years old).

Although some heterosexual people try to maintain a progressive image, the fear of being associated with LGB people and criticized by others contributes to distance and lack of awareness about LGB people (Herek & McLemore, 2013). Sometimes the idea of same-sex relationships as an "illness" appeared, as in the experience shared by Elisabeth, a 20-year-old lesbian participant: "I went to a psychologist, [and] they [my parents] kept me in rehabilitation, because [being lesbian] was seen as some kind of illness." In line with social perceptions in Ecuador, focus group participants described LGB people (especially gay men) as loud and promiscuous people who dress as women and wear makeup and high heels. They also described the behavior of visible LGB people as disrespectful and considered jokes and negative comments against LGB people as a consequence of their behaviors (and visibility). It is possible that LGB workers have internalized negative attitudes (internalized homophobia) toward "loud" or visible LGB people: Many of them talked about the need to "respect heterosexual people" as a basic condition to receive fair treatment. Such respect means distancing themselves from heterosexual people of the same sex and maintaining a low profile.

Modern sexual prejudice is quite evident when heterosexual participants explained discriminatory acts (e.g., not getting a promotion at work) by offering work-related justifications (e.g., if LGB workers do not get a job, it is because they are not good enough, or their self-esteem is low). Jokes, negative comments, rumors, and insults are negative acts experienced frequently by LGB workers. Taken together, these forms of (modern) sexual prejudice manifested in covert and overt discrimination are still present in Ecuadorean society.

Consequences on LGB People's Well-Being

Although minority stress theory (Meyer, 1995, 2003) was developed in North America, we believe that it is possible to apply it to the Ecuadorean context to explain factors associated with LGB individuals' well-being. According to

Meyer (1995, 2003), hiding sexual orientation, expecting discrimination, and internalizing homophobia are proximal stressors that, together with distal stressors such as past discriminatory experiences, can affect LGB people's health in terms of physical, psychological, and social well-being (World Health Organization, 2014). Therefore, it is reasonable to expect negative consequences for Ecuadorean LGB workers' well-being. However, exploring health consequences for LGB participants was challenging because generally interviewees tried to minimize the effects of negative acts, particularly regarding subtle discrimination, possibly as a coping strategy.

As we saw in Lucio's story at the beginning of the chapter, concealing sexual orientation at work and trying to lead a double life might produce adverse results. Concealment may affect LGB people's well-being negatively and increase depressive symptoms (Riggle, Rostosky, Black, & Rosenkrantz, 2017). Gloria, a 37-year-old lesbian participant who maintained a relationship with a man for a short time to quell rumors at work, described her affective state: "I felt bad because you try to lead a double life, you [try to be] somebody different." Not being authentic produces negative feelings because people do not feel that they are acting according to their "true self" (Riggle et al., 2017). "Feeling bad" for not being authentic might evolve into depression and perceived stress, as demonstrated in past research (Riggle et al., 2017). On the contrary, authenticity might foster self-esteem, satisfaction, and well-being (Wood, Linley, Maltby, Baliousis, & Joseph, 2008).

Ecuadorean LGB people who concealed their sexual orientation perceived that they were wasting energy because of the need to invent and maintain their second life. Anxiety about being discovered and anger for not showing their real self were also widespread among the Ecuadorean LGB participants. As a participant stated,

> For me it's horrible because people think that you're alone and you're not. . . . People don't know how one suffers every day, it's a trauma that you have to fight every day. And when you're older the trauma is still there. . . . With my supervisors [I think] "Oh my God, will I say something that I don't have to say? If I do will they fire me?" This pressure is always there. (Carlos, gay, 24 years old)

The dilemma between being consistent with their true self and the fear of discrimination following disclosure creates tension in Ecuadorean LGB people's daily life. The expectation of discrimination is related to fear and uncertainty. Some believed that they might be fired for disclosing their sexual orientation. But when a researcher asked about the consequences of such expectations on well-being, LGB people minimized the impacts. It is worth noting that subtle discrimination is quite normalized by LGB people in Ecuador, who perceive jokes and negative comments as part of workplace dynamics. Perhaps the recent recognition of LGBT rights has reduced overt and stronger forms of discrimination. Thus, jokes and negative comments, although not welcomed, might be interpreted as a "minor problem."

Witnessing or experiencing discrimination also produces negative effects. LGB workers tried to minimize the effect of discrimination, yet heterosexuals discussed cases in which rejection led to suicide. In many cases, heterosexuals blamed low self-esteem among LGB people for an inability to cope with external stressors. In other cases, by considering LGB people as people who "talk about sexual orientation in a non-appropriate context" and considering their behaviors as "too loud," heterosexual participants projected the problem onto LGB people, not taking into account the role played by heterosexual individuals' stigma.

CONCLUSION

The aim of this chapter was to understand how Ecuadorean LGB people manage their sexual orientation at work. We also explored the flip side of the coin by examining the attitudes of heterosexual workers toward LGB workers. Data presented in this chapter suggest that, on the whole, Ecuadorean LGB people conceal their sexual orientation at work because of the perception of potentially risky and discriminatory coworkers' reactions. At several points, cultural factors tied to the culture of honor (e.g., masculinity, gender roles) and connected to heteronormative beliefs were presented to explain rejection by heterosexual coworkers. Findings align with the minority stress theory (Meyer, 1995, 2003). In Ecuadorean workplaces, LGB people perceive distal and proximal stressors that decrease their psychological well-being. Focus groups confirmed the presence of such stressors and the existence of negative attitudes among heterosexuals.

Organizations can stimulate a positive change for the inclusion of LGB people by promoting an organizational culture that bans every form of discrimination (Di Marco et al., 2018). According to LGB participants, the main organizational problem is the lack of awareness about LGB people. Gaining more visibility with the support of supervisors might help to create a climate of trust in which LGB people could feel free to manage their sexual orientation (Di Marco et al., 2017). The involvement of supervisors is also essential in trying to overcome and challenge unconscious biases (Di Marco et al., 2017). Caring about LGB workers' well-being and health has positive outcomes for people and organizations: LGB workers who are not afraid of disclosing their sexual orientation are more motivated and satisfied, and teamwork improves along with relationships with coworkers (Ragins, 2004).

Minority (proximal and distal) stressors in the Ecuadorean context, modern sexual prejudice, and specific cultural features should be considered by health professionals when they work with LGB people. Primarily, any professional should take into account potential therapeutic biases (Pachankis & Goldfried, 2013). Those cultural elements that affect LGB daily experiences might be shared by those therapists who grew up in the same culture: Traditional gender roles, religious beliefs, masculinity norms, and heteronormativity might affect the relationship between the LGB client and the therapist. This might lead to treating sexual orientation as an aspect to overcome, or to adopt an approach that blames clients' sexual orientation instead of recognizing the damage that the heteronormative society is causing (Pachankis & Goldfried, 2013). The feeling of living a double life and not being authentic could produce anxiety, shame, and guilt. Therapists should be able to recognize when homophobia has been internalized to help in shaping a positive image of an LGB person's self and identity.

REFERENCES

Chakrapani, V., Vijin, P. P., Logie, C. H., Newman, P. A., Shunmugam, M., Sivasubramanian, M., & Samuel, M. (2017). Understanding how sexual and gender minority stigmas influence depression among trans women and men who have sex with men in India. *LGBT Health, 4*, 217–226. http://dx.doi.org/10.1089/lgbt.2016.0082

Clair, J. A., Beatty, J. E., & MacLean, T. L. (2005). Out of sight but not out of mind: Managing invisible social identities in the workplace. *Academy of Management Review, 30*, 78–95. http://dx.doi.org/10.5465/amr.2005.15281431

Cortina, L. M. (2008). Unseen injustice: Incivility as modern discrimination in organizations. *Academy of Management Review, 33*, 55–75. http://dx.doi.org/10.5465/amr.2008.27745097

Cromptone, L. (2003). *Homosexuality and civilization*. Cambridge, MA: Harvard University Press.

Day, S. D. (2005). *Sexual orientation and human rights: The use of human rights law to address sexual orientation-based discrimination and violence in Ecuador* (Unpublished master's thesis). University of Florida, Gainesville.

Deschamps, M. (2017, June 1). *Private clinics in Ecuador exposed as gay 'conversion clinics.'* Available from https://www.telesurenglish.net/opinion/Private-Clinics-in-Ecuador-Exposed-as-Gay-Conversion-Clinics-20170601-0027.html

Dietrich, D. M., & Schuett, J. M. (2013). Culture of honor and attitudes toward intimate partner violence in Latinos. *SAGE Open, 3*(2). http://dx.doi.org/10.1177/2158244013489685

Di Marco, D., Hoel, H., Arenas, A., & Munduate, L. (2018). Workplace incivility as modern sexual prejudice. *Journal of Interpersonal Violence, 33*, 1978–2004. http://dx.doi.org/10.1177/0886260515621083

Di Marco, D., Munduate, L., Arenas, A., & Hoel, H. (2017). *Quién queda en el armario? La experiencia de personas gais y lesbianas en el trabajo* [Who is in the closet? The experience of gay and lesbian people at work]. Madrid, Spain: Ediciones Pirámide.

Ecuadorean Constitution. (2008, October 20). Official Diary n. 449. Quito, Ecuador.

Einarsdóttir, A., Hoel, H., & Lewis, D. (2016). Fitting the bill: Disclosure and embodiment. *Work, Employment and Society, 30*, 489–505. http://dx.doi.org/10.1177/0950017014568136

Goffman, E. (1963). *Stigma: Notes on the management of spoiled identity*. Englewood Cliffs, NJ: Prentice-Hall.

Griffin, P. (1992). From hiding out to coming out: Empowering lesbian and gay educators. In K. M. Harbeck (Ed.), *Coming out of the classroom closet* (pp. 167–196). Binghamton, NY: Harrington Park Press.

Griffith, K. H., & Hebl, M. R. (2002). The disclosure dilemma for gay men and lesbians: "coming out" at work. *Journal of Applied Psychology, 87*, 1191–1199. http://dx.doi.org/10.1037/0021-9010.87.6.1191

Herek, G. M., & McLemore, K. A. (2013). Sexual prejudice. *Annual Review of Psychology, 64*, 309–333. http://dx.doi.org/10.1146/annurev-psych-113011-143826

Hoel, H., Lewis, D., & Einarsdóttir, A. (2014). *The ups and downs of LGBs' workplace experiences*. Manchester, England: Manchester Business School.

Hofstede, G., Hofstede, G. J., & Minkov, M. (2010). *Cultures and organizations: Software of the mind revised and expanded* (3rd ed.). New York, NY: McGraw-Hill USA.

Instituto Nacional De Estadísticas Y Censos. (2013). *Estudio de caso sobre condiciones de vida, inclusión social y cumplimiento de derechos humanos de la población LGBTI en el Ecuador* [Case study on living conditions, social inclusion and compliance with human rights of the LGBTI population in Ecuador]. Quito, Ecuador: Author.

Jones, K. P., Arena, D., Nittrouer, C. L., Alonso, N. M., & Lindsey, A. P. (2017). Subtle discrimination in the workplace: A vicious cycle. *Industrial and Organizational Psychology: Perspectives on Science and Practice, 10*, 51–76. http://dx.doi.org/10.1017/iop.2016.91

King, N. (2004). Using templates in thematic analysis of text. In C. Cassell & G. Symon (Eds.), *Essential guide to qualitative methods in organizational research* (pp. 256–270). London, England: Sage. http://dx.doi.org/10.4135/9781446280119.n21

Kurian, G. T. (2011). Ecuadorian Christianity. In G. T. Kurian (Ed.), *The encyclopedia of Christian civilization* (pp. 787–801). Malden, MA: Blackwell. http://dx.doi.org/10.1002/9780470670606.wbecc0473

Labor Code. (2015, April 20). Official Diary n. 167. Quito, Ecuador.

Losert, A. (2008). Coping with workplace heteronormativity among lesbian employees: A German study. *Journal of Lesbian Studies, 12*, 47–58. http://dx.doi.org/10.1300/10894160802174300

Luyten, C., Corveleyn, J., & Fontaine, J. R. J. (1998). The relationship between religiosity and mental health: Distinguishing between shame and guilt. *Mental Health, Religion & Culture, 1*, 165–184. http://dx.doi.org/10.1080/13674679808406507

Madill, A., Jordan, A., & Shirley, C. (2000). Objectivity and reliability in qualitative analysis: Realist, contextualist and radical constructionist epistemologies. *British Journal of Psychology, 91*, 1–20. http://dx.doi.org/10.1348/000712600161646

McGivern, M. (2012). Encountering culture through gender norms in international education: The case of volunteers in Ecuador. *Research in Comparative and International Education, 7*, 105–114. http://dx.doi.org/10.2304/rcie.2012.7.1.105

Mealy, M., Stephan, W. G., & Abalakina-Paap, M. (2006). Reverence for mothers in Ecuadorean and Euro-American culture. *Journal of Cross-Cultural Psychology, 37*, 465–484. http://dx.doi.org/10.1177/0022022106288481

Meyer, I. H. (1995). Minority stress and mental health in gay men. *Journal of Health and Social Behavior, 36*, 38–56. http://dx.doi.org/10.2307/2137286

Meyer, I. H. (2003). Prejudice, social stress, and mental health in lesbian, gay, and bisexual populations: Conceptual issues and research evidence. *Psychological Bulletin, 129*, 674–697. http://dx.doi.org/10.1037/0033-2909.129.5.674

Miles, M. B., & Huberman, A. M. (1994). *Qualitative data analysis* (2nd ed.). Thousand Oaks, CA: Sage.

Morse, J. M. (2000). Determining sample size. *Qualitative Health Research, 10*, 3–5.

Pachankis, J. E., & Goldfried, M. R. (2013). Clinical issues in working with lesbian, gay, and bisexual clients. *Psychology of Sexual Orientation and Gender Diversity, 1*(S), 45–58.

Ragins, B. R. (2004). Sexual orientation in the workplace: The unique work and career experiences of gay, lesbian and bisexual workers. *Research in Personnel and Human Resources Management, 23*, 35–120. http://dx.doi.org/10.1016/S0742-7301(04)23002-X

Ragins, B. R. (2008). Disclosure disconnects: Antecedents and consequences of disclosing invisible stigmas across life domains. *Academy of Management Review, 33*, 194–215. http://dx.doi.org/10.5465/amr.2008.27752724

Riggle, E. D. B., Rostosky, S. S., Black, W. W., & Rosenkrantz, D. E. (2017). Outness, concealment, and authenticity: Associations with LGB individuals' psychological distress and well-being. *Psychology of Sexual Orientation and Gender Diversity, 4*, 54–62. http://dx.doi.org/10.1037/sgd0000202

Rodriguez Mosquera, P. M., Manstead, A. S. R., & Fischer, A. H. (2002). The role of honour concerns in emotional reactions to offences. *Cognition and Emotion, 16,* 143–163. http://dx.doi.org/10.1080/02699930143000167

Wood, A. M., Linley, P. A., Maltby, J., Baliousis, M., & Joseph, S. (2008). The authentic personality: A theoretical and empirical conceptualization and the development of the authenticity scale. *Journal of Counseling Psychology, 55,* 385–399. http://dx.doi.org/10.1037/0022-0167.55.3.385

World Health Organization. (2014). *Basic documents* (48th ed.). Geneva, Switzerland: Author.

Worthen, M. G. F. (2013). An argument for separate analysis of attitude toward lesbian, gay, bisexual men, bisexual women, MtF and FtM transgender individuals. *Sex Roles, 68,* 703–723. http://dx.doi.org/10.1007/s11199-012-0155-1

4

"It's Because of Our Culture"

Navigating Gender Norms and Coping With Sexual Stigma Among Lesbian, Bisexual, and Queer Women in Jamaica

Natania L. Marcus, Carmen H. Logie, Nicolette Jones, Nicolette Bryan, and Kandasi Levermore

The following is an amalgamation of quotes from a number of participants in our study that represents a typical story of Jamaican lesbian, bisexual, and queer young women in our study.

> When I was younger it was really hard; I didn't know what it meant to be gay in high school, but I was bullied a lot all throughout high school until a few months or shortly before I graduated, and even when I went to college I was still bullied. My family is increasingly homophobic, as in everyday it gets worse. So, at home it was a very difficult environment to be in. At church, well I go to church when I go home to visit my family and I sing and read the Bible and teach the kids and wear the dress, comb my hair, and everything so they don't really know [that I'm gay]. And yes, people might think it's wrong for me to pretend to be a Christian, but you have to understand that you have to make your family happy to the extent where they feel comfortable enough to want to be around you. Discrimination is a part of being a lesbian overall. It comes with it, and we have to learn to deal with it. It's because of our culture and how it has been for a long time. For me, access to opportunities is not a levelled [*sic*] playing field. Based on how I dress, people look down on me. So, if there is an opportunity, they will give the job to someone else who dresses more feminine. Most of the times, I wish I could express myself freely. It limits me in what I do, where I go and how I behave. I am scared of sharing my life story with people that I don't know . . . and many other things. But I just encourage myself because I know why I am like this. I love myself and I love my orientation. I just love myself. Other people are unhappy and that's why they are picking on me.

Pervasive stigma, family rejection, and socially sanctioned violence from the community and police targeting lesbian, gay, bisexual, and transgender

http://dx.doi.org/10.1037/0000159-005
LGBTQ Mental Health: International Perspectives and Experiences, N. Nakamura and C. H. Logie (Editors)

(LGBT) persons are reported in Jamaica (Logie, Lacombe-Duncan, et al., 2018). Jamaica is one of 72 countries in which same-sex practices are criminalized, and this law is used to justify state and socially sanctioned violence and discrimination against LGBT individuals, irrespective of specific sexual practices (Carroll, 2016). Many historians, lawyers and postcolonial theorists have traced pervasive sexual stigma back to British colonialism and plantation slavery (Campbell, 2005; LaFont, 2001; Lovell, 2016; Tielman & Hammelburg, 1993). The British, who colonized and controlled the island from the early 18th century until 1962 (Smith & Kosobucki, 2011), imported both Christian homophobic theology and strict Victorian sexual mores (Campbell, 2005; Lovell, 2016). According to LaFont (2001), many Jamaicans who were brought to the island as slaves accepted Christianity as a means of salvation and preservation, a necessary support and belief system during slavery. After the British abolished slavery in 1833, Christian and Victorian values translated into the criminalization of "buggery" (i.e., anal intercourse) as a way of targeting nonprocreative sexual practices (Human Rights Watch, 2014; Lovell, 2016). Even though analyses linking all Jamaican laws, values, and norms to colonial power may risk undermining the agency in Jamaican communities, it remains important to examine Jamaican society through a postcolonial lens. As one lesbian study participant articulated, "We live in a generation where slavery is abolished for race, but slavery is now in our sexual orientation."

Sexual stigma—social and structural processes of devaluation, mistreatment, and constrained power and opportunities of sexual minorities (Herek, 2007)—can be further broken down into *perceived stigma*, the awareness and fear of negative attitudes and norms, and *enacted stigma*, acts of violence, mistreatment, or discrimination (Herek, Gillis, & Cogan, 2009). Stress resulting from both forms of sexual stigma contributes to mental health disparities among LGBT populations (Hatzenbuehler, Phelan, & Link, 2013; Meyer, 2003). A systematic review of 199 studies found that LGBT individuals are at elevated risk of many mental health challenges, including depression, anxiety, suicide, and substance use (Plöderl & Tremblay, 2015). Yet the vast majority of these studies were conducted in North America. Less is known about the impacts of stigma on mental health among LGBT individuals in Jamaica. Preliminary cross-sectional research in Jamaica revealed that sexual stigma is associated with negative mental health outcomes (Logie, Wang, et al., 2018), sex work involvement (Logie et al., 2017), decreased social support, and sexual health disparities (Logie, Wang, et al., 2018) among gay and bisexual men and transgender women. Findings from a qualitative study with LGBT young persons in Kingston, Jamaica, indicated multiple types of violence experienced across social ecological sites (e.g., family, employment, health care), which contributed to social isolation and poor mental health and to lower health-related quality of life. Lesbian, bisexual, and queer (LBQ) women in Jamaica face pervasive, and at times life-threatening, stigma (West & Cowell, 2015). Yet little is known about the cultural, community, and well-being impacts of experiences of stigma and discrimination among LBQ women in Jamaica. This chapter focuses on the experiences of LBQ women in Jamaica.

METHODS

LBQ women were recruited for in-depth semistructured interviews in Kingston, Jamaica. We collaborated with Jamaica AIDS Support for Life, a national community-based AIDS service organization in Jamaica, in study design, data collection, analysis and interpretation, and manuscript preparation. Self-identified lesbian and bisexual women were hired as peer research assistants (PRAs). PRAs contributed to the interview guide, participant recruitment, and data collection. For the qualitative interviews, the PRA identified participants through her social networks and advertised the study by word of mouth at LGBT and/or HIV community services. Inclusion criteria were as follows: 18 to 29 years of age; self-identification as lesbian, bisexual, or queer; current residence in Jamaica; and ability to provide informed consent. Participants who met the inclusion criteria were invited to participate in a 60-minute individual interview in Kingston, Jamaica. Individual interview questions were semistructured, open-ended, and developed in collaboration with Jamaican-based community agencies. Interview guides included questions about typical experiences of lesbian/bisexual women in Jamaica. For instance, participants were asked, "Can you describe some common experiences that lesbian youth face here in Jamaica?" and "What are some ways that lesbians resist the challenges of being gay?" Participants were provided with USD$15 for their time and to cover the cost of transportation. Research ethics approval was granted from the University of Toronto, Canada, and the University of the West Indies, Mona Campus, Jamaica.

Individual interviews were recorded and transcribed verbatim. The transcriptionist provided interpretations of Jamaican patois dialect that was verified by the research coordinator. Personal identifying information was removed from all transcripts. Study participants are identified using the acronyms W01 to W18 for the purposes of anonymity. Conventional content analysis, which is used "with a study whose aim is to describe a phenomenon" (Hsieh & Shannon, 2005, p. 1279), allowing the categories and names for the categories to flow from the data. Each segment of text was in turn assigned a label or "code." As the analysis progressed, and new categories were identified, each segment of text was reanalyzed to determine if it fit within the new category, as it was possible to have multiple codes occur within a given segment of text.

RESULTS

Qualitative interview participants' ($n = 20$) mean age was 23.4 years ($SD = 3.42$, range = 19–28), and most participants ($n = 16$; 80%) identified as lesbian, followed by bisexual ($n = 3$; 15%) and other sexualities ($n = 1$; 5%). A focus group (FG) was conducted with five women who identified as LBQ. For the FG, the mean participant age was 23.8 years (*SD* = 3.0, range = 18–29). The majority of participants (80%) reported that they are lesbian, and 20% reported that they are bisexual. Interviews and the FG both took place in Kingston, Jamaica.

Data were collected between February and October 2014. Overarching themes included (a) hegemonic gender norms and stereotypes; (b) stigma, discrimination, and minority stress; (c) sources of discrimination; (d) emotional and behavioral impacts of discrimination; (e) navigating outness; (f) coping, strength, and resiliency; and (g) need for services.

Hegemonic Gender Norms and Stereotypes

When FG participants were asked what it means to be a woman in Jamaica, the majority responded by describing stereotypical and patriarchal ideals that centered on physical appearance, housework, and child-rearing. Common responses describing expectations for women in Jamaica included "having a child; wearing false nails; false hair; knowing how to cook," "damsels in distress," "dependent," "pretty," "taking care of the kids," "curls and heels," "staying at home, being a housewife," and "make sure the house is clean and when they come home, food is on the table." One participant challenged these narratives by stating,

> being strong, being independent, having a mind of your own, of course boobs and ass and looking sexy, but . . . being a woman is being what you want to be; so if you want to do construction work it shouldn't matter; that is how you perceive yourself. . . . I don't care about society. (FG participant)

Other participants stressed the rigidity of gender norms. For instance, a participant explained how any characteristics or behaviors typical for women should not be exhibited by men: *"man cya do dem supm dere* [men cannot do those things]" (FG participant). Some women in the FG who did not conform to gender norms positioned themselves as "not female" based on the gender role expectations for women within Jamaican society. The FG participants also described never being exposed to "masculine women" growing up, indicating a lack of representation and visibility of women who do not conform to highly feminine gender norms. Overall, participants described unyielding and pervasive gender norms that prescribe how to be a "proper" man or woman in Jamaican society.

Gender Norms Within the Lesbian Community

Participants also described how gender expression impacted experiences of discrimination within and outside the lesbian community. Differences in enacted stigma against "butch" (gender-nonconforming women) and "femme" (gender-conforming women) couples were frequently articulated. The majority of participants stated that two femme women experience less discrimination compared with butch and femme couples: "If it's two femmes, they can do whatever . . . but I know it couldn't have happened if one of them was a stud [gender-nonconforming woman], because they would say they don't want to see that *batty man ting* [gay behavior]" (FG participant). Multiple FG participants seemed averse to the idea of two butch women dating, as this pairing represented excessive gayness or gender nonconformity. For example, participants stated that "two femmes is okay; but two studs or butches is kinda too much" and that "two butches would be extra gay." Some participants articulated the privilege of invisibility that femme women have, as others are unable to perceive their sexual orientation. For example,

> I think that lipstick lesbians, those that like to dress up and be girly, have it better because no one will automatically think that they are a lesbian. If you are dressed up in guy clothing and wearing a cap, people will say that you are a lesbian. When they know that you are a lesbian, it is different. (W13)

However, one participant expressed the opposite sentiment, noting how others may respond with alarm, confusion, and judgment when feminine-presenting women disclose their sexual orientation:

> If you don't appear to be a gay person but identify as that it is harder than if you just look gay; if you look that way it is easier for people to wrap their head around it. [Otherwise] it confuses them and they are much harsher, and their comments are meaner; people tend to attack not just your [sexual] identity but your personality and you as a person. (FG participant)

Although many participants described a relationship between gender nonconformity and discrimination, this quote reveals that feminine-presenting LBQ women may also face challenges related to sexual identity disclosure.

Stigma, Discrimination, and Minority Stress

LBQ women in our sample described pervasive experiences of stigma and discrimination and resulting minority stress. Stigma and discrimination ranged from verbal and physical harassment to more insidious forms of institutional stigma, such as school, church, and workplace discrimination. LBQ women in our sample described a range of emotional impacts of stigma and discrimination that were consistent with minority stress.

Enacted Stigma

LBQ women living in Jamaica described experiencing overwhelming sexual minority stigma at the community level, often in the form of enacted stigma. Of the women who participated in individual interviews, the vast majority described experiencing enacted sexual minority stigma on a daily basis. For example, "everyday. They say we are abnormal" (W02) and "almost every day. People will say, 'you're not normal, something is wrong with you'" (W18). Participants also described frequently experiencing other verbal harassment based on their sexual orientation, including name-calling: "People call you names like sodomite, and faggot and *batty gyal* [derogatory term for lesbian]"

(FG participant). Another participant describes how she experiences violent threats: "They will curse and call me sodomite gal, and say that they should rape me. All sorts of things" (W11).

Participants also described how verbal harassment was frequently sexual in nature; for example, "Some people think you're a slut if you're a lesbian. People have said that to me, that I'm a slut that's why I am a lesbian" (FG participant). Another participant described how sexual harassment from men can be motivated by the desire to "turn" queer women straight:

> Before you use to hear a lot about women getting raped. I mean I've had a lot of guys trying to sex me straight. Like two days ago I had to block this dude from WhatsApp, and he started texting me—"*Yuh know seh if yuh gimme di chance you wouldn't want back nuh more ooman*" [You know if you gave me the chance (to have sex with you) you wouldn't want women anymore]. And I was like, I wasn't always gay though I know what sex with a man is like and he said "*yuh jus neva did a get it good jus gimme the chance*" [You just weren't getting it good enough, just give me the chance]. [laughter] . . . Every guy I meet who tries to hit on me and finds out that I am gay wants to try to sex me straight. (FG participant)

Physical violence based on sexual orientation was also frequently described:

> You hear of a woman walking home who gets raped and killed because she is a lesbian. Two girls were walking into a place, celebrating some great achievement, probably gyrating in some way, and you hear of them getting shot up just because they were too close. (W18)

Similarly, "When I walk on the road, people say things, people *buss blanks* [shoot an unloaded gun in order to threaten], throw stones and many other things" (W02). One woman sums up the experience of discrimination and violence against LBQ in Jamaica:

> We face a lot of criticism; we face a lot of stress. We also face a lot of discrimination. Like, if they see us, they would just start cussing us. They will pick on us and we haven't done anything to them. We face a lot of brutality; people abuse us. (W08)

Participants described an alarming amount of enacted stigma in the form of verbal harassment, threats, and physical violence in public realms, frequently from strangers. The following section outlines more specific sources of discrimination described by Jamaican LBQ women.

Sources of Discrimination: Who Discriminates and How?

LBQ women in our sample described experiencing discrimination and stigma from multiple sources. Although some participants recounted their experiences, others tried to explain how common ideologies in Jamaica, such as hegemonic masculinity and Christianity, shape heterosexist beliefs. Participants' descriptions of their experiences of family rejection and discrimination were particularly common and emotionally charged.

Hegemonic Masculinity and Discrimination

When participants were prompted as to who instigates the harassment and violence, responses were similar, with the vast majority of women stating that men are the aggressors of homophobic violence. For example, one participant stated that "males are often the aggressors, especially if they are approaching the female and she doesn't respond in a way that they would like. It usually starts as a verbal attack and usually escalates to more than that" (W17). Some women indicated that the male ego incited homophobic violence and discrimination: "Some people have a problem, mostly males, because they know they can't get a certain female, and most females look good. So, the male ego is hurt" (W12). Similarly, "most times there is a male in there. Like I said, it's about male insecurity" (W18). These participants almost unanimously stated that men initiate violence as a result of LBQ women threatening their own masculinity, which is explored further in the Discussion section.

Structural Discrimination: Schools and Workplaces

At the structural level, sexual minority stigma was described across various institutions. Many participants told of experiencing discrimination beginning in grade school and extending into the workplace. One participant described being denied accolades in high school because of her sexual orientation:

> When I was in Grade 7, my teachers would tell me that I am a good student, that I would make the prefect body. In Grade 10 they were giving me the prefect badge and on the day when I was supposed to go in the devotion and collect it, the principal called me in her office and told me that I would not get it because no lesbian will be a prefect in her school. (W19)

Multiple participants described how the school system is especially homophobic and how this can impact choice of profession, opportunity, and ability to be "out" in the workplace:

> It influences the jobs that we choose. As a female, you could get away with being a gay police, but there are some occupations that you may have a problem with. Teaching, for example. As a teacher, you can't tell others that you teach and you are gay. You have influence on students and people believe that students are going to look up to you and emulate you. If a parent hears that a lesbian teacher is teaching her child, they will move them to another school. (FG participant)

Echoing the sentiment of the previous quote, another participant articulated how employers fear sexual orientation "contagion," deterring them from hiring LBQ/LGBT individuals: "In some cases, if people recognize your sexual orientation, they won't hire you. They will feel that you want to bring your sexual orientation unto others in the workplace" (W04). Many participants described losing their jobs because of others discovering their sexual orientation, revealing inequities and a lack of employee protections against harassment and for job security.

> I had a job driving a truck for a company, and unfortunately, I had to leave. I reapplied for the job and later on found out that the owner said that he didn't want "them sort of people in his workplace." So no gays and lesbians. (W06)

One participant articulated how she experienced decreased access to employment based on her appearance, which violated traditional gender norms:

"For me, access to opportunities is not a levelled [*sic*] playing field. Based on how I dress, people look down on me. So, if there is an opportunity, they will give the job to someone else who dresses more feminine" (W01). Participant descriptions reveal the economic cost of their sexual identities through loss of recognition, job opportunities, and employment.

Discrimination, Christianity, and the Church

Participants in both the FG and the interviews overwhelmingly described the church as a source of discrimination. One woman described the structural influence of the church: "Because Jamaica is so set between . . . church and the state . . . here we don't really have the separation between church and state we just kinda have church" (W03). Similarly,

> They see it as taboo. It comes from way, way back where it is not right; it's against God's will. Here in Jamaica, Christians are deeply rooted in Christianity, or they think they are. So, they will forever bash it. They may think of it as an experiment, or something that's not real, or an illness. So, they don't like it. (W09)

Women mentioned how verbal harassment and discrimination was frequently colored with biblical references, such as "People say you're a sinner" (FG participant). Many participants also described the biblical origins of heterosexism:

PARTICIPANT: They say that the Bible says that woman and woman and men and men [*sic*] that lay together will burn. . . . God didn't make Eve and Eve.

INTERVIEWER: So you think that it's religion why you are given a hard time?

PARTICIPANT: Yes. (W08)

Some participants' answers revealed conflicting sentiments about believing in God and wanting to go to church while fearing that discrimination by churchgoers and by God: "People say we should burn up in hell's fire and things like that. I want to go to church but I am afraid to because of the discrimination" (W07). Similarly, "I feel bad, I feel ignorant, I feel left out, I feel like I am not God's child. I just feel like I am on another level, not in this book, here" (W02). Women's narratives revealed complex conundrums regarding their relationships to God and Christianity, as they frequently connected heterosexist and homophobic societal perspectives to the church.

Family Discrimination

Participants described experiencing interpersonal stigma based on their sexual orientation, which manifested most frequently in familial settings. One participant stated she would change her sexual orientation to please her family: "I would change it because of my mother and my family. I have tried not to be who I am because of them and because I am pressured into not being that type of person" (W12). Sexual minority stigma within familial settings also led to ostracism for some participants: "A lot [of children] keep [sexual orientation] a secret because of what they think they will say. A lot of parents cut off their children because of their sexual orientation" (W14). One participant described how she perceives that her experience of homophobia in the family has gotten worse, which reflected increasingly intolerant attitudes in society:

> My family is increasingly homophobic, as in everyday it gets worse. When I was a kid it was like "yeah gay people moving on" now it is like "kill all *batty man dem*" [derogatory term for gay men]. I'm not really out to my family, but they might know, they might suspect. Every now and again my mom brings up the conversation, asking "are you gay"? And I ask why do you care, is it important? She cries and then I hang up and we don't speak for like a week. (FG participant)

Another participant poignantly described the emotional impact of her mother's rejection: "[The worst was] the time when my Mommy just found out. I felt that the world had sunk, because she didn't like it at first, she wasn't into it, she didn't accept it. That was the worst feeling" (W02). Descriptions of family discrimination and rejection were laden with emotions as participants described internalized homophobia and negative affect as a result of family attitudes. The following section elaborates the psychological impact of continued discrimination.

Emotional and Behavioral Impacts of Discrimination

When LBQ women were asked for their feelings about stigma and discrimination, many described experiencing a range of negative emotions. Fear, anger, and sadness were common. For example, "I generally feel an adrenaline rush. We want to fit in, not stand out. I feel sad and depressed at times" (W20). Similarly,

> I generally have mixed feelings [about discrimination that LGBT people face in Jamaica]. If I should examine how I feel, it's mostly anger. There is also a bit of disgust and I also feel some amount of pity and sympathy on what I consider to be a narrow-minded view of life that facilitates this kind of behavior towards gays, lesbians, bisexuals and transgender people. (W17)

Participants also described how perceived stigma can restrict their behavior, such as the ability to freely express love to another woman:

> Most of the times [*sic*], I wish I could express myself freely. It limits me in what I do, where I go and how I behave. It would not be like the typical attraction an adolescent feels towards a person; I can't display certain behaviors. (W20)

Another participant described how frequently enacted stigma leads to expectation for rejection. She articulated a self-protective, reciprocal process of adapting her behavior based on her perception of the person with whom she interacts:

> It's all about how they [the larger society] treat us. If they treat us a certain way, we will behave and react in a certain way. We tend to pull away or draw closer based on their behaviour. How they react to our personality influences us a lot . . . the things that these people say turns you off and so you get reserved. You will just look at their behaviour and just listen. (W12)

Another participant described how discrimination can lead to avoidance of support structures:

> For one, we shy away from most things that we are to participate in and it's because we are scared of what might happen. For example, some things are being kept in my community and I would like to participate, but when you know how they are going to deal with me, I just don't bother. (W07)

For some participants, the inability to cope with the constant stigma led to depression:

> Sometimes I feel "a way." My face is made up. I feel bad because I am in that category too. So, when I hear them "licking out" [speaking badly] and chatting about lesbians and *batty man* [gay men], I take my time and get out. I don't let people see that I am depressed, but they can still tell. I don't cope with it well. I feel down, depressed, stressed out. (W08)

A few participants described that LGBT persons in Jamaica may engage in substance use to cope:

> INTERVIEWER: What are some of the ways that lesbian youths resist the challenges faced by them in society? What do they do when faced with discrimination?
>
> PARTICIPANT: I think that's where drugs come in. I think they take up smoking and alcohol. (W06)

The psychological impact of discrimination that many women described was indicative of minority stress. LBQ women not only described experiencing negative emotions but also articulated a process wherein societal attitudes shape personality and behavioral coping such as avoidance, isolation, and substance use.

Navigating Outness: Staying in the Closet for Self-Protection

When participants spoke about their experiences with homophobia and discrimination and were asked to give advice to lesbian youth, many participants mentioned the self-protective function of staying "in the closet." For example, "Keeping something like that [your sexual orientation] from people isn't always the worst idea; it's just something to protect yourself" (W03). Another participant advised that youth who live with homophobic family members gain economic stability before coming out:

> Choose your battles wisely; for example, you are in a situation where you live in the country or an area that is very homophobic . . . you wouldn't walk up and down and say oh I am a lesbian or gay. Or for example if you are living with family or you have nowhere else to go and they are very homophobic . . . you will end up homeless; so wait until you are able to support yourself before declaring your status; then you can say oh, I am gay; but you would have another outlet. (FG participant)

Many participants described developing a balance of freedom to express themselves and monitoring their behavior to avoid violence:

You know the society that you are in. Don't put yourself out there so that certain things happen to you. You can express yourself in ways that are not outrageous. We want freedom, just to be ourselves, a bit of peace, no war, but at the same time, you can't push it. (W18)

These narratives reveal another contradiction that LBQ women must navigate: hiding their identities to stay safe and freedom of self-expression.

Coping, Strength, and Resiliency: Self-Acceptance and Community Support

Intrapersonally, self-acceptance based on sexual orientation was cited by many of the women as an adaptive way of coping with sexual minority stigma. Responses such as "I would not change. I love being a lesbian" (W14) and "For one, accept yourself. Once you accept yourself, a lot of the waste and burden of having to deal with everybody else and the dictator society has been lifted" (W17) were common. Participants were asked for advice they would give to lesbian youth in Jamaica, and their advice focused on fostering self-love and not internalizing antigay attitudes—for example, "Just know who you are, be comfortable with yourself" (FG participant) and "As you hear somebody saying something about gays you automatically take it on your head [feel like you have to defend all the gays]. . . . It's about who you are and how comfortable you are" (FG participant). Many women also described channeling strength and courage to build resilience to stigma. Their answers included detaching from negative emotions that result from discrimination by ignoring what others say, generating positive emotions such as courage, and focusing on thinking positively—for example, "I always say that if you are going to be a lesbian, you have to have a backbone. Most lesbians do have a backbone. They will go out there and not care" (W13) and "If I am walking on the road and someone says something discriminatory, it takes a lot of strength and courage for me not to answer or resort to physical violence" (W01).

Many women also described using friends and other LGBT individuals as supports to cope with discrimination: "Well, I have my friends. If I am having LGBT problems, they are the only ones that I turn to" (W14). Solidarity and finding support within the lesbian community were described by many of the women.

I have to say that there is a kind of niche in Jamaica. If you know one lesbian, then you know five, then you know everybody. So it's sort of a little clique where you walk up and down and see one another and greet each other saying "Hey." They are friends. (W04)

Similarly,

We are defensive as lesbians and if someone is cursing a lesbian, we will get into the mix and question it. We stand up for each other and when it comes to certain things, we get upset together. We are not really attached, but when it comes to numbers, especially when there is discrimination, we will be there. (W13)

Despite persistent discrimination, participants described resilient narratives that were indicative of bravery, self-acceptance, and community connectedness.

Need for Confidential, Nonjudgmental Counseling Services

When FG participants were asked about current access to professional support and what ideal counseling supports would look like, some people described barriers to accessing mental health care specifically targeted toward lesbians:

> No [support resources] that I know of. I know of J-FLAG [Jamaica Forum for Lesbians, All-Sexuals and Gays, a LGBT advocacy group] but I have never talked to them. I have never heard any of my lesbian friends or associates talk about them. I think J-FLAG is more concerned about gay men rather than gay women because they think that we are okay. (W13)

FG participants described wanting confidential, nonjudgmental counselors for suicidality, domestic violence, and couples' counseling. One participant also raised the issue of wanting more discreet services that aren't necessarily located within an LGBT-specific organization:

> Open-minded professionals; not necessarily females, someone who is under-standing, cool to talk to, discreet; well trained; people don't want to be identified and don't want their orientation to be public and sometimes they won't go to a particular centre because they don't want anyone to know. (FG participant)

Although these participants described a willingness to seek professional support, they noted a number of barriers to accessing such supports.

DISCUSSION

LBQ women in our study described pervasive and multilevel *enacted stigma* on a daily basis in the form of name-calling, threats, rejection from family, the church, and limited access to employment. These experiences led to *perceived stigma*, wherein LBQ women described high expectations for stigma and rejection and subsequently eschewed certain areas, traditions, events, or people to avoid discrimination. This supports Meyer's (2003) conceptualization of minority stress, wherein distal experiences of discrimination, prejudice, and violence may be psychologically appraised in the form of stigma, leading to concealment of one's sexual orientation or gender identity and internalized homophobia. The intersection of both female gender and queer identities among our study participants involved a complex navigation of multiple, intersecting forms of stigma, including sexism and homophobia. Despite this, very few women in our study described experiencing internalized stigma, or self-directed negative societal attitudes. Instead, women's narratives revealed strength, resiliency, and coping through self-acceptance, social support, and community connectedness. This is consistent with previous research, as LGBT individuals often develop the resources necessary to respond adaptively to minority stress (Hatzenbuehler, 2009). A theoretical framework of resilience in LGB individuals by Kwon (2013) indicates that social support can buffer stress by lowering reactivity to prejudice. Research in North America has also found that self-acceptance mediates the relationship between discrimination and distress among LBG individuals (Woodford, Kulick, Sinco, & Hong, 2014) and that LGBT connectedness is protective against poor mental health among Israeli LGB youth (Shilo, Antebi, & Mor, 2015). Our study builds on these findings by presenting a nuanced understanding of how LBQ women experience and navigate intersectional stigma in Jamaica.

Many women in our study attributed pervasive stigma to rigid gender norms in Jamaican society and hegemonic expressions of masculinity among Jamaican men. Adherence to traditional gender norms has been found to be the most reliable predictor of LGBT prejudice in Jamaica, over and above income, education, religiosity, and age (West, 2018; West & Cowell, 2015). Some theorists indicate that Jamaica's sexual restrictiveness primarily functions to police gender norms (especially masculinity) rather than same-sex sexual practices and identities specifically (Hope, 2006; Pinnock, 2007; West, 2018). Academic work has also traced the intersections of hegemonic masculinity and homophobia in the Caribbean to colonialism and slavery (Carbado, 1997; Pinnock, 2007; Wilets, 2010). Wilets (2010) noted that the "tenuous socioeconomic position of men in the Caribbean fuels homophobia and anti-feminism, as men respond, sometimes violently, to their perception of diminished status" (p. 666).

Findings from our study have clinical implications for mental health practice. First, LBQ women in Jamaica have developed adaptive ways of coping with pervasive sexual stigma, and clinicians working with this population may aid in bolstering support systems and promoting self-acceptance and compassion to decrease internalized homophobia. Moreover, clinicians may highlight ways in which perceived stigma impacts behavior, validate the protective nature of avoiding discriminatory contexts, and ensure that LBQ women create spaces wherein they feel safe to express themselves freely. Some participants in our study cautioned other LGB youth not to come out until they have the social and financial resources to do so. Much research from the global North indicates mental health, physical health, and social support benefits of outness (see Kwon, 2013, for a review), but these findings may not be generalizable to low- and middle-income countries or to other cultural contexts where stigma is more severe. Indeed, one study found the relationship between outness and well-being to be moderated by the degree to which one's social network supports autonomy (Legate, Ryan, & Weinstein, 2012). Thus, clinicians should carefully and collaboratively assess their clients' social context and supports to examine the costs and benefits of disclosure. Finally, many women in our study emphasized a need for confidential and discreet support services, as stigma may prevent some LBQ women from accessing supports that are overtly a part of LGBT rights organizations in Jamaica.

These findings represent a preliminary step in understanding how gender norms, stigma, and discrimination impact the lives of LBQ women in Jamaica. In-depth questions regarding mental health symptoms were not directly asked during interviews; thus, future research may aim to understand more specific mental health impacts of stigma in this population. As many participants cited men and fragile masculinity to be sources of discrimination, future qualitative research could also examine relationships between masculinity, heterosexism, and homophobia among heterosexual Jamaican men. Moreover, multiple LBQ women cited a need for LBQ/LGBT-affirmative couples' counseling. Future research may examine the romantic and relational impact of discrimination on lesbian and queer couples in Jamaica. Recruitment through a community-based organization may have biased our sample toward those more likely to access support services; however, PRAs also recruited participants through their own networks, with the potential to include participants who may not regularly access services. Despite these limitations, we highlight how LBQ women experience intersecting stigmas based on gender and sexual orientation and the importance of examining sexual stigma in Jamaica from a postcolonial lens. Although women in our study described multiple emotional and behavioral impacts of discrimination, they also articulated multiple ways in which they actively cope with daily stigma. Mental health clinicians can bolster these strengths by helping LBQ women to build support networks and self-acceptance. Structurally, a need for discreet service provision for LGBT individuals in Jamaica was demonstrated so that individuals accessing services will not be placed at further risk of violence and discrimination.

REFERENCES

Campbell, H. (2005). Reflections on the post-colonial Caribbean state in the 21st century. *Social and Economic Studies, 54*, 161–187.

Carbado, D. W. (1997). The construction of O.J. Simpson as a racial victim. *Harvard Civil Rights–Civil Liberties Law Review, 32*, 49–103.

Carroll, A. (2016). *State-sponsored homophobia 2016: A world survey of sexual orientation laws: Criminalisation, protection and recognition* (11th ed.). Geneva, Switzerland: International Lesbian, Gay, Bisexual, Trans and Intersex Association. Retrieved from http://ilga.org/downloads/02_ILGA_State_Sponsored_Homophobia_2016_ENG_WEB_150516. pdf

Hatzenbuehler, M. L. (2009). How does sexual minority stigma "get under the skin"? A psychological mediation framework. *Psychological Bulletin, 135*, 707–730. http://dx.doi.org/10.1037/a0016441

Hatzenbuehler, M. L., Phelan, J. C., & Link, B. G. (2013). Stigma as a fundamental cause of population health inequalities. *American Journal of Public Health, 103*, 813–821. http://dx.doi.org/10.2105/AJPH.2012.301069

Herek, G. M. (2007). Confronting sexual stigma and prejudice: Theory and practice. *Journal of Social Issues, 63*, 905–925. http://dx.doi.org/10.1111/j.1540-4560.2007.00544.x

Herek, G. M., Gillis, J. R., & Cogan, J. C. (2009). Internalized stigma among sexual minority adults: Insights from a social psychological perspective. *Journal of Counseling Psychology, 56*, 32–43. http://dx.doi.org/10.1037/a0014672

Hope, D. P. (2006). *Passa passa*: Interrogating cultural hybridities in Jamaican dancehall. *Small Axe, 10*, 125–139. http://dx.doi.org/10.1215/-10-3-125

Hsieh, H. F., & Shannon, S. E. (2005). Three approaches to qualitative content analysis. *Qualitative Health Research, 15*, 1277–1288. http://dx.doi.org/10.1177/1049732305276687

Human Rights Watch. (2014). *Not safe at home: Violence and discrimination against LGBT people in Jamaica*. Retrieved from https://www.hrw.org/report/2014/10/21/not-safe-home/violence-and-discrimination-against-lgbt-people-jamaica

Kwon, P. (2013). Resilience in lesbian, gay, and bisexual individuals. *Personality and Social Psychology Review, 17*, 371–383. http://dx.doi.org/10.1177/1088868313490248

LaFont, S. (2001). Very straight sex: The development of sexual mores in Jamaica. *Journal of Colonialism and Colonial History, 2*(3). http://dx.doi.org/10.1353/cch.2001.0051

Legate, N., Ryan, R. M., & Weinstein, N. (2012). Is coming out always a "good thing"? Exploring the relations of autonomy support, outness, and wellness for lesbian, gay, and bisexual individuals. *Social Psychological and Personality Science, 3*, 145–152. http://dx.doi.org/10.1177/1948550611411929

Logie, C. H., Lacombe-Duncan, A., Kenny, K. S., Levermore, K., Jones, N., Baral, S. D., . . . Newman, P. A. (2018). Social-ecological factors associated with selling sex among men who have sex with men in Jamaica: Results from a cross-sectional tablet-based survey. *Global Health Action, 11*, 1424614. http://dx.doi.org/10.1080/16549716.2018.1424614

Logie, C. H., Wang, Y., Lacombe-Duncan, A., Jones, N., Ahmed, U., Levermore, K., . . . Newman, P. A. (2017). Factors associated with sex work involvement among transgender women in Jamaica: A cross-sectional study. *Journal of the International AIDS Society, 20*, 21422. http://dx.doi.org/10.7448/IAS.20.01/21422

Logie, C. H., Wang, Y., Marcus, N. L., Levermore, K., Jones, N., Ellis, T., . . . Newman, P. A. (2018). Pathways from sexual stigma to inconsistent condom use and condom breakage and slippage among MSM in Jamaica. *Journal of Acquired Immune Deficiency Syndromes, 78*, 513–521. http://dx.doi.org/10.1097/QAI.0000000000001712

Lovell, J. S. (2016). 'We are Jamaicans': Living with and challenging the criminalization of homosexuality in Jamaica. *Contemporary Justice Review, 19*, 86–102. http://dx.doi.org/10.1080/10282580.2015.1101687

Meyer, I. H. (2003). Prejudice, social stress, and mental health in lesbian, gay, and bisexual populations: Conceptual issues and research evidence. *Psychological Bulletin, 129*, 674–697. http://dx.doi.org/10.1037/0033-2909.129.5.674

Pinnock, A. M. (2007). "A ghetto education is basic": (Jamaican) dancehall masculinities as counter-culture. *The Journal of Pan African Studies, 1*(9), 47–84. Retrieved from https://www.jpanafrican.org/docs/vol1no9/AGhettoEducationIsBasic.pdf

Plöderl, M., & Tremblay, P. (2015). Mental health of sexual minorities. A systematic review. *International Review of Psychiatry, 27*, 367–385. http://dx.doi.org/10.3109/09540261.2015.1083949

Shilo, G., Antebi, N., & Mor, Z. (2015). Individual and community resilience factors among lesbian, gay, bisexual, queer and questioning youth and adults in Israel. *American Journal of Community Psychology, 55*, 215–227. http://dx.doi.org/10.1007/s10464-014-9693-8

Smith, C. L., & Kosobucki, R. (2011). Homophobia in the Caribbean: Jamaica. *Journal of Law and Social Deviance, 1*, 1–55.

Tielman, R., & Hammelburg, H. (1993). World survey on the social and legal position of gays and lesbians. In A. Hendriks, R. Tielman, & E. van der Veen (Eds.), *The third pink book: A global view of lesbian and gay liberation and oppression* (pp. 150–151). Buffalo, NY: Prometheus.

West, K. (2018). Understanding and reducing sexual prejudice in Jamaica: Theoretical and practical insights from a severely anti-gay society. *Journal of Sex Research, 55*, 472–485. http://dx.doi.org/10.1080/00224499.2017.1416055

West, K., & Cowell, N. M. (2015). Predictors of prejudice against lesbians and gay men in Jamaica. *Journal of Sex Research, 52,* 296–305. http://dx.doi.org/10.1080/00224499.2013.853725

Wilets, J. D. (2010). From divergence to convergence—A comparative and international law analysis of LGBTI rights in the context of race and post-colonialism. *Duke Journal of Comparative and International Law, 21,* 631–686.

Woodford, M. R., Kulick, A., Sinco, B. R., & Hong, J. S. (2014). Contemporary heterosexism on campus and psychological distress among LGBQ students: The mediating role of self-acceptance. *American Journal of Orthopsychiatry, 84,* 519–529. http://dx.doi.org/10.1037/ort0000015

5

The Return of Repression

Mental Health Concerns of Lesbian, Gay, Bisexual, and Transgender People in Russia

Sharon G. Horne and Lindsey White

As a U.S. college student majoring in Slavic Languages and Literature, I (Sharon G. Horne) was part of a small cohort of U.S. citizens who were permitted to study in the Soviet Union in 1987 and 1988. I was mesmerized by a place so different from my own upbringing, and I returned in 1990. I expected the Soviet Union to remain fixed in its ways, despite the emerging sense of *glasnost* (greater openness and dissemination of information) and *perestroika* (less restricted government planning and the move away from Soviet-style central governing). It was hard to imagine the country ever wavering from its reliable disposition: the only color in the ad-free streets the red swatches of political slogans; the simple cursive signs designating stores precisely by what they sold—*Bread, Milk, Products*; the efficient and pristine metro and train cars; the not-so-surreptitious black market; and the ubiquitous state-run radio blaring out consistent government propaganda in public and private spaces. The true openness and hope for change weren't exhibited on the streets but openly expressed in small kitchens where people shared their hopes and fears around endless pots of tea or bottomless vodka bottles—if they could find them during the restrictive years of the Gorbachev alcohol policy. Dissent and discontent were voiced in the nomadic underground music scene that would pop up in basement apartments through word of mouth; in the country dachas, where people let loose and shed their Soviet skins on the weekends; and on the trains, when they knew they could speak openly to a foreigner who would never see them again.

http://dx.doi.org/10.1037/0000159-006
LGBTQ Mental Health: International Perspectives and Experiences, N. Nakamura and C. H. Logie (Editors)

But then the Soviet Union dissolved in a major way, breaking apart into 16 separate nations by 1991. I was coming out as bisexual about the time that Russia emerged from the former Soviet Union. The change for the country was of course far more dramatic and rapid than my own personal transformation. My emerging sexual orientation occurred in fits and starts as I navigated the heteronormative expectations of the U.S. South in the early '90s, and I identified as lesbian by the mid-1990s.

During the '90s, when I spent nearly every summer in the new post-communist country, Russia developed in leaps and bounds. For the first time, it was acknowledged that there was domestic violence and sexual assault, and that these were not just problems that existed in the West (Horne, 1999). Organizations and shelters developed to serve survivors. Private businesses began to take root, and with them an onslaught of color billboards began to line the streets and sidewalks. Merchandise flowed freely—and Russians wore Western-style jeans and pastel turtlenecks, sported Ray-Bans and stylish skinny Italian shoes. Nongovernmental organizations (NGOs) took root in services not only for nonviolence but also for HIV, disability, and eventually lesbian, gay, bisexual, and transgender (LGBT) concerns. One of the first organizations founded specifically for LGBT concerns was MOLLI, the Moscow Organization for Lesbian Literature and Art, founded in 1991. In major cities, LGBT bookstores, nightclubs, and other LGBT organizations followed suit, including the Lesbian Archives, hosted in a Moscow apartment by one of the icons of the lesbian community with its weekly salons; the lesbian journal *Ostrov* [Island]; and the slick gay men's magazine *Kvir*. Gay men claimed the term *goloboi* [the color light blue] and lesbian women *rozovoi* [light pink], terms in the Russian language for gay and lesbian identities.

Throughout the '90s and through the 2000s, it seemed that Russian queer life was coming out of the shadows. But then it changed.

This chapter describes the development of Russian LGBT identities and communities and current challenges and concerns related to mental health for LGBT Russians. We share the trajectory of what seemed to be a forward march toward greater justice for and awareness of LGBT people in Russia, and how this progress has come to a lurching halt during the last 6 to 8 years.

Although the Bolshevik Revolution of 1917 was accompanied by a climate open and receptive to sexual freedom, including more versatile family structures, an easing of divorce rights, and a greater openness to nontraditional sexual relations (Clements, 1979; Healey, 2001), this atmosphere of sexual liberty ended with the rise of Josef Stalin, who instituted new repressive Bolshevik codes. In 1933, Article 121 was passed, and consensual sex between men became criminalized, with sentencing of up to 5 years of hard labor. Same-sex relations were characterized as emanating from capitalist (i.e., Western) influences, a charge that persists to this day. Due to the repression that began in the 1930s, the use of labor camps for imprisonment for even minor offenses, and the existence of Article 121, the discussion of sexuality was off limits. In particular, same-sex sexuality was considered taboo and was the "unmentionable sin" (Kon, 1993,

p. 93). Social attitudes reflected these repressive practices; during the final years of the Soviet Union, a poll using a representative sample found that 27% of Russians reported favoring liquidation of "homosexuals" (*liquidation* was a term to indicate killing or disposing of people), 32% endorsed isolation, 12% reported that they thought "homosexuals" should be left alone, and only 6% favored support for them (Kon & Riordan, 1993).

Soon after the founding of the post-communist Russian Republic, in 1993, same-sex sexuality was decriminalized, and it seemed that the new country would be moving toward a stance of greater openness for LGBT individuals common to many countries in Europe. As an example of the significant progress in the new Russia, in 1994 I had the pleasure of serving on a U.S. Agency for International Development project as the chief trainer as we welcomed 55 women leaders from the former Soviet Union who had established the first NGOs to address social services, including the leaders of MOLLI and other shelter and crisis center leaders from as far east as Kamchatka in Siberia, to Armenia, Azerbaijan, and Georgia in the south, to St. Petersburg in the north. Our Russian colleagues attended the 1995 Beijing Women's Conference representing women's concerns, including bisexual and lesbian women, and more NGOs were forming regularly throughout Russia. Despite the disjointed and austere measures that took place during the economic change from a Soviet system to an open market, throughout the 1990s, among those working in nonprofit organizations there was a sense of optimism and belief that an open society supported by free market policies and founded in a forward march for civil rights was bound to emerge.

I didn't encounter heterosexism exclusively in Russia, but within U.S. borders as well. By 1999 I was living in Tennessee, which also had a long way to go in LGBT rights. In truth, Moscow and Memphis didn't seem all that different. Our city had no nondiscrimination policies based on sexual orientation or gender identity, the university health club still restricted family memberships to other-sex married couples, the nation's largest live-in conversion therapy center for teens was housed within our city limits, and the health community restricted fertility care to women married to men. In Memphis, most LGBT professionals were not out, and there was a thriving LGBT bar scene serving African American and European American patrons, in separate establishments for the most part, who ranged in degrees of outness. When I would visit Russia, I felt that both contexts were similar in their sluggish progress on LGBT rights.

My partner and I began research with Russian individuals in the mid-2000s, at a time when optimism prevailed and there was a cautious expectation that civil rights were advancing and would fall in line with Europe and the United States, and that greater recognition of human rights would follow (Horne, Ovrebo, Levitt, & Franeta, 2009). In our interviews, we found LGBT people describing the obstacles they experienced and the caution they shared in "asking for too much, too quickly" (Horne et al., 2009, p. 12). Couched in all of these discussions was a looming backdrop of caution of not moving too fast or asking for any "special" rights. In almost every interview, the Soviet gulags or labor camps were brought up, which were a primary mechanism of social control used against millions of Soviet citizens. Individuals were imprisoned sometimes for minor or fabricated offenses, and millions perished under the horrendous conditions (Applebaum, 2003). Our participants noted the dangers of being perceived as different in any way and the historical ways that any difference was repressed, punished, ostracized, or extinguished in the former Soviet Union. In our study, we determined the core category of our grounded theory analysis to be *leaving the herd: the lingering threat of difference for same-sex desires in Russia.* Although we remarked upon the phenomenal organizing that was occurring, the development of the nonprofit support network for LGBT people, and the advocacy and risks that these LGBT leaders were taking, we couldn't dismiss the threatening context and the impact of the looming historical oppression and marginalization of LGBT people. We certainly wish that our findings had not been so prescient.

POST-SOVIET RUSSIAN LGBT CONTEXT

Following the dissolution of the Soviet state in 1991, the new established Russian government led by Boris Yeltsin fostered greater market reforms and privatization of state institutions, as well as movement toward expanding civil rights to be in line with European and Western standards. Sexual relations between men were decriminalized in 1993, and in 1999 the Ministry of Health officially removed *homosexuality* as a mental disorder. Increasingly, Russian LGBT people came out about their sexual and gender identities; however, disclosure was typically limited to family and friendship networks and rarely extended to the workplace or to public disclosures of LGBT identities (Essig, 1999; Healey, 2002; Horne et al., 2009). Nonprofit organizations emerged to serve the LGBT communities, and many international partnerships were formed to support affirming LGBT initiatives during the 1990s (Dufalla, 2014; Kondakov, 2013). There was a burgeoning civil society taking root, and social services for many different stigmatized communities were developed.

Unfortunately, the economic reforms instituted by the new Russian government under the leadership of Boris Yeltsin created instability through rapid privatization, referred to as "shock therapy," and periods of hyperinflation and fluctuations in the market followed. In an attempt to consolidate power and reduce the impact of the chaotic economic reforms of the Yeltsin years, Vladimir Putin introduced greater restrictions on the press, cultivated a closer relationship with the Russian Orthodox Church, and took a political position that diverged from Europe and the United States, including in social concerns. For example, NGOs that had been funded by international partnerships were perceived as threatening to the state and were characterized as acting as "foreign agents" (Dufalla, 2014). Thus, limitations were placed on NGO activity through the 2006 Russian NGO Law and the 2013 "Foreign Agent Law."

The 2006 Russian NGO law set parameters for Russian NGO activity and led to a reduction in NGO activity and a curtailment of civil society, resulting in the dominance of state-funded and controlled organizations (Crotty, Hall, & Ljubownikow, 2014). The "Foreign Agent Law," officially "On Amendments to Legislative Acts of the Russian Federation regarding the Regulation of the Activities of Non-profit Organizations Performing the Functions of a Foreign Agent," has taken these restrictions to a new level; any organization receiving funding or maintaining political activity is required to register as a foreign agent. This law has curtailed LGBT supports, as organizations that are identified as foreign agents are required to list this designation on any materials they produce and be more closely supervised by the state, and they are vulnerable to harassment and pressure. Numerous LGBT organizations have been designated foreign agents, essentially shutting them down or rendering them ineffective, as organizations in Russia cannot depend on local funds to support them because of a lack of a structure for philanthropy as well as long-standing negative attitudes toward LGBT individuals.

It may be that the decades of sexual repression during the Soviet era, combined with the slow progress on LGBT concerns in the 1990s and 2000s, contribute to the persistence of stigma related to LGBT identities in contemporary Russian society (Horne, Maroney, Zagryazhskaya, & Koven, 2017; Khazan, 2013). Among democratic countries, Russia ranks high in anti-LGBT attitudes (Pew Research Center, 2013), and research suggests that attitudes may be worsening; for example, in 1998, 54.2% of Russians in a representative cross-national sample reported that same-gender sexuality was "always wrong," and 10 years later, the percentage that reported the same was 64.2% (Pew Research Center, 2013).

In 2015, a Russian study of 800 participants in a national sample gauged public opinion toward same-sex relationships, using the common (but outdated, and often considered offensive in other global regions) terms of *homosexual* and *homosexuality*. Results showed that 37% believed homosexuality to be an illness requiring medical treatment, 26% believed that homosexuality was the manifestation of a bad upbringing or promiscuity, and 13% believed that homosexuality was caused by sexual seduction or abuse (Levada Center, 2015). A mere 11% reported that homosexuality was a sexual orientation that warranted the same rights as a heterosexual orientation. More alarming, 18% of the sample reported that homosexual people should be prosecuted, an increase from prior surveys (Levada Center, 2015). Similar to other research on attitudes, a recent study found that being a college student living in an urban area versus a rural area, being a woman versus a man, having low levels of Neuroticism and Conscientiousness, and personally knowing LGBT individuals were all factors associated with affirming attitudes. Only being female and living in an urban setting were associated with a belief in LGBT civil rights (Horne, Maroney, Zagryazhskaya, & Koven, 2017). Transnational research suggests that, compared with many countries, Russia is less accepting; when measured against residents of many other democracies, greater proportions of Russians report that same-gender sexual relations are not acceptable (Andersen & Fetner, 2008).

Such a discrepancy from the global trend among democratic societies toward greater acceptance for LGBT people may be a result of the increased negative media attention toward LGBT people reported over the past decade. The moderate increase in LGBT tolerant attitudes, visibility, and activism in the 1990s and early 2000s incited a backlash from opponents who broadcast messages depicting same-sex relationships as immoral, perverse, and a threat to traditional values. Buyantueva (2018) argued that LGBT depictions in the media both influence individual-level appraisals of LGBT people and queerness and critically provide individuals with an awareness of how LGBT people are perceived by various others. As such, media consumers are feeling the pulse of common negative attitudes toward LGBT persons within greater society and within powerful interests who are provided a platform to offer commentary on LGBT concerns (e.g., journalists, religious leaders, politicians; Buyantueva, 2018).

The stance of the Putin administration, as well as local governments, on LGBT concerns has only amplified the expression of negative attitudes and damaging media portrayals. In 2012, Pride parades in Moscow were banned for 100 years, sending a strong message that being out as an LGBT person is unacceptable (Clemons, 2012). In 2013, the federal law called "For the Purpose of Protecting Children from Information Advocating for a Denial of Traditional Family Values," otherwise known as the *Propaganda Ban on Non-Traditional Sexual Relations*, was passed with a majority (435 of 436 members voting for, and one abstention) in the Russian Parliament. This bill makes criminal any actions that treat same-sex relationships and LGBT identities to be equivalent to other-sex relationships in the presence of minors, in person, or on the Internet. For example, Elena Klimova, a journalist who established a website for LGBT youth seeking information on sexual orientation and gender identity, was charged in 2013, and again in 2014, with violating this ban; the charges were ultimately dropped because the content was deemed not to constitute propaganda. However, in 2015 she was again charged and convicted, and then won on appeal in 2016. It remains to be seen whether the website she has sponsored, Deti 404, which has been blocked by authorities in the past, will be allowed to continue in Russia; it is currently active on Facebook and continues for the time being on Russian social media. Other important legislation was passed in 2014 restricting adoption by international same-sex couples and single Russian LGBT people (and because same-sex marriage is not permitted, this means it bans adoption by LGBT couples; Human Rights Campaign, 2014). Essentially, these laws concomitant with negative media—combined with the anti-LGBT rhetoric of President Putin toward LGBT people, such as his statement that Russia needs to "cleanse itself" from "homosexuality" if it wants to increase its birth rate, as well as his equating of "homosexuality" with pedophilia—have created a hostile and increasingly dangerous society for LGBT people.

IMPACT OF SOCIOCULTURAL CONTEXT ON
LGBT INDIVIDUALS IN CONTEMPORARY RUSSIA

The leader of a lesbian organization, whom I have known since 1993, contacted me through Facebook Messenger earlier this year. She had changed her name out of concerns for her safety and attached a picture of a diploma from an art school; her surname had changed to one that matched a popular Western term. She wrote that because of being seen as an out lesbian in the 1990s, she had continued to be "beaten by men, simply because I am known for Lesbian." Her story is not unusual. Russian people who were formerly out have emigrated to Europe, Canada, or the United States; married other sex partners; or tried to return to the closet and keep a low profile.

Five NGOs in Russia serving LGBT concerns—the Coming Out LGBT Group, the Moscow LGBT initiative group Stimul, Phoenix Plus, the Russian LGBT Network, and the Transgender Legal Defense Project—formed a coalition to draft *Written Submission Related to the Situation of Lesbian, Gay, Bisexual and Transgender Persons and Men who Have Sex with Men in Russia* (Coalition of Civil Society Organizations, 2017) for consideration by the United Nations Committee on Economic, Social, and Cultural Rights to supplement the sixth periodic report of the Russian Federation. The Coalition concluded that in Russia the following concerns continue to prevail: (a) discrimination of LGBT persons in employment, (b) hate crimes on the grounds of sexual orientation and gender identity, (c) a lack of HIV prevention programs among men who have sex with men and transgender persons, and (d) discrimination against transgender persons. The Coalition reported the results of a study of 3,759 LGBT persons: 17.3% encountered problems related to employers or colleagues, and 13.9% were victims of dismissal motivated by homophobia or transphobia (Coalition of Civil Society Organizations, 2017). The Coalition documented an additional 78 cases of discrimination in hiring due to sexual orientation and gender identity between 2013 and 2016, as well as 33 cases in which LGBT people were forced out of their employment due to homophobia or transphobia (Coalition of Civil Society Organizations, 2017). In particular, teachers and educators were being singled out; the report documented in detail 18 cases of forced resignation from schools, primarily due to outing by anti-LGBT people.

The increase in hate crimes on the grounds of sexual orientation and gender identity (SOGI) since the Propaganda Ban is particularly concerning (Coalition of Civil Society Organizations, 2017; Kondakov, 2017). Although the Russian Federation does not collect information on crimes related to these identities, NGOs reported that from 2015 to 2016, 18 victims reported hate crimes related to SOGI to police departments; in nine other cases, police departments declined to initiate criminal proceedings due to SOGI hate crimes. There has been such an increase in hate crimes that the Coalition of Civil Society Organizations (2017) categorized hate crimes into four types: (a) state-sponsored violence in the Chechen Republic, (b) hate crimes committed by nonfamily perpetrators, (c) hate crimes perpetrated by the victim's family, and (d) hate crimes related to Internet dating stings. In 2016, it was reported widely that more than 200 Chechen men purported to have engaged in same-sex practices were rounded up; detained; and repeatedly beaten, starved, and tortured with electricity in an effort to find other men. Following their release, the men were returned to their families, and they often faced further violence from family members who believed that their family honor had been violated. The Chechen Republic denied the accusations, and to this day there has been no federal investigation conducted by the Russian government (Coalition of Civil Society Organizations, 2017). In January 2019, the Russia LGBT Network reported in Chechnya a new wave of violence against LGBT people, resulting in at least two deaths.

In addition, hate crimes committed by strangers are common; from 2015 to 2016 there were 67 attacks reported, as well as five documented homicides. Violence from family members is also widespread. In both the cases of family and stranger-perpetrated hate crimes, the reported incidence is much lower than likely because of the stigma and risk of further violence in reporting assaults. Finally, one of the most heinous ways that hate crimes are perpetrated in Russia is through extortion in online dating. In these cases, gay men respond to an online dating inquiry and are invited to meet their prospective date at a specific location; instead, they are met by a gang of men who threaten violence or to out the victim at their workplace or to their family, as well as threaten to report pedophilia to the police, if they don't pay. In 2016, 65 crimes of this nature were reported (Coalition of Civil Society Organizations, 2017); perpetrators depend on the fear of their victims' disclosure to police to keep them safe from prosecution. Therefore, such hate crimes are likely greatly underestimated.

In addition, the "Foreign Agent Law" and the negative attitudes toward LGBT people have greatly reduced services for HIV prevention for sexual and gender minorities (European Region of the International Lesbian, Gay, Bisexual, Trans and Intersex Association, 2016). Russia has the largest HIV epidemic in Europe, with more than 1 million cases of HIV (European Centre for Disease Prevention and Control & World Health Organization Regional Office for Europe, 2016). Due to the Propaganda Ban, prevention information for men who have sex with men and transgender people has been severely curtailed (Coalition of Civil Society Organizations, 2017).

TRANSGENDER AND NONBINARY INDIVIDUALS IN RUSSIA

Transgender and nonbinary people in the Russian Federation face particular vulnerabilities due to a lack of access to transparent and accessible processes to gain legal gender recognition (Transgender Legal Defense Project, 2018). Exploring the impact of legal identification-related discrimination in a sample of 242 transgender individuals in Russia, the Transgender Legal Defense

Project found that 74% of participants experienced denials in employment, postal services, bank services, transportation services, medical services, or government and public services (Yashenkova & Kirichenko, 2016). Furthermore, participants reported avoiding instances in which they anticipated discrimination, including choosing to not apply for new jobs (62%), avoiding medical and public health services (41%), not enrolling in university/school (34%), avoiding bank services (33%), and avoiding traveling between cities (30%) and foreign countries (23%; Yashenkova & Kirichenko, 2016).

Recent reforms to the legal process by which transgender individuals can access gender-affirming documentation offer a promising step toward reducing opportunistic discrimination that arises when individuals cannot provide identification that reflects their gender identity. In January 2018, the Russian Ministry of Health signed an order that established a transparent process for transgender individuals to obtain legal gender-recognition documentation. The order was drafted in response to calls from LGBT organizations and the Committee on Economic, Social, and Cultural Rights to increase access to legal gender recognition in hopes of reducing documented instances of widespread institutional discrimination against the transgender community. Under the new process, transgender individuals can no longer be required to have undergone gender-affirming surgeries or hormone replacement therapy before obtaining documentation, nor can individuals be denied documentation on the basis of marriage or having children. Individuals can apply for a medical certificate directly from the Ministry of Health, bypassing inconsistent civil registry officials and avoiding prohibitive court costs and lengthy processes.

Despite streamlining the application process, transgender individuals are still required to receive a diagnosis of *transsexualism* following a psychiatric evaluation in order to receive their documentation (Transgender Legal Defense Project, 2018). The ultimate gatekeeping role of psychiatrists and medical professionals for transgender and nonbinary individuals in search of legal gender recognition is colored by strong anti-LGBT stigma, as evidenced by the history of LGBT psychiatric treatment in Russia. Therefore, transgender individuals are vulnerable to maltreatment by medical professionals and health care specialists, and for these reasons, many transgender people access hormone replacement treatment illegally, exposing them to health risks including contaminated needles.

CURRENT MENTAL HEALTH CONCERNS

By promoting a biological deterministic basis for same-gender attraction, psychiatrists and other medical professionals played an instrumental role in the eventual decriminalization of homosexuality in 1993 (Healey, 2002). Homosexuality was officially removed from consideration as a mental disorder upon adoption of the ICD-10 in 1999, though reports indicate that the outdated Soviet system of psychiatric diagnoses continued to be used, and schizophrenia diagnoses have been commonly misapplied to transgender and nonbinary individuals (Essig, 1999; Sitnikova, 2015). Deeply entrenched anti-LGBT stigma persists in Russian psychiatry; in one survey of 450 psychiatrists in the Rostov Region, 62.5% reported that they considered homosexuality to be a disease (Savenko & Perekhov, 2014). Psychiatrists' anti-LGBT attitudes fuel the continued pathologization and marginalization of LGBT individuals.

In addition, psychiatrists, psychologists, and mental health professionals do not receive training in working with LGBT people and often rely on outdated psychological theories of homosexuality and gender identity when treating LGBT people who have mental health concerns. Increasingly, conversion therapies are employed to target Russian LGBT people (Golubeva, 2017), including hypnosis procedures that draw on psychoanalysis to extinguish a person's same-sex attractions and approaches that require a client to sexually objectify a person of another gender and then have sexual intercourse with a person of the other gender. Other therapies are religiously based and offered by faith leaders affiliated with the Russian Orthodox Church, which views homosexuality as a sin. The roles of environment and sociocultural factors in psychological theories in Russia are woefully underdeveloped.

Given the perpetual hostile environment for LGBT people, it remains to be seen whether Russia will be a safe or welcoming country for LGBT people in the near future. Many LGBT people who have the opportunity and resources seek refuge in other countries. Based on data obtained from the U.S. Department of Homeland Security, RadioFreeEurope/RadioLiberty reported that 2017 Russian asylum applications in the United States reached a 24-year high with 2,444 new applications, a number that has increased by nearly 40% since 2016 and continues an upward trend that began in 2012 after Putin returned to office (Schreck, 2018). Asylum applications in the United States do not indicate the basis for asylum claims, though rights activists and immigration attorneys indicate that the increasingly hostile atmosphere for LGBT individuals has largely contributed to the surge in Russian applicants (Schreck, 2016). The United States received the second highest number of Russian asylum applications in 2017; Germany lead with 4,885 first-time applications, mostly from ethnic Chechens (Schreck, 2018).

Many Russian LGBT people do not have the desire or the means to emigrate. Many LGBT individuals are committed to their communities, are deeply loyal to their families and/or country, and want to work toward progress on LGBT human rights. Until greater protections for LGBT people are put in place, however, physical safety concerns will remain of paramount importance for Russian LGBT people. Given the high incidence of hate crimes and violence against LGBT people, posttraumatic stress disorder and other mental concerns, such as stress and depression, will continue to be significant mental health issues for many LGBT people. Indeed, in a longitudinal study from 2010 to 2015 that sampled 1,367 Russian men who have sex with men, Hylton and colleagues (2017) found that participants experiencing stigma related to sexual orientation reported increased depression symptoms after the passage of the

Propaganda Ban. Russian LGBT people who face constant fears for their safety will need additional support for their minority stressors.

The impact of such negative media messages and a general anti-LGBT atmosphere undoubtedly contribute to internalized homonegativity and internalized trans-stigma (Gulevich, Osin, Isaenko, & Brainis, 2016, 2018; Horne, Maroney, Geiss, & Dunnavant, 2017). Russian LGBT people are limited in opportunities to build community and be out, which have been shown to be inversely related to internalized homonegativity (Herek, Cogan, Gillis, & Glunt, 1998; Puckett, Levitt, Horne, & Hayes-Skelton, 2015). LGBT Russian people need access to positive representations of LGBT people to counter such images; therefore, freedom of information and access to Internet resources are vital. Unfortunately, increasingly Russian authorities are censoring information related to sexual orientation and gender identity, particularly for youth (Human Rights Watch, 2018; U.S. Department of State, 2015).

Mental health professionals working in Russia need to make explicit their affirmative stances for LGBT individuals. Given the struggle to find supportive services that many Russian LGBT people have experienced, and the widespread presence of conversion therapies, clarifying LGBT-inclusive and affirmative policies is critical. Providers will need to take precautions to ensure that any materials they provide to prospective clients do not put them at risk for censure by the Propaganda Ban; some LGBT organizations have resorted to stamping their brochures and documents with "18+" for that reason. At the same time, providing information that is easily accessible and accurate remains an important aspect of LGBT mental health support. Advocating for accurate and accessible information for LGBT youth is a necessary and critical component of LGBT rights, and this advocacy by professionals includes overturning the Propaganda Ban.

Mental health professionals should also know legal rights in Russia that will assist them to make a case to maintain affirmative LGBT practices. For example, although sexual orientation and gender identity are not considered protected classes in the Russian constitution, the Russian Constitutional Court has ruled that Article 19 protects *social groups* from discrimination, including those of a particular sexual orientation ("On Amendments," 2013). This article states the following:

> Article 19 (Section 2) . . . guarantees protection equally to all persons, irrespective of their sexual orientation, and sexual orientation as such cannot serve as a lawful criterion for establishment of distinctions in the legal status of human and citizen.

Therefore, the legal case can be made in mental health treatment that LGBT individuals cannot be discriminated against or receive inferior treatment due to their sexual orientation or gender identity. Although there do not appear to be court cases brought by LGBT people against practitioners of conversion therapy practices, it may be that Russian law, under different leadership, could eventually be used to rule against therapies that cause harm or attempt to change sexual orientation. For the time being, however, the current leadership appears to find stigmatizing LGBT people and communities politically expedient.

CONCLUSION

During the early years of the Russian Federation, there was a gradual thaw in repression as same-sex practices were decriminalized and then depathologized, and it is true that LGBT sexual and gender expressions and identities have not returned to Soviet-era levels of criminal designation or pathologization. However, modern forms of repression through the Propaganda Ban, adoption laws, and other legal restrictions have imposed new infringements on LGBT Russian people, which may have implications that are just as severe (e.g., in Chechnya). Moreover, these measures have created a sociocultural climate permissible for hate crimes targeting LGBT people that are not recognized as such by law enforcement. At the same time, the Russian government has conducted no official investigation into the Chechen purge of gay men, giving tacit approval to severe acts of torture and structural violence in regions not under direct federal supervision. It is more dangerous to be Russian and LGBT than it was a decade ago, making the political repression and labor camps where thousands of LGBT people served time during the Soviet era seem not so distant after all. In terms of mental health treatment and support, for many Russian LGBT people, there may be no distance at all.

REFERENCES

Andersen, R., & Fetner, T. (2008). Economic inequality and intolerance: Attitudes toward homosexuality in 35 democracies. *American Journal of Political Science, 52*, 942–958. http://dx.doi.org/10.1111/j.1540-5907.2008.00352.x

Applebaum, A. (2003). *Gulag: A history*. New York, NY: Doubleday.

Buyantueva, R. (2018). LGBT rights activism and homophobia in Russia. *Journal of Homosexuality, 65*, 456–483. http://dx.doi.org/10.1080/00918369.2017.1320167

Clements, B. C. (1979). *Bolshevik feminist: The life of Alexandra Kollontai*. Bloomington: Indiana University Press.

Clemons, S. (2012, June 8). Not the Onion: Moscow bans gay pride parades for next 100 years. *The Atlantic*. Retrieved from https://www.theatlantic.com/international/archive/2012/06/not-the-onion-moscow-bans-gay-pride-for-next-100-years/258296/

Coalition of Civil Society Organizations. (2017, August). *Written submission related to the situation of lesbian, gay, bisexual and transgender persons and men who have sex with men in Russia*. Retrieved from https://tbinternet.ohchr.org/Treaties/CESCR/Shared%20Documents/RUS/INT_CESCR_CSS_RUS_28824_E.pdf

Crotty, J., Hall, S. M., & Ljubownikow, S. (2014). Post-soviet civil society development in the Russian Federation: The impact of the NGO law. *Europe-Asia Studies, 66*, 1253–1269. http://dx.doi.org/10.1080/09668136.2014.941697

Dufalla, J. (2014). Non-Governmental Organizations in Russia: Adapting for success. *Vestnik, 15*.

Essig, L. (1999). *Queer in Russia: A story of sex, self, and the other*. Durham, NC: Duke University Press.

European Centre for Disease Prevention and Control and World Health Organization Regional Office for Europe. (2016). *Surveillance report: HIV/AIDS surveillance in Europe 2015*. Retrieved from http://www.euro.who.int/__data/assets/pdf_file/0019/324370/HIV-AIDS-surveillance-Europe-2015.pdf?ua=1

European Region of the International Lesbian, Gay, Bisexual, Trans and Intersex Association. (2016). *Annual review of the human rights situation of Lesbian, Gay, Bisexual, Bisexual, Trans, and Intersex people in Europe*. Retrieved from https://www.ilga-europe.org/sites/default/files/2016/full_annual_review.pdf

Golubeva, A. (2017, May 3). *Hypnosis and holy water: Russian 'cures' for gay people*. Retrieved from http://www.bbc.com/news/world-europe-39777612

Gulevich, O., Osin, E., Isaenko, N., & Brainis, L. (2016). Attitudes to homosexuals in Russia: Content, structure, and predictors. *Psychology: Journal of the Higher School of Economics, 13*, 79–110.

Gulevich, O. A., Osin, E. N., Isaenko, N. A., & Brainis, L. M. (2018). Scrutinizing homophobia: A model of perception of homosexuals in Russia. *Journal of Homosexuality, 65*, 1838–1866. http://dx.doi.org/10.1080/00918369.2017.1391017

Healey, D. (2001). *Homosexual desire in revolutionary Russia: The regulation of sexual and gender dissent*. Chicago, IL: University of Chicago Press. http://dx.doi.org/10.7208/chicago/9780226922546.001.0001

Healey, D. (2002). Homosexual existence and existing socialism: New light on the repression of male homosexuality in Stalin's Russia. *GLQ: A Journal of Lesbian and Gay Studies, 8*, 349–378. http://dx.doi.org/10.1215/10642684-8-3-349

Herek, G. M., Cogan, J. C., Gillis, J. R., & Glunt, E. K. (1998). Correlates of internalized homophobia in a community sample of lesbians and gay men. *Journal of the Gay and Lesbian Medical Association, 2*, 17–25.

Horne, S. (1999). Domestic violence in Russia. *American Psychologist, 54*, 55–61. http://dx.doi.org/10.1037/0003-066X.54.1.55

Horne, S. G., Maroney, M. R., Geiss, M., & Dunnavant, B. (2017). The reliability and validity of a Russian version of the Lesbian Internalized Homophobia Scale. *Psychology in Russia: State of the Art, 10*(2), 5–20. http://dx.doi.org/10.11621/pir.2017.0201

Horne, S. G., Maroney, M. R., Zagryazhskaya, E. A., & Koven, J. (2017). Attitudes toward gay and lesbian individuals in Russia: An exploration of the interpersonal contact hypothesis and personality factors. *Psychology in Russia: State of the Art, 10*(2), 21–34. http://dx.doi.org/10.11621/pir.2017.0202

Horne, S. G., Ovrebo, E., Levitt, H. M., & Franeta, S. (2009). Leaving the herd: The lingering threat of difference for same-sex identities in postcommunist Russia. *Sexuality Research & Social Policy, 6*, 88. http://dx.doi.org/10.1525/srsp.2009.6.2.88

Human Rights Campaign. (2014, February 14*). Russia officially bans LGBT international adoption*. Retrieved from http://www.hrc.org/blog/russia-officially-implements-anti-lgbt-international-adoption-ban

Human Rights Watch. (2018). *Russia: Events of 2017*. Retrieved from https://www.hrw.org/world-report/2018/country-chapters/russia

Hylton, E., Wirtz, A. L., Zelaya, C. E., Latkin, C., Peryshkina, A., Mogilnyi, V., . . . Beyrer, C. (2017). Sexual identity, stigma, and depression: The role of the "Anti-gay Propaganda Law" in mental health among men who have sex with men in Moscow, Russia. *Journal of Urban Health, 94*, 319–329. http://dx.doi.org/10.1007/s11524-017-0133-6

Khazan, O. (2013, June 12). Why is Russia so homophobic? Communist-era justifications for bigotry doesn't make sense anymore. What's behind lawmakers' opposition to gays? *The Atlantic*. Retrieved from https://www.theatlantic.com/international/archive/2013/06/why-is-russia-so-homophobic/276817/

Kon, I. (1993). Sexual minorities. In I. Kon & J. Riordan (Eds.), *Sex and Russian society* (pp. 89–115). Bloomington: Indiana University Press.

Kon, I., & Riordan, J. (1993). *Sex and Russian society*. Bloomington: Indiana University Press.

Kondakov, A. (2013). Resisting the silence: The use of tolerance and equality arguments by gay and lesbian activist groups in Russia. *Canadian Journal of Law & Society/La Revue Canadienne. Droit Social, 28*, 403–424.

Kondakov, A. (2017). *Prestupleniya na pochve nenavisti protiv LGBT v Rossii: Otchet* [Hate crimes against LGBT in Russia: Report]. St. Petersburg, Russia: Centre for Independent Social Research, Renome.

Levada Center. (2015, October 6). Homophobia. Retrieved from http://www.levada.ru/en/20 15/06/10/homophobia/

On amendments to Article 5 of the federal law "On Protecting Children from Information Harmful to their Health and Development." (2013, July 2). No. 135-FZ. *Rossiskaya Gazeta*. Retrieved from http://www.rg.ru/2013/06/30/deti-site-dok.html

Pew Research Center. (2013, June 4). *The global divide on homosexuality: Greater acceptance in more secular and affluent countries*. Retrieved from http://www.pewglobal.org/2013/06/04/the-global-divide-on-homosexuality

Puckett. J. A., Levitt, H. M., Horne, S. G., & Hayes-Skelton, S. A. (2015). Internalized heterosexism and psychological distress: The mediating roles of self-criticism and community connectedness. *Psychology of Sexual Orientation and Gender Diversity, 2*, 426–435. http://dx.doi.org/10.1037/sgd0000123

Savenko, Y. S., & Perekhov, A. Y. (2014, February 13). The state of psychiatry in Russia. *Psychiatric Times, 31*(2).

Schreck, C. (2016, December 6). Russian applications for U.S. asylum surge again in 2016. *RadioFreeEurope/RadioLiberty*. Retrieved from https://www.rferl.org/a/russia-increase-seeking-us-asylum-in-2016/28159435.html

Schreck, C. (2018, May 2). Russian asylum applications in U.S. hit 24-year record. *RadioFreeEurope/RadioLiberty*. Retrieved from https://www.rferl.org/a/russian-asylum-applications-in-u-s-hit-24-year-record/29204843.html

Sitnikova, Y. (2015, March 13). Psychiatric abuse of transgender people in Russia. *openDemocracy*. Retrieved from https://www.opendemocracy.net/en/odr/psychiatric-abuse-of-transgender-people-in-russia/

Transgender Legal Defense Project. (2018, January 24). *The Russian Ministry of Health approved the Legal Gender Recognition procedure*. Retrieved from http://pravo-trans.eu/the-russian-ministry-of-health-approved-the-legal-gender-recognition-procedure/

U.S. Department of State. (2015). *Russia 2015 human rights report: Country reports on human rights practices*. Retrieved from https://www.state.gov/documents/organization/253105.pdf

Yashenkova, D., & Kirichenko, K. (2016). *Violation of transgender people's rights in Russia: Research results*. Saint Petersburg, Russia: Transgender Legal Defense Project. Retrieved from http://pravo-trans.eu/files/violation_of_the_rights_of_transgender_people_in_Russia-en.pdf

6

LGBT Mental Health in Mongolia

A Brief History, Current Issues, and Future Directions

Julie M. Koch, Douglas Knutson, and Anaraa Nyamdorj

Batchimeg and Tsetsegmaa[1] are cisgender lesbian women living together in Ulaanbaatar, Mongolia. They are both in their mid-40s and have been romantic partners for more than 20 years. Batchimeg was married briefly in her early 20s and has a daughter in college. Batchimeg's family, including her daughter, view Batchimeg and Tsetsegmaa as "roommates" and lifelong friends. Batchimeg has stable employment as a manager with an international mining corporation based in Ulaanbaatar. She is not out to anyone at work. She reports that she is frequently stressed, has difficulty sleeping, and has high blood pressure and kidney problems.

Tsetsegmaa never married; her parents kicked her out of the house when she was a teenager after they saw her kissing a girl. She has been estranged from her immediate and extended family ever since. In her late teens and early 20s she was intermittently homeless and engaged in sex work to survive. She has experienced considerable physical and emotional trauma and has attempted suicide twice. She reports struggling with depression and fears for her safety on a daily basis. Tsetsegmaa currently works at a local coffee shop but struggles to maintain stable employment; she is more out in public and social circles, and this creates friction between Batchimeg and Tsetsegmaa.

Batchimeg and Tsetsegmaa frequently discuss the possibility of moving to another country where they can be themselves more authentically, but

---

[1] All case examples are fictional and/or have been deidentified to protect confidentiality.

http://dx.doi.org/10.1037/0000159-007
LGBTQ Mental Health: International Perspectives and Experiences, N. Nakamura and C. H. Logie (Editors)

Batchimeg worries about leaving her daughter, and they are not sure there is anyplace that is completely safe for them. Batchimeg and Tsetsegmaa enjoy going to museums and supporting local artists. Recently they contributed to the LGBT Centre (Mongolia) to support its upcoming Pride Days. The youth they have met through the LGBT Centre give them hope that the climate for lesbian, gay, bisexual, and transgender (LGBT)[2] people will improve.

HISTORY AND CONTEXT

To fully understand the experiences of LGBT people, it is important to understand the history and context of Mongolia in the post-Soviet era and how the country's relationship with Russia has shaped the experiences of members of the LGBT community. Next we discuss the role of the economy in Mongolia, the rise of anti-LGBT sentiment, groups who actively target LGBT people, and a system of legal policies and law enforcement that offer LGBT people few protections. There is very little published scholarship related to the experiences of LGBT people in Mongolia, and throughout this chapter we rely largely on reports from the LGBT Centre (a nongovernmental organization in Ulaanbaatar) and reports by international organizations such as the United Nations Development Programme (UNDP) and the U.S. Agency for International Development (USAID; 2014), as well as some unpublished studies. Some reports and data come from studies of men who have sex with men (MSM) or of people living with HIV. Very few studies have specifically focused on lesbian or bisexual women or on transgender populations.

Mongolia is in Asia, bordered by China to the south and Russia to the north. Its population is approximately 3 million. Traditionally a livestock-based nomadic society with shamanistic and Buddhist religious practices, Mongolia began an intensive modernization and industrialization push in the early 1960s, leading to the gradual urbanization and decline in its livestock-based nomadic practice that continues to this day (World Bank, 2017). Mongolia was a satellite state of the Soviet Union from 1939 to 1990 (Weatherford, 2005). When the Soviets withdrew from Mongolia, the economy experienced a transitional recession (Weatherford, 2005). With political and economic strife over the past 20 or more years, and gaps growing between the rich and the poor (Casey, 2015), the environment has been rich for extreme right-wing and nationalist views that promote hatred against "outsiders." Outsiders may include foreigners, interracial couples, binational couples, and members of the LGBT community (Casey, 2015). As the transition from an authoritarian socialist country to a democratic system has led to increased visibility and awareness of human rights, particularly LGBT rights, it has also led to increased intolerance, discrimination, and anti-LGBT sentiment that the media has

[2]Throughout the chapter, *LGBT* is used as an umbrella term to refer to lesbian, gay, bisexual, transgender, intersex, queer, gender expansive, and other identities.

often perpetuated (LGBT Centre, 2016b). The attitudes within Mongolia may also reflect its long-standing relationship with Russia, where anti-LGBT sentiment has increased in recent years (Schaaf, 2014).

Historically, due to economic limitations and other social forces, Mongolians raised livestock in tight-knit family-based microcosms to survive in the country's vast swaths of land and harsh climatic conditions. Anthropologically and socially speaking, there were no *extra people*. In other words, regardless of who one was, not a single person was considered expendable and/or outcast. Oral histories and traditional sayings confirm that all people were valued and that minority groups within the country had not been *othered* yet. This traditional Mongolian social acceptance of queer identities is analogous with Native American and other preindustrial, presettlement societies in which queer people were a firm and accepted part of the social fabric, often thought of as shamans and medicine people. Although queer identities were unarticulated, they were well recognized historically and called *khootsgon* (and its variations such as *khiosgon* in Buryat dialect), a term that denotes a person who presents both male and female characteristics. The word fell out of use during the socialist period and is now considered archaic and inappropriate given that the term references gender identity alone and is generally considered derogatory (LGBT Centre, 2010a).

Until 2015, there were no comprehensive laws against LGBT discrimination in Mongolia (Kaleidoscope Human Rights Foundation [KHRF], 2015; LGBT Centre, 2016b). In 2015, following years of LGBT Centre advocacy at the United Nations (UN) and at the domestic level with the Mongolian government, a new Criminal Code, which came into effect on July 1, 2017, outlawed discrimination based on sexual orientation or gender identity (KHRF, 2015; LGBT Centre, 2016b). In 2008, the Mongolian government added an amendment to the Law on Civil Registration to make it easier for people to change gender markers on identity documents (KHRF, 2015; LGBT Centre, 2016b). The State Ikh Khural, or the parliament, is currently (as of October 2017) also near the end of deliberations on a draft of a Law on Labour that includes protection from discrimination based on sexual orientation and gender identity. This is a direct result of the LGBT Centre's advocacy work.

According to the LGBT Centre, the Mongolian government has passed a number of other initiatives supportive of LGBT people, such as resolutions to implement recommendations from the Universal Periodic Review (a review process of the UN Human Rights Council) and the National Human Rights Commission (LGBT Centre, 2016b), as well as including nondiscrimination clauses inclusive of both sexual orientation and gender identity in health care policy, specifically in the Medical Practitioners' Ethical Guidelines section 2 (Mongolian Government, 2013), and State Policy on Health section 2.2.1 (Mongolian Government, 2017). However, it appears that in actual practice, the Mongolian government either has not implemented these provisions or has implemented them inconsistently (KHRF, 2015; LGBT Centre, 2016b).

At present, the Mongolian government defines marriage as between a man and a woman (KHRF, 2015). Thus, same-sex marriage is illegal (KHRF, 2015; UNDP & USAID, 2014). In addition, same-sex couples are barred from adopting, from maintaining shared property rights, and from engaging in procedures that would follow the legal dissolution of a relationship (UNDP & USAID, 2014). For LGBT people in Mongolia, the most cited concern is legal service access given that problems with law enforcement are strikingly common (UNDP & USAID, 2014). In fact, 77.4% of LGBT people in Mongolia reported abuse from law enforcement (UNDP & USAID, 2014). The second most cited concern of LGBT people is day-to-day discrimination (UNDP & USAID, 2014). LGBT youth, in particular, report discrimination and physical assaults at school because of their sexual orientation or gender identity (LGBT Centre, 2016a).

Within the context just described, there have been few studies of mental health conducted with LGBT people in Mongolia (KHRF, 2015). KHRF (2015) reported that the National Center of Mental Health in Mongolia provides some mental health services to the LGBT community, but there is a low staff-to-patient ratio and, across Mongolia, a lack of counseling services. At the same time, LGBT people have higher rates of mental health issues, including anxiety, depression, and suicidal ideation (LGBT Centre, 2015). One study of MSM stated that a "large majority" of these men reported symptoms of clinical depression (KHRF, 2015; see also UNDP & USAID, 2014). Current data suggest that 73.3% of LGBT people in Mongolia have considered suicide (KHRF, 2015; UNDP & USAID, 2014).

Further, visibility or being out remain difficult for LGBT Mongolians. Given the aversive climate, 82% of LGBT people report being in the closet at work, and 70% of all LGBT people surveyed stated that they hide their sexual orientation or gender identity when seeking health care (UNDP & USAID, 2014). Fear of being outed to others may affect health care use. Of MSM who reported depression, most did not seek help from a professional (UNDP & USAID, 2014). In response, the LGBT Centre has been active in advocating for LGBT mental health through trainings, a crisis helpline, and outreach to the LGBT community (LGBT Centre, 2016b, 2017).

TRADITIONAL MONGOLIAN VALUES

Historically, LGBT Mongolian identities were largely accepted prior to the 20th century, but toward the latter part of that century, LGBT people became "othered." This shift resulted in the eventual criminalization and pathologization of same-sex identities and practices in Mongolia that were introduced through the country's political alignment with the USSR in 1961 (Schaaf, 2014). The USSR made same-sex identities and practices a crime in its 1926 criminal code and expanded upon this in its 1960 criminal code Section 121 (Schaaf, 2014). This was mirrored in Mongolia in its 1961 criminal code.

LGBT identities came to be unacceptable within Mongolian families (UNDP & USAID, 2014).

As Mongolia has shifted toward becoming a more urbanized democracy, external pressures have been exerted on the country in an effort to shape its policies to fit Western ideals. For example, the World Health Organization has admonished the Mongolian leadership to provide more support for mental health and more protections for LGBT people. As a result of this pressure, policymakers began to pay closer attention to mental health in the early 2000s, which resulted in the creation of two National Mental Health Programs. The first, Government Resolution 59, was implemented between 2002 and 2007, and the second, Government Resolution 303, was implemented between 2010 and 2015 (Mongolian Government, 2002, 2009). Unfortunately, mental health services are concentrated in the largest urban area, Ulaanbaatar, and are scarce in rural areas of the country, which means that primary care physicians are often the providers who end up treating mental health concerns outside of Ulaanbaatar (Erdenetuul, 2010).

Historically, Mongolian people have relied on their close relationships or turned to Buddhist monks and shamans for mental health care. It appears that some may turn to substances such as alcohol to manage negative emotions. This may be why rates of alcohol use are troublingly high in Mongolia (Lim, 2009). In the current Westernized climate, it is unclear whether Mongolian people have become more open to seeking formal mental health services, but there is some evidence indicating that gay and bisexual Mongolians may be less likely to seek health care when they experience discrimination from health care providers (Yasin et al., 2013). It is plausible that the more stigma Mongolians experience, the less likely they are to value their own health and to seek support from mental health professionals. Given the high rates of alcoholism in Mongolia, it is also possible the LGBT Mongolians self-medicate with substances and alcohol (Lim, 2009). More research is needed to determine how LGBT Mongolians cope with stigma and how they understand and seek treatment for mental health concerns.

As mentioned earlier, modern Mongolian families may pressure LGBT individuals to conform to traditional gender roles, pursue heterosexual marriages, and produce children (KHRF, 2015; UNDP & USAID, 2014). This environment is further reinforced by media that, on the whole, depicts LGBT people in a negative light as either worthy of pity or worthy of contempt (UNDP & USAID, 2014). Still, major media outlets are showing signs of positive change, and some have started to provide affirmative coverage of LGBT issues. This was especially the case during the Equality and Pride Days event in 2017.

As a result of traditional family values, lesbian women and gay men may enter into heterosexual marriages while maintaining extramarital same-sex relationships (UNDP & USAID, 2014). Given the difficulty of coming out to loved ones, 86.7% of Mongolians who have been surveyed reported that they are not out to their families. Many LGBT people who are out to their families have reported that they are estranged (32%) from family, whereas 43% have stated that they are excluded from family gatherings (UNDP & USAID, 2014). Within Mongolian society, individuals are expected to be married by their mid-20s, and if one does not get married within this window, pressure from family may begin to increase significantly (UNDP & USAID, 2014), although this trend may be changing at least for some heterosexual Mongolians (Yasin et al., 2013).

Religious observance does not have a unified or definitive impact on Mongolian values and cultural perspectives such as gender roles or mental health stigma in the same way that it may in other countries around the world. In the 1930s, Mongolia underwent a purge of religious objects and books, and only recently, in the post-Soviet context, have surviving artifacts of the religious history of Mongolia prior to the 20th century started to surface (Weatherford, 2005). However, as a consequence of the tumultuous history of Mongolia, Buddhism does not currently play a dominant role in the country, and other influences, such as Christian proselytism and shaman traditions, also impact the religious makeup of Mongolia. Any one of these religious traditions may impact LGBT people at an individual or familial level, but it is difficult to speak to the comprehensive impact of religion on the majority of LGBT people. Current shared cultural mores that impact LGBT Mongolians may be more rooted in political ideologies and cultural transformations than by long-standing religious traditions.

INTERSECTIONALITY

In this section we discuss *intersectionality*, or the overlapping, interconnected roles that urban and rural location, socioeconomic status, religion, gender, ethnicity, age, and traditional Mongolian family values play in the lives of LGBT people in Mongolia. Intersectionality refers to an examination of the ways that multiple minority identities may interact in unique ways (Crenshaw, 1993). In Mongolia, individuals may experience a variety of oppressions that intersect with their LGBT identity. There is not enough research to understand how religious or ethnic identities may intersect with LGBT identities in Mongolia, but with the wide religious and ethnic diversity within Mongolia, we imagine these may play a role as well.

As an example, Temir is an ethnic Kazakh gay man in his mid-30s. Kazakhs are an ethnic minority within Mongolia; most Kazakhs are Muslim, and ethnic Kazakhs are mostly Sunni Muslim. Since the time he came out in his 20s, Temir has been working with gay men's health organizations that work on raising awareness around HIV among MSM. As a gay man who grew up in rural Mongolia within an ethnic, linguistic, and religious minority group, Temir has faced numerous struggles and many instances of violence in his life. Temir remains closeted to his family, who are still living in the country-side. Here we see sexual orientation, ethnicity, rural location, religion, language, and age all intersecting to make Temir's life experience unique.

Location

There are significant differences between resources available to Mongolians living in urban areas, such as Ulaanbaatar, and those in rural areas. At present, no statistics are available regarding the number or percentages of LGBT people living in Ulaanbaatar versus the more rural provinces. In one online study of LGBT people in Mongolia related to poverty, approximately 80% of the respondents reported living in Ulaanbaatar, whereas 14% lived in the provinces (the other 6% reported being out of the country at the time of the survey; LGBT Centre, 2014). However, these figures do not necessarily reflect the actual geographic distribution of LGBT persons. Instead, the low percentage of rural respondents may be a reflection of limited Internet access and few urban social networks and connections.

In the city of Ulaanbaatar, there are some LGBT-focused services and events organized through the LGBT Centre. As of June 2017, there was one gay bar in Mongolia, located in Ulaanbaatar. This bar, and other bars, have been closed in the past because of issues with discrimination, police raids, and lack of attendance (Seidman, 2016). Another resource in Ulaanbaatar is the Youth for Health Centre, which is a nongovernmental organization that focuses on HIV-related health issues faced by MSM (KHRF, 2015). There is no information about LGBT organizations, resources, or events for LGBT people outside of Ulaanbaatar. However, the LGBT Centre does operate a crisis helpline that is available for anyone in the country to call.

Socioeconomic Status

With Mongolia recovering from an economic recession over the past 20 years, socioeconomic status plays a major role in the lives of Mongolians who identify as LGBT. In 2014, the unemployment rate for the whole country was 7.9% (Census and Economic Information Center, 2017), whereas the unemployment rate of LGBT people was higher than 10% (LGBT Centre, 2014). Approximately 14% of respondents reported earning less than 140,000 MNT (2017 equivalent of USD$60) monthly, which is below the Mongolian poverty line (LGBT Centre, 2014). Many responded that they rely on their parents or other family support for financial difficulties. At the time the survey was conducted in 2014, LGBT participants reported that poverty and unemployment were affecting everyone in their community (LGBT Centre, 2014). Participants reported that their ability to acquire a job and earn an income was related to whether they were closeted at work rather than on their qualifications or on other situational factors.

More broadly, participants reported that being LGBT affected their ability to pursue education, acquire employment, and afford health care that is necessary for interventions such as gender affirmation or transition. They also expressed concern that there were no laws in effect to protect LGBT persons from work discrimination. Some stated that poverty and inability to pursue education and find employment affected self-esteem, promoted substance abuse, and pushed LGBT people, especially transgender women, to turn to sex work for income (LGBT Centre, 2014).

Gender

There is not any research directly comparing experiences of gay men and lesbian women in Mongolia. However, according to the LGBT Centre (2016b), there is "widespread societal and institutional discrimination against, and intolerance of, lesbian and bisexual women and transgender persons in Mongolia" (p. 3). Based on focus group discussions with lesbian and bisexual women and transgender (LBT) persons, the Centre reported that generally, LBT people do not disclose experiences of discrimination or violence for fear of repercussions or additional trauma from law enforcement personnel, health care workers, or social workers/psychologists. Focus group participants shared concerns particularly related to health care, including gynecological, reproductive, and transition-related health care. For example, transgender persons cannot receive hormone replacement therapy through the publicly funded health care system in Mongolia (KHRF, 2015). Health issues for LBT individuals are exacerbated by lack of awareness or training, outright refusal to provide services to LBT persons, and heteronormative and cis-normative approaches to health care among health professionals (LGBT Centre, 2016b). LBT persons report pressure from society and family to enter into heterosexual marriages; discrimination in the realm of housing and employment (KHRF, 2015); and discrimination based on their hairstyle, clothing, or other markers of appearance (LGBT Centre, 2016b).

Age

The authors identified one study that focused on the intersection of age and lesbian, gay, bisexual, and transgender, and intersex (LGBTI) identity in Mongolia. The study focused on the experiences of children younger than age 18 and was conducted in 2016 by the LGBT Centre. In total, 19 children and youth were interviewed (LGBT Centre, 2016a). Of the children interviewed, 26% identified as gay or lesbian, 63% identified as bisexual, and 11% identified as straight in terms of sexual orientation. Regarding gender identity, 84% identified as cisgender and 16% identified as transgender. Although the sample size for this study was relatively small, the results are striking. To begin with, only one of the participants reported feeling safe to be out at home, and only two reported feeling safe to be out at school. As many as 80% of the participants reported general discrimination or ostracism because of their identity; 45% reported discrimination, ostracism, or violence at home/from family; and 42% reported discrimination, ostracism, or violence in their education environment from teachers and peers.

In general, interviewees reported problems with discrimination, ostracism, and violence in their homes and at school. Meanwhile, they reported that they did not have access to accurate information on sexual orientation or gender identity to counteract the negative messages they encountered on a regular basis. For example, all of the children who identified as transgender also reported that mental health professionals told them that their "transgender feelings" would go away (LGBT Centre, 2016a). The impact of such an aversive climate for young people has yet to be studied in Mongolia. The first author's perception from her brief stay in Mongolia was that there was a large generation-based gap between youth (who were curious, open, and active) and older generations who previously lived under Soviet control and were more closed and resistant to acceptance of LGBT people.

FUTURE DIRECTIONS

We conclude with recommendations for culturally relevant interventions and prevention work in Mongolia that may have implications for other post-Soviet countries. Although we separate these recommendations into the categories of health, education, law enforcement, and legislation and policy, these guidelines are appropriate for all educators, human rights advocates, law enforcement personnel, government officials, mental health practitioners, and physicians.

Health

LGBT people in Mongolia need access to culturally and technically competent health care and knowledgeable physical and mental health providers. Barriers to seeking services in Mongolia include invisibility, fear of judgment, fear of being outed as LGBT, fear of harassment or insults, outright refusal of services, and providers who are not knowledgeable (LGBT Centre, 2016b). We recommend specific and ongoing training and education for health providers in every arena, including instruction in best practices, ethics, and scholarship specific to LGBT issues and concerns. Governmental health care systems may benefit from offering specialized providers for the LGBT community who are familiar with lesbian, gay, bisexual, transgender, and queer/questioning (LGBTQ) affirmative work, an approach that embraces a positive view of LGBTQ identities and relationships and addresses the negative influences that homophobia, transphobia, and heterosexism have on the lives of LGBTQ clients (Edwards-Leeper, Leibowitz, & Sangganjanavanich, 2016).

In 2013, the Mongolian Ministry of Health added a new Code of Ethics for health professionals, which guides practitioners to not discriminate based on sexual orientation or gender identity (KHRF, 2015; UNDP & USAID, 2014). However, it is unclear whether training is provided to health care providers regarding ethical practice with LGBT people, which is problematic. There are several international standards and guidelines, such as the World Professional Association for Transgender Health (2011) Standards of Care; the American Psychological Association (APA) *Guidelines for Psychological Practice with Lesbian,*

Gay, and Bisexual Clients (APA, 2011); and the APA *Guidelines for Psychological Practice With Transgender and Gender Nonconforming People* (APA, 2015). Some of these have been translated into Mongolian by the LGBT Centre but have not been used widely. We recommend that practitioners within Mongolia develop their own culturally relevant standards to guide practice with LGBT persons.

Education

Professionals who work with children and youth, particularly teachers, social workers, and counselors, must be educated on providing culturally competent and affirmative services to LGBT youth younger than age 18 in Mongolia. LGBTI youth reported that perpetrators of violence toward them were family members (45%), peers (26%), teachers (16%), and psychologists (13%; LGBT Centre, 2016a). These numbers also indicate that prevention of violence and antibullying work must be done in educational settings at early ages. Educators should also engage in activities that promote education of the public through social media or other outlets.

We suggest that national and local initiatives should include education aimed at reducing societal discrimination and misguided prejudice against LGBT people. For example, efforts toward this end may include the creation of working groups and community discussions that may increase acceptance and understanding of LGBT issues. In regard to education systems at every level, we recommend that curricula be revised to include LGBT representation. Educational materials that take an approach to education that incorporates sensitivity to diversity and that removes heteronormative, sexist, and cisnormative biases may assist with reducing anti-LGBT bias.

Law Enforcement

Regarding law enforcement officials, we suggest that hate crimes trainings, civil rights trainings, diversity education, and briefings on best practices are imperative if conditions are to improve for LGBT people. Because LGBT Mongolians may be afraid to approach law enforcement officials, specific actions may create alliances between the LGBT community and law enforcement personnel. For example, law enforcement personnel may benefit from attending support groups or open discussion forums designed to place them in contact with the narratives of LGBT people. By creating opportunities for open and safe contact between law enforcement officials and LGBT community members, greater trust may be fostered that may result in increased rates of reporting and use of law enforcement services. This could lead to the maintenance of more accurate statistics regarding assaults and crimes perpetrated against LGBT people.

Legislation and Policy

Change will be most successful when it is supported on the national level through legislation and amendments that provide protections and equality for LGBT individuals. Without the cooperation of national and local govern-mental agencies, LGBT people remain vulnerable to work, school, and insti-tutional discrimination, as well as other forms of prejudice. Comprehensive, broad-based antidiscrimination legislation should include protections against workplace discrimination and a definition of human rights that includes gender identity and sexual orientation. Specific legislation is warranted not only to address discrimination more broadly but also to attend to rampant sexual violence and sexual assault against LGBT people.

The LGBT Centre (Ulaanbaatar, Mongolia)

In 2015, the LGBT Centre in Ulaanbaatar, Mongolia, hosted a Fulbright Spe-cialist to focus on mental health and prevention of violence, both familial and societal. The development of this chapter was influenced by the personal experiences of the first author (Koch) as a White, queer, cisgender, female psychologist who traveled to Ulaanbaatar to work with the LGBT Centre. The third author (Nyamdorj) is the cofounder of the LGBT Centre of Mongolia. He identifies as an Asian, queer, transgender male, and mental health issues for LGBT people are close to his heart. Most of the collaborative work between Koch and Nyamdorj has focused on the prevention of violence and treatment of trauma in LGBT people in Mongolia. During Koch's time in Ulaanbaatar, she developed and implemented crisis intervention training for Crisis Helpline volunteers at the Centre. She also developed and implemented training work-shops for local practitioners and university faculty members in social work, psychology, and psychiatry.

The LGBT Centre of Mongolia was initially established in 2007 but was not officially registered until 2009 due to resistance from the Mongolian government (Casey, 2015; LGBT Centre, 2010b). Since its establishment, it has sponsored awareness events, fund-raisers, and international artists and scholars. The LGBT Centre has a Legal Programme, Youth Programme, and Health Programme. It advocates for LGBT rights with the UN and other inter-national human rights organizations. It has actively solicited external funding to support development of awareness, educational programs, and mental health for LGBT people. For example, in early 2015, artist Nathan Stoneham was an artist-in-residence at the Centre who assisted with the organization of the performance art piece titled "Love Bus." Stoneham's project centered on a bus tour around Ulaanbaatar that made stops at locations significant to the LGBT community to facilitate dialogue and to build awareness about LGBT rights in Mongolia (Khishigjargal, 2015). This project attracted media attention and was well received by participants; one participant called it "life changing" (Khishigjargal, 2015).

The LGBT Centre held its first Pride Week in 2013 and has sponsored Equality and Pride Days in following years. The Equality Walk, one of the Pride events, has had increasing public participation and support despite historical attempts to block such programs. For example, municipality and law enforcement officials have restricted pedestrian traffic in areas in which the walk was preapproved to occur, in violation of event permits properly filed and approved by the government and law enforcement (LGBT Centre, 2017). In 2016 and 2017, LGBT Centre activities included trainings for staff of youth development centers, gynecologists, social workers, human resources specialists, psychiatrists, and psychologists; a queer film festival; Voices-4-Equality public concert; a series of training sessions for disability rights civil society organizations; participation in and organization of a workshop on international advocacy and LGBTI rights during the Asia Europe People's Forum; advocacy to obtain recommendations on improving the situation of LGBTI people from the UN Committees on Elimination of Discrimination Against Women and the Committee against Torture; and numerous other art functions and public education events (LGBT Centre, 2017).

CONCLUSION

As specific issues arise in the LGBT community, it is important that these issues not be treated as pathological but that reasonable, nonjudgmental services be provided to address the needs of this unique and diverse population. Ultimately, our recommendations must be actually implemented for change to occur. In report after report, the LGBT Centre has written about the fact that although the Mongolian government has adopted laws, provisions, or amendments, many of these have yet to be fully enforced. The Mongolian government appears to be invested in placating the UN regarding human rights concerns that have been brought to light but has been slower when it comes to actually enforcing these laws. The government must not only enact policies but also provide funding and infrastructure for implementation.

REFERENCES

American Psychological Association. (2011). *Guidelines for psychological practice with lesbian, gay, and bisexual clients.* Washington, DC: Author.

American Psychological Association. (2015). *Guidelines for psychological practice with transgender and gender nonconforming people.* Washington, DC: Author.

Casey, K. (2015, June 11). *Yes we khaan: Fighting for equality in Mongolia.* Retrieved from www.postpravdamagazine.com/yes-we-khaan/

Census and Economic Information Center. (2017). Mongolia household income per capita. Retrieved from https://www.ceicdata.com/en/country/mongolia

Crenshaw, K. W. (1993). Beyond racism and misogyny: Black feminism and 2 Live Crew. In M. J. Matsuda, C. R. Lawrence, R. Delgado, & K. W. Crenshaw (Eds.), *Words that wound: Critical race theory, assaultive speech, and the First Amendment* (pp. 111–132). Boulder, CO: Westview.

Edwards-Leeper, L., Leibowitz, S., & Sangganjanavanich, V. F. (2016). Affirmative practice with transgender and gender nonconforming youth: Expanding the model. *Psychology of Sexual Orientation and Gender Diversity, 3*, 165–172. http://dx.doi.org/10.1037/sgd0000167

Erdenetuul, N. (2010). Where there's no psychiatrist—Mongolia. *Asia-Pacific Psychiatry*, *2*, 127. http://dx.doi.org/10.1111/j.1758-5872.2010.00074.x

Kaleidoscope Human Rights Foundation. (2015, April). *Shadow report to the UN Committee on Economic, Social and Cultural Rights regarding Mongolia's protection of the rights of LGBTI persons.* Unpublished report, Kaleidoscope Human Rights Foundation, Clayton, Victoria, Australia.

Khishigjargal, E. (2015, April 14). Where can the Love Bus take you? *The UB Post.* Retrieved from ubpost.mongolnews.mn/?p=14187

LGBT Centre. (2010a). *How to write about sexual orientation and gender identity: A handbook for media* [Mongolian]. Unpublished paper, LGBT Centre of Mongolia, Ulaanbaatar, Mongolia.

LGBT Centre. (2010b). *The LGBT Centre report on the human rights situation of the lesbian, gay, bisexual and transgender (LGBT) people in Mongolia—For the 101st session of the UN Human Rights Committee (CCPR).* Unpublished report, LGBT Centre of Mongolia, Ulaanbaatar, Mongolia.

LGBT Centre. (2014). *Poverty and the lesbian, gay, bisexual and transgender community in Mongolia: Survey report.* Unpublished report, LGBT Centre of Mongolia, Ulaanbaatar, Mongolia.

LGBT Centre. (2015). *Report on Mongolia—Twenty second round of the Universal Periodic Review.* Unpublished report, LGBT Centre of Mongolia, Ulaanbaatar, Mongolia.

LGBT Centre. (2016a). *Findings of the research done for the UN Committee on the Rights of the Child: LGBTI children and youth in Mongolia.* Unpublished report, LGBT Centre of Mongolia, Ulaanbaatar, Mongolia.

LGBT Centre. (2016b). *The status of lesbian, bisexual women and transgender persons in Mongolia: Shadow report for the 63rd Convention on the Elimination of all Forms of Discrimination Against Women (CEDAW) session 2016.* Unpublished report, LGBT Centre of Mongolia, Ulaanbaatar, Mongolia.

LGBT Centre. (2017). *LGBT Centre activities report, 1 August 2016 to 31 January 2017.* Unpublished report, LGBT Centre of Mongolia, Ulaanbaatar, Mongolia.

Lim, L. (2009, September 7). Mongolians seek fortune in gold, but at a cost. *National Public Radio Morning Edition.* Retrieved from https://www.npr.org/2009/09/07/112516360/mongolians-seek-fortune-in-gold-but-at-a-cost

Mongolian Government. (2002). Government resolution number 59. Retrieved from http://www.legalinfo.mn/annex/details/1502?lawid=3681

Mongolian Government. (2009). Government resolution number 303. Retrieved from http:/emg.to.gov.mn/upload/shilendans/580fbb9bc87fbeb6173fbc523103d4dd.pdf

Mongolian Government. (2013). Medical Practitioners' Ethical Guidelines Section 2. Retrieved from http://www.legalinfo.mn/annex/details/6084?lawid=9583

Mongolian Government. (2017). State Policy on Health Section 2.2.1. Retrieved from http://www.legalinfo.mn/annex/details/7663?lawid=12536

Schaaf, M. (2014). Advocating for equality: A brief history of LGBT rights in Russia. *Harriman Magazine*, pp. 23–27. Retrieved from http://www.columbia.edu/cu/creative/epub/harriman/2014/winter/advocating_for_equality.pdf

Seidman, L. (2016, June 3). Inside Mongolia's only gay bar. *Gawker.* Retrieved from gawker.com/inside-mongolia-s-only-gay-bar-1778436860

United Nations Development Programme, & U.S. Agency for International Development. (2014). *Being LGBT in Asia: Mongolia country report.* Bangkok, Thailand: United Nations Development Programme.

Weatherford, J. (2005). *Genghis Khan and the making of the modern world.* New York, NY: Crown.

World Bank. (2017). *Rural population (% of total population)* [Figure]. Retrieved from https://data.worldbank.org/indicator/SP.RUR.TOTL.ZS?end=2015&locations=MN&sta=1960&view=chart

World Professional Association for Transgender Health. (2011). *Standards of care for the health of transsexual, transgender, and gender nonconforming people.* Retrieved from https://www.wpath.org/publications/soc

Yasin, F., Delegchoimbol, A., Yamiyanjamts, N., Sovd, T., Mason, K., & Baral, S. (2013). A cross-sectional evaluation of correlates of HIV testing practices among men who have sex with men (MSM) in Mongolia. *Aids Behavior, 17,* 1378–1385. http://dx.doi.org/10.1007/s10461-013-0412-5

7

Stigma Toward and Mental Health of Hijras/Trans Women and Self-Identified Men Who Have Sex With Men in India

Venkatesan Chakrapani, Peter A. Newman, and Murali Shunmugam

"Doctor, can you change me?" AJ (pseudonym), a gay-identified college student asked the lead author of this chapter. I asked AJ to clarify what he meant by "change" just to make sure I got the meaning right. "To become normal, like other men," he replied. Before meeting AJ, I had seen several *kothi*-identified males (i.e., feminine gender expression and primarily adopt a receptive sexual role), but never did they request that I "change" them. So I asked AJ what prompted him to ask this. AJ revealed that he felt guilty about being attracted to men and that he felt responsible for having "seduced" his male lover who was otherwise "normal"—meaning he "was dating girls." He was also in a dilemma about his family's reactions if they found out about his sexuality. I still remember having asked AJ one question, which apparently provided some clarity for him: "Would you still want to 'change' if the society and your family accepted you as who you are?" He took a moment and then responded, "No." But that moment of clarity became shrouded by his worries about being his parents' only son, what would happen to his family line, and the possibility that his parents could not "show their face" to their relatives because of him.

HISTORICAL AND CULTURAL CONTEXT

Several sources of evidence indicate the presence of sexual and gender minorities in India for centuries—the Kama Sutra and other written traditions,

http://dx.doi.org/10.1037/0000159-008
LGBTQ Mental Health: International Perspectives and Experiences, N. Nakamura and C. H. Logie (Editors)

sculptures in ancient Indian monuments and temples, and Indian mythology. The Kama Sutra dedicates a specific chapter for "oral sex," in which it describes males with a "third nature" (*Tritiya prakriti*) who perform oral sex on other men (Vatsyayana, ca. 400 BCE/1994). The text describes two types of such persons: those in female dress and those in male dress—that is, essentially describing persons who would now be labeled as transgender women and same-sex attracted men, respectively. The Kama Sutra casually mentions marriage between two men and uses the term *svairini* (literally translated by scholars as "virile or independent women") to refer to lesbian women. History scholars show that homonegative texts began to appear during the 19th century, during British rule (Vanita & Kidwai, 2006). Other evidence of sexual and gender minority representations emerges from stone sculptures in ancient monuments and temples, such as Khajuraho, Ajanta, and Ellora, which have several statues depicting sexual acts between two men and between two women. Similarly, the great Indian epics, such as the Ramayana and Mahabharata, describe same-sex relations, as well as trans persons (e.g., Shikhandi, a warrior princess who became a man, in the Mahabharata; Custodi, 2007; Pattanaik, 2014). All of these examples illustrate the centuries-old presence of same-gender-attracted people and trans people in India and suggest peaceful coexistence of sexual and gender minorities with other citizens in ancient India.

Despite this substantial historical evidence, arguments are still made in Indian mainstream media that Western influence contributed to homosexuality in India. Thus, ironically, Section 377 of the Indian Penal Code, which was introduced by the British to criminalize consensual same-gender relations between adults, was reinstated by the Indian Supreme Court in December 2013, after a brief period of decriminalization of adult same-gender relations from July 2009. In its judgment, the Supreme Court argued that lesbian, gay, bisexual, and transgender (LGBT) communities constitute a "miniscule fraction" (*Koushal v. Naz Foundation*, 2013, p. 83) and that the majority view needed to be heeded. Also, it opined that only Parliament can enact laws to decriminalize or legalize sex between consenting same-gender adults—not the courts. However, elected representatives in India generally avoid discussion of sexual and gender minorities. A member of Parliament who openly supported the rights of sexual minorities was ridiculed as being a same-gender-attracted person himself. In contrast, the Supreme Court rendered a progressive judgment in relation to transgender people in the case of *National Legal Services Authority v. Union Government* (2014), in which it allowed trans people to choose the gender with which they identified, waived the need for medical diagnosis to certify a person as transgender, and regarded the terms *third gender* and *transgender* as legally valid gender identity terms. Nevertheless, that judgment was silent about the sexual lives of trans people, as any such discussions would have created a conflict with the judgment related to Section 377 and the Immoral Trafficking Prevention Act (1986), which criminalizes soliciting clients for sex work. Overall, this situation has been characterized as "India's U-turn on LGBTQ rights" (Mitra, 2014), and "one step forward, two steps back." As aptly described in the *Hindustan Times* (Jyoti, 2015), "the noose of Section 377 hangs over it all—a festering weapon of harassment, intimidation and violence" (para. 11). However, on September 6, 2018, 4 years subsequent to the National Legal Services Authority, the Supreme Court declared that sex between consenting same-gender adults is not illegal. However, it will take considerable time to see the implementation of this decision, to change negative societal attitudes toward same-gender attracted people, and to achieve rights equal to those of other citizens in India.

CONSTRUCTIONS OF SEXUALITY AND GENDER WITHIN COMMUNITIES OF SAME-SEX-ATTRACTED MEN AND TRANS WOMEN IN INDIA

Although the mental health issues of lesbian women and trans men in India are equally important, due to the near wholesale lack of academic publications about these populations, we focus on mental health issues of men who have sex with men (MSM) and trans women in India in this chapter. Although the English language terms *gay* and *bisexual* are commonly used by middle and upper socioeconomic class sexual minorities in India, several indigenous self-identity terms are used by same-sex-attracted men who are primarily of lower or lower-middle socioeconomic status. In academic and social policy, including HIV program literature, MSM refers to any men who have sex with other men, regardless of their sexual orientation or identity. Those from lower/middle socioeconomic classes are usually categorized as kothi, *double-decker*, or *panthi*—primarily based on their sexual role. Typically, kothis are described as "feminine and receptive," panthi as "masculine and insertive," and double-deckers as both insertive and receptive with their male partners (e.g., Chakrapani, Newman, Mhaprolkar, & Kavi, 2007). However, a discordance between identity and sexual role (especially among kothis) has been reported in several studies (e.g., Chakrapani, Newman, Mhaprolkar, & Kavi, 2007; Phillips et al., 2008; Stief, 2017). These identities or labels are largely unknown to the general public, as kothis and *hijras* (a visible subculture of trans women in India) were apparently the creators of these terms and used them as a code language, at least to start with, before they became understood in broader circles as identities. The terms kothi, panthi, and double-decker have been called "gender/sexual identities" (Asthana & Oostvogels, 2001, used *danga* instead of *kothi*, probably reflecting the terminology at that time), MSM sexual identities (Phillips et al., 2008), gender-role-based identities (Chakrapani et al., 2002), and identities based on gender expression and sexual role (Chakrapani, Shunmugam, Newman, Kershaw, & Dubrow, 2015).

Over the past 15 to 20 years, the meanings and nuances of the self-identifications used by same-sex-attracted men in India have evolved significantly (e.g., Asthana & Oostvogels, 2001; Bose & Bhattacharyya, 2007; Chakrapani, Kavi, et al., 2002; Chakrapani, Shunmugam, et al., 2015; Cohen,

2006). Heated arguments emerge when sexual minority community leaders, with the same or different identities, come together in consultations and conferences to debate what their identities mean. Accordingly, the descriptions offered here should be approached with an understanding of their inherent limitations, including disagreements within sexual minority communities, variations across India's vast geography, and inevitable changes over time.

In Indian mainstream society, there are not equivalent cultural concepts of heterosexuality and homosexuality as in Western societies; although technical terms have been coined to refer to "heterosexual," there are apparently no lay language terms for "heterosexual" in any of the many Indian languages. However, most Indian languages have several derogatory terms to refer to men who are "not men" or who are "woman-like."

From the point of view of kothis and hijras, men are seen as either "man" or "not man." A "real man" (or panthi/*giriya*) is defined by his presumably almost exclusive attraction toward cisgender women and his insertive sexual role. However, sex with men largely does not impact on his presumed sexual identity if such a "real man" chooses to have sex with feminine men. Nevertheless, if he states that he is attracted to other masculine men, or if he adopts a receptive sexual role, then he is not considered to be a "real man" by kothis/hijras.

These ideas are similar to the conceptualizations of homosexuality among the general public, who suspect a man to be a homosexual if he appears feminine. Thus, an ostensibly masculine man will not be suspected to be engaging in same-gender sexual behaviors, and even if he is found to have had sex with another man, he will still be not considered a "homosexual" as long as his sexual role is perceived to be that of a "man" (i.e., insertive). That is, the conceptualization of homosexuality among both the general public and kothis/hijras is derived from the expected gender roles of man and woman: man—masculine and insertive; woman—feminine and receptive. This conceptualization, however, becomes problematic, as kothis and hijras often see sex between two masculine men or two feminine men as inappropriate. This means that even sex between two kothis remains a taboo; if other kothis found out about such a relationship, those kothis would be teased and mocked for having engaged in "lesbian sex." This may have implications for how kothis conceptualize their own sexuality, links with internalized homonegativity, and for their mental health.

Trans women in India also have several indigenous identities; a widely known and visible trans community is that of hijras, especially in North and Western India. Other indigenous self-identification terms of trans women vary by regions: *kinnars* in North India, *thirunangai* in Tamil Nadu, *mangalmukhi* in Karnataka, *shivshakti* in Andhra Pradesh, and *jogappa* or *jogta* in parts of Karnataka and Maharashtra (Chakrapani, Newman, Mhaprolkar, & Kavi, 2007; Chakrapani, Newman, & Noronha, 2018). Trans men too are now using locally relevant terms to reflect the indigenous nature of their self-identity (e.g., *thiru nambi* in Tamil Nadu). However, many trans activists, irrespective of their indigenous trans identities, also use the English term *transgender* to refer to themselves or their communities, particularly during discussions in national and international forums.

High Prevalence of Mental-Health-Related Problems

Studies that focus on mental health challenges of sexual and gender minorities in India are very limited. The prevalence of moderate or severe depression among 300 MSM and 300 trans women in a sample recruited through community agencies was 35.3% and 42.0%, respectively (Chakrapani, Newman, Shunmugam, Logie, & Samuel, 2017), compared with 13.9% prevalence of depression among 12,557 heterosexual cisgender men (general population) sampled from household surveys (Poongothai, Pradeepa, Ganesan, & Mohan, 2009). Similarly, the prevalence of suicidal ideation was 44.9% among 150 MSM (Sivasubramanian et al., 2011). High levels of stigma and discrimination, including sexual violence faced by MSM and trans women (Chakrapani, Newman, et al., 2017; Shaw et al., 2012), have been shown to contribute to depression (Chakrapani, Vijin, et al., 2017; Logie, Newman, Chakrapani, & Shunmugam, 2012). These problems may be compounded by the lack of sufficient mental health services with competence in working with sexual and gender minority populations.

MENTAL HEALTH ISSUES IN THE LIVES OF MSM AND TRANS WOMEN IN INDIA

Given the limited research on mental health issues on MSM and trans women, for this section we primarily use qualitative data conducted by our team in different parts of India, in collaboration with community-based agencies working with MSM and trans women. Wherever data are available, we cite other studies and mainstream newspaper articles as well.

Growing Up in a Patriarchal Environment and Understanding One's Sexuality or Gender Identity

Studies among kothis and trans women have reported that as they grew up, they were treated just like any other children—until their family members noticed mannerisms or behaviors that were stereotypically seen as feminine or if boys expressed interest in girls' dresses or accessories (Chakrapani & Dhall, 2011; Reddy, 2007). Parents and elder brothers may resort to physical punishment in their attempt to enforce "gender-appropriate" behavior. Some gender-variant children thus leave their families on their own and may find supportive hijra community in cities. Thus, during adolescence many of these youth face turmoil in understanding and dealing with their gender identity, which in turn may affect their mental health. Often there is a lack of family and peer support and constrained access to mental health professionals. Psychological stress experienced during adolescence may be so severe that suicidal ideation and attempts have been reported by both MSM and trans people during their teenage years (Chakrapani, Samuel, Shunmugam, & Sivasubramanian, 2013; Gwalani, 2015). A mother of a trans woman described a suicide attempt by her adult child:

> He used to come home late at night. I used to ask why he was coming home late. But he never opened his mouth. One day I got angry and I shouted at him badly. He took a lot of sleeping pills [a suicide attempt]. We admitted him in a private hospital and spent around 50,000 rupees for his treatment. Again he attempted suicide. We took him to [government hospital]. Somehow we were able to save him. Only after that we came to know about [the gender identity of their son]. (Chakrapani & Dhall, p. 14)

Despite these frequently described negative experiences, studies have also documented that gender-diverse children may develop friendships with gender-variant peers and schoolmates and support one another—especially when they were teased or called names by other students (Chakrapani & Dhall, 2011; Munoz-Plaza, Quinn, & Rounds, 2002). Family members also may be supportive, although they are generally concerned about negative reactions of the larger society to their child's sexuality or gender expression more so than their experiences of stress by virtue of a hostile community and society (Chakrapani & Dhall, 2011).

Disclosing One's Sexuality or Gender Identity

Studies have found that gay or transgender persons often did not want to disclose their sexual orientation or gender identity because of fear of negative consequences from their family members—for example, eviction, isolation, or rejection (Chakrapani & Dhall, 2011; Chakrapani et al., 2013). Suicidal ideation and attempts because of fear of rejection from one's family have been reported (Tomori, McFall, et al., 2016). Some youth did not want to bring shame upon their family or pose problems to their siblings—especially sisters or other female relatives whose marriage proposals might be affected. For example, in a multisite qualitative study on the impact of stigma on mental health of MSM, a kothi dancer said the following:

> Once I went to a family's home taking the marriage proposal for my sister-in-law. They refused the proposal stating that they don't want to have any relations with the family that has a "dancing and singing" background. [They said] "You dance and sing and we don't approve of it." So I said "I dance and sing. My sister-in-law doesn't sing and dance. She is from other house." They said that you will have to change yourself and this is not approved of in the society we live in. (Chakrapani et al., 2013, p. 51)

In a qualitative study in Chennai and Mumbai that explored family acceptance of MSM and trans women (Chakrapani & Dhall, 2011), parents of gender-variant children reported always suspecting that "something was wrong" (p. 14) or wishing that things would eventually become "normal" (p. 18). In that study, MSM (ages 19–27) and trans women (ages 19–34) also reported violence from fathers and elder brothers once they found out that their son or brother preferred to wear girls' clothing. As sex, in general, is a taboo subject in most homes—regardless of the gender of one's partner—it is most often not discussed openly. An indirect way by which parents handle this situation is to start looking for a girl to introduce to their son in an attempt to "cure" his problem.

Recently, stories of acceptance by family members have been documented as well, as in some Pride marches (e.g., in Mumbai) in which parents and siblings jointly participated with their same-sex-attracted or gender-diverse child or sibling (Uttamchandan, 2016). Until disclosure to family members, many gay, bisexual, and trans persons experience stress in hiding their sexuality or gender identity and lack support from other people in dealing with such situations. Sometimes after disclosure to family members, parents may choose to take their son to a psychiatrist in an attempt to "cure" his homosexuality (Narrain & Chandran, 2016). In the author's own clinical practice, a father brought his doctor son with him for a counseling session, as he felt that his son was lying about his inability to have sex with a woman. The father wanted the author (VC) to check if his son was impotent. He also thought that a doctor would listen to another doctor's advice. This reaction may be common among parents and siblings who may misunderstand that a man's lack of attraction to women means there is a problem with his masculinity or "potency" and thus a "cure" is possible. Rarely do resources exist in most Indian cities for parents of same-gender-attracted children in terms of providing accurate information or counseling or access to support groups of parents of sexual/gender minority children. Thus, disclosure-related issues pose challenges to the mental health of gay/bisexual and trans persons as well as their family members, and discomfort in discussing sex-related matters in general within the family remains a barrier.

Love and Marriage

MSM and trans people often report having different types of male partners, including regular, casual, paying, and/or paid (e.g., National AIDS Control Organisation [NACO], 2015). Important to note, some MSM may make a conscious decision not to seek a steady male partner, as many men, including same-sex attracted men, eventually get married in response to familial and social pressure and expectations, and MSM anticipate that this may leave them heartbroken. For example, in a mainstream newspaper article, a gay man explained his breakup with his boyfriend:

> He too was a closeted gay, but was far too petrified to ever come out. When he refused to commit to a future with me just because his family would not accept it, and he'd ultimately have to marry a girl as all Indian men are expected to do, I broke up with him. Our relationship lasted only a few months, but it left me

emotionally scarred and broken in spirit. But I also realized that it was not totally his fault.

AJ, the gay college student, eventually left his male lover and married a woman to comply with his parents' wishes and deeply rooted familial and societal norms. Now, a decade later, although the situation has not changed drastically, one may also hear rare stories of two men getting married in a traditional ceremony (Gupta, 2015) and a mother posting an advertisement in the classifieds section of a newspaper for a groom for her gay son (Cumming, 2016).

Among hijras and other trans women, too, finding a male lover is often difficult. A decade ago, the first author knew of an incident in which a panthi who loved a hijra and wanted to live with her had to pay a huge amount to the guru of that hijra so that she could be allowed to go with him. These days, stories of hijras and trans women getting married to a man are reported, although the legal validity of that marriage is yet to be tested. A trans activist from Tamil Nadu even started a matrimonial website for trans people (Amir, 2009). Although that website is now inactive, it at least attracted the attention of mainstream media and contributed to sensitizing the general public about a right that is denied to trans people. Not all same-sex-attracted people may desire to get married to a same-gender partner, as they may have the opinion that marriage is a heterosexual institution and gay men need not follow it. However, for those people who desire to get married to the partner of their choice, regardless of their gender, lack of legal recognition of same-sex marriage may be a psychological stressor (Vanita, 2005).

Discourses surrounding marriage of self-identified MSM have most often been couched in terms of family pressure to get married or using marriage as a cover to hide their sexuality (Mayer et al., 2015; Pandya, 2011; Shahani, 2008). However, it has also been documented that self-identified MSM may choose whether to get married to a woman in more practical terms (Chakrapani, Boyce, & Dhanikachalam, 2011; Closson et al., 2014). For one, a small proportion of MSM, including kothis, may also be attracted to women; bisexual orientation has been stated as a reason for voluntarily getting married to a woman. For example, in a multisite qualitative study on female partners of MSM, a married man with bisexual sexual practices reported, "When I was young I looked better. We fell in love with each other and finally got married. I met her only two months before the day we eloped to get married" (Chakrapani, Boyce, & Dhanikachalam, 2011, p. 9). For many other MSM, however, marrying a woman is a duty to one's family in terms of sustaining the family lineage, and one's sexual life and family life are often seen as separate (Chakrapani, Boyce, & Dhanikachalam, 2011).

Facing Oppression Within One's Own Community

Within MSM and trans communities, both covert and overt discrimination against other MSM and trans people have been documented in relation to presumed or actual HIV status, engagement in sex work, marital status, and gender identity/expression. The extent to which there are any MSM, gay, or kothi communities in India may reasonably be questioned, both in the sense of geography and in terms of solidarity, given a largely stigmatizing environment. There seem to be at least sexual and social networks of MSM, with some networks cutting across socioeconomic classes, self-identities, or age differences, though some networks are restricted to people from within particular classes. For example, kothis and trans people complain about certain gay parties that explicitly state "no CDs [cross-dressers] or trans persons" (Chakrapani, Kaur, Newman, Mittal, & Kumar, 2019, p. 421). This might reflect both discomfort with trans persons and other gender-diverse people within MSM communities and apparent class differences. Kothis allege that sometimes it is not explicitly stated that kothis and trans people are not allowed, but the entry fees for the party will be so exorbitant that it would not be affordable to most kothis, double-deckers, or trans persons.

Other forms of discrimination take place within kothi and hijra communities, in which sometimes those who engage in sex work may be stigmatized by other kothis and hijras. In some instances, kothis engaged in sex work disapprove of other kothis' casual unpaid sex with panthis, as the former are worried that panthis would then not pay them but expect free sex. Within MSM and trans communities, those living with HIV often face discrimination, and this is amplified for those who continue to engage in any sex or who engage in sex work (Chakrapani, Newman, & Shunmugam, 2008; Chakrapani et al., 2015). These discriminatory experiences from within one's own community are likely to exacerbate the mental health challenges faced by MSM and trans people who are HIV-positive, those who are married, and/or who engage in sex work. Fear of discrimination from other MSM and trans women also prevents HIV-positive MSM and trans women from accessing even free HIV treatment-related services (Chakrapani, Newman, Shunmugam, & Dubrow, 2011).

Getting Support and Being Resilient

Many MSM and trans people, seemingly despite all odds, maintain good mental health. According to Meyer's (2003) minority stress model, social support and coping mechanisms may buffer the effect of stigma on mental health. Evidence for the positive impact of social support on mental health has been documented in qualitative studies from India. After disclosure of one's sexuality or gender identity, the availability of psychological, emotional, and financial support from family members generally contributes to decreasing the impact of discrimination from other sources (e.g., general public, relatives) and fosters self-acceptance (Chakrapani et al., 2013; Safren et al., 2014). Sometimes, although there is not a complete welcoming of sexual or gender minority children, there is a conditional acceptance by parents. For example, trans women may be asked to show up in men's clothing when they visit their family and not to disclose their gender identity to relatives (Chakrapani & Dhall, 2011). The presence of a supportive employer and some supportive coworkers has been reported by trans women to have helped them to continue their jobs despite discriminatory incidents that occurred in their workplaces (VHS & C-SHaRP, 2015). For kothis and gay men who are open about their sexuality, their peers often serve as support groups (Tomori, Srikrishnan, et al., 2016), with some of these groups facilitated by community agencies working with and oftentimes run by MSM.

Trans communities in India often have well-established support systems of their own. Among hijra communities, there may be several *chelas* (disciples) under a *guru* (master), both of which belong to one of several *gharanas* (Clans or Houses; Chakrapani, Newman, Mhaprolkar, & Kavi, 2007; Reddy, 2007). Within each clan, gurus and chelas take care of and support one another psychologically, emotionally, and financially. Sometimes, as in other traditional systems with social hierarchy and power structures, exploitation of chelas by gurus (Reddy, 2007) and violence within hijra communities have been reported (Prabhugate, Noronha, & Narang, 2014). However, trans communities often show solidarity when it comes to fighting discrimination faced by trans people from police or the general public. Currently, a variety of community-based organizations managed by trans communities themselves are implementing HIV interventions and engaging in social, political, and economic advocacy activities, mostly in urban areas in India.

Community solidarity events for MSM and trans people offer platforms for social connections and opportunities to support resilience. Several Pride marches have taken place in different parts of India, not only in major cities such as Mumbai, Delhi, Chennai, and Kolkata but also in smaller cities such as Nagpur. These Pride marches; observation of certain international days such as international day against homophobia, transphobia, and biphobia; queer film festivals; and other similar events help in mobilizing LGBT communities and foster solidarity among diverse sexual and gender minority communities, indirectly providing support that may improve mental health.

ASSOCIATIONS BETWEEN PSYCHOSOCIAL HEALTH PROBLEMS AND HIV RISK

Disparities in HIV prevalence is perhaps the most well-documented health gap between the general population and MSM and trans women: National average HIV prevalence among MSM is 4.3% (NACO, 2015) to 7% (Solomon et al., 2015) and among trans women is 7.5%, nearly 15 to 25 times higher than that among the general population (0.3%; NACO, 2013). HIV-related sexual risk among MSM in India is associated with various psychosocial health problems, including depression (Safren et al., 2009; Sivasubramanian et al., 2011), sexual violence (Chakrapani, Newman, Shunmugam, McLuckie, & Melwin, 2007; Shaw et al., 2012), and alcohol use (Mimiaga et al., 2011;

Yadav et al., 2014). These psychosocial health problems may co-occur and mutually reinforce one another, producing syndemics among MSM and trans women in India (Chakrapani, Kaur, et al., 2019; Chakrapani, Lakshmi, et al., 2019; Chakrapani, Newman, et al., 2017). Thus, to effectively address HIV burden among MSM and trans women, structural issues, discrimination, and mental health issues need to be addressed (Operario & Nemoto, 2010). As a gay participant said in a mixed methods study on stigma and mental health in Chennai,

> [MSM] face a lot of discrimination. Mentally it is a harrowing experience for them and they are made to feel it during each day. I can recall a particularly disturbing incident when a father of a son, who . . . was effeminate, severely beat up his son and made him to stay out in the freezing night with a flimsy *ganjee* [thin inner garment] on. How would [we tell him to use] a condom? He would rather—as he said to me crying—prefer ending his life than live . . . [not] use a condom to keep himself safe from HIV. (Chakrapani et al., 2013, p. 52)

IMPLICATIONS FOR MENTAL HEALTH PROFESSIONALS

Mental health professionals need to develop a solid understanding of sexuality and gender diversity among Indian LGBT communities. Given that medical and mental health field curricula typically do not include adequate, if any, information on sexual and gender minorities, mental health professionals need to educate themselves about LGBT issues if it is to happen at all. Despite the ostensibly supportive positions of the Indian Medical Association and Indian Psychiatric Society on homosexuality, many health care practitioners and mental health professionals are still not even aware that same-sex sexuality was removed from the list of psychiatric disorders a decade ago in the 10th edition of the *International Classification of Diseases* of the World Health Organization. Famous yoga gurus have been reported to make claims to having a "cure" for homosexuality, whereas any such sexual orientation change efforts are considered unethical and unscientific by several major mental health professional organizations, including the Indian Medical Association and Indian Psychiatric Society in India.

In 2016, the World Health Organization was conducting a field trial in India to test the newly proposed gender incongruence category instead of the gender identity disorder category from the *International Classification of Diseases* (10th ed.). During the first author's interactions with mental health professionals, he noted that many professionals prefer to retain the power to diagnose "transgenderism" as a medical condition so that people who require medical procedures (hormonal therapy or gender reassignment surgery) need to first consult mental health professionals. This view persists despite the recent Indian Supreme Court judgment that trans people have the right to choose their gender identity and that self-declaration of gender identity alone is sufficient to obtain a legal gender identity document (*National Legal Services Authority v. Union Government*, 2014). The Transgender Persons (Protection of

Rights) Bill 2016 approved by the Indian cabinet ("Cabinet Approves Bill," 2016) mentions the need for a district screening committee, which will have a psychologist or psychiatrist, to authorize a district magistrate to provide a "certificate of identity" to a transgender person. We hope that national guidelines will soon be available on transgender health care, which should clarify issues such as the need for a mental health professional's diagnosis to receive a legal gender identity document and a requirement for a surgical team to provide postoperative follow-up care, an internationally recommended standard of care (Coleman et al., 2011), which is often not done at present (Chakrapani, 2016; Singh et al., 2014).

People in India are generally hesitant to consult with a mental health professional due to stigma. This scenario is exacerbated for LGBT people who worry that their mental health issues will be attributed solely to their sexuality or gender identity. Even if certain mental health issues are related to one's sexuality or gender identity, many LGBT people expect that these will be approached absent an understanding of powerful social-structural challenges that pose obstacles to health and well-being for sexual minorities and rather as a personal failing or "disease." Finding LGBT-affirmative and competent mental health professionals is even more challenging. Several community organizations working with LGBT people, however, have created informal networks of mental health professionals in their cities; this helps to ensure that if an individual needs professional help, a provider can refer them with some confidence that their client will be treated with respect and by a competent provider. Even then, a large proportion of LGBT people are unable to afford the even nominal fees charged by LGBT-affirmative therapists from these networks, so their only resort is government hospitals or clinics that most often lack such LGBT-competent professionals (Ministry of Social Justice and Empowerment Expert Committee, 2014).

Accordingly, one promising pathway toward provision of LGBT-affirmative mental health services is through further introduction and strengthening of mental health services in community agencies working with sexual and gender minorities. Many people, including sexual and gender minorities—who are disproportionately represented among people living with HIV—are currently reached through HIV prevention projects delivered through community organizations. These could also serve as valuable resources for mental health care and referrals. Enhancement of such services in the HIV sector is another productive inroad to reaching sexual and gender minority communities, some of whom may need mental health services.

Finally, at the structural level, the recent decriminalization of adult consensual same-gender relations provides a significant opportunity, necessitating the introduction and implementation of antidiscrimination laws targeting family, educational, employment, and government sectors, and stigma reduction programs targeting the general public. These are vital measures to support implementation of this landmark legal decision amidst enduring social and political resistance to equal rights for sexual and gender minority populations.

Sustained efforts to promote broad social acceptance of sexual and gender minorities along with multisectoral antidiscrimination laws may begin to dismantle mechanisms that present barriers to achieving social inclusion and human rights. Advancing the mental health of sexual and gender minorities, including lesbian women and trans men, in India also requires development and investment in a national LGBT health research agenda to inform competent and effective mental health policies and programs.

REFERENCES

Amir, I. (2009, August 27). World's first matrimonial site for transsexuals. *India Times.* Retrieved from https://timesofindia.indiatimes.com/india/Worlds-first-matrimonial-site-for-transsexuals/articleshow/4937887.cms

Asthana, S., & Oostvogels, R. (2001). The social construction of male 'homosexuality' in India: Implications for HIV transmission and prevention. *Social Science & Medicine, 52,* 707–721. http://dx.doi.org/10.1016/S0277-9536(00)00167-2

Bose, B., & Bhattacharyya, S. (2007). *The phobic and the erotic the politics of sexualities in contemporary India*. Calcutta, India: Seagull Books.

Cabinet approves bill to empower transgenders: Harassment will entail punishment, proposes draft law. (2016, July 22). *The Indian Express*. Retrieved from http://indianexpress.com/article/india/india-news-india/transgender-persons-bill-passed-approve-empowerment-2926551/

Chakrapani, V. (2016). Sex change operation and feminizing procedures for transgender women in India: Current scenario and way forward. In A. Narrain & V. Chandran (Eds.), *Nothing to fix: Medicalisation of sexual orientation and gender identity: A human rights resource book* (pp. 137–159). New Delhi, India: Sage Yoda.

Chakrapani, V., Boyce, P., & Dhanikachalam, D. (2011). *Women partners of men who have sex with men in India* (India MSM Situation Paper Series, Technical Brief 2). New Delhi, India: DFID AIDS TAST of Futures Group and National AIDS Control Organisation.

Chakrapani, V., & Dhall, P. (2011). *Family acceptance among self-identified men who have sex with men (MSM) and transgender people in India*. Mumbai: Family Planning Association of India.

Chakrapani, V., Kaur, M., Newman, P. A., Mittal, S., & Kumar, R. (2019). Syndemics and HIV-related sexual risk among men who have sex with men in India: Influences of stigma and resilience. *Culture, Health & Sexuality, 21,* 416–431. http://dx.doi.org/10.1080/13691058.2018.1486458

Chakrapani, V., Kavi, A. R., Ramakrishnan, L., Gupta, R., Rappoport, C., & Raghavan, S. S. (2002, April). *HIV prevention among men who have sex with men (MSM) in India: Review of current scenario and recommendations*. Retrieved from http://www.indianlgbthealth.info/Authors/Downloads/MSM_HIV_IndiaFin.pdf

Chakrapani, V., Lakshmi, P. V. M., Tsai, A. C., Vijin, P. P., Kumar, P., & Srinivas, V. (2019). The syndemic of violence victimisation, drug use, frequent alcohol use, and HIV transmission risk behaviour among men who have sex with men: Cross-sectional, population-based study in India. *SSM–Population Health, 7,* 100348. http://dx.doi.org/10.1016/j.ssmph.2018.100348

Chakrapani, V., Newman, P. A., Mhaprolkar, H., & Kavi, A. R. (2007). *Sexual and social networks of MSM and hijras in India: A qualitative study*. Mumbai, India: The Humsafar Trust.

Chakrapani, V., Newman, P. A., & Noronha, E. (2018). Hijras/transgender women and sex work in India: From marginalization to social protection. In L. Nuttbrock (Ed.), *Transgender sex work and society* (pp. 214–235). New York, NY: Harrington Park Press.

Chakrapani, V., Newman, P. A., & Shunmugam, M. (2008). Secondary HIV prevention among kothi-identified MSM in Chennai, India. *Culture, Health & Sexuality, 10*(4), 313–327. http://dx.doi.org/10.1080/13691050701816714

Chakrapani, V., Newman, P. A., Shunmugam, M., & Dubrow, R. (2011). Barriers to free antiretroviral treatment access among kothi-identified men who have sex with men and aravanis (transgender women) in Chennai, India. *AIDS Care, 23*, 1687–1694. http://dx.doi.org/10.1080/09540121.2011.582076

Chakrapani, V., Newman, P. A., Shunmugam, M., Logie, C. H., & Samuel, M. (2017). Syndemics of depression, alcohol use, and victimisation, and their association with HIV-related sexual risk among men who have sex with men and transgender women in India. *Global Public Health, 12*, 250–265. http://dx.doi.org/10.1080/17441692.2015.1091024

Chakrapani, V., Newman, P. A., Shunmugam, M., McLuckie, A., & Melwin, F. (2007). Structural violence against kothi-identified men who have sex with men in Chennai, India: A qualitative investigation. *AIDS Education and Prevention, 19*, 346–364. http://dx.doi.org/10.1521/aeap.2007.19.4.346

Chakrapani, V., Samuel, M., Shunmugam, M., & Sivasubramanian, M. (2013). *Modelling the impact of stigma on depression and sexual risk behaviours of men who have sex with men and hijras/transgender women in India: Implications for HIV and sexual health programmes.* Chennai, India: MCC, Humsafar Trust, C-SHaRP.

Chakrapani, V., Shunmugam, M., Newman, P. A., Kershaw, T., & Dubrow, R. (2015). HIV Status disclosure and condom use among HIV-positive men who have sex with men and *hijras* (male-to-female transgender people) in India: Implications for prevention. *Journal of HIV/AIDS & Social Services, 14*, 26–44. http://dx.doi.org/10.1080/15381501.2013.859113

Chakrapani, V., Vijin, P. P., Logie, C. H., Newman, P. A., Shunmugam, M., Sivasubramanian, M., & Samuel, M. (2017). Understanding how sexual and gender minority stigmas influence depression among trans women and men who have sex with men in India. *LGBT Health, 4*, 217–226. http://dx.doi.org/10.1089/lgbt.2016.0082

Closson, E. F., Sivasubramanian, M., Mayer, K. H., Srivastava, A., Safren, S. A., Anand, V. R., . . . Mimiaga, M. J. (2014). The other side of the bridge: Exploring the sexual relationships of men who have sex with men and their female partners in Mumbai, India. *Culture, Health & Sexuality, 16*, 780–791. http://dx.doi.org/10.1080/13691058.2014.911960

Cohen, L. (2006). The kothi wars: AIDS cosmopolitanism and the morality of classification. In S. L. Pigg & V. Adams (Eds.), *Sex in development: Science, sexuality, and morality in global perspective* (pp. 269–304). Durham, NC: Duke University Press.

Coleman, E., Bockting, W., Botzer, M., Cohen-Kettenis, P., DeCuypere, G., Feldman, J., . . . Zucker, K. (2011). Standards of care for the health of transsexual, transgender, and gender-nonconforming people, version 7. *International Journal of Transgenderism, 13*, 165–232.

Cumming, L. (2016, February 23). *Proud mom posts India's first gay marriage ad to prove a point about her son's happiness.* Retrieved from http://www.theplaidzebra.com/proud-mom-posts-indias-first-gay-marriage-ad-to-prove-a-point-about-her-sons-happiness/

Custodi, A. (2007). 'Show you are a man!' Transsexuality and gender bending in the characters of Arjuna/Brhannada and Amba/Sikhandin(i). In S. Brodbeck & B. Black (Eds.), *Gender and narrative in the Mahabharata* (pp. 208–229). London, England: Routledge.

Gupta, A. (2015, June 27). *Why Indian opponents of same-sex marriage are so horrified at the US verdict.* Retrieved from https://scroll.in/article/737216/why-indian-opponents-of-same-sex-marriage-are-so-horrified-at-the-us-verdict

Gwalani, P. (2015, November 17). High rate of suicides haunts LGBT youths. *Times of India*. Retrieved from https://timesofindia.indiatimes.com/city/nagpur/High-rate-of-suicides-haunts-LGBT-youths/articleshow/49808926.cms

Jyoti, D. (2015, December 19). "The law has to go: It's time to walk the talk on Section 377." *Hindustan Times*. Retrieved from http://www.hindustantimes.com/opinion/this-law-has-to-go-it-s-time-to-walk-the-talk-on-section-377/story-6AkU6dRU3w9YRK9RbjoAPK.html

Koushal v. Naz Foundation. (2013). Civil Appeal No. 10972 of 2013. Retrieved from https://www.sci.gov.in/jonew/judis/41070.pdf

Logie, C. H., Newman, P. A., Chakrapani, V., & Shunmugam, M. (2012). Adapting the minority stress model: Associations between gender non-conformity stigma, HIV-related stigma and depression among men who have sex with men in South India. *Social Science & Medicine*, *74*, 1261–1268. http://dx.doi.org/10.1016/j.socscimed.2012.01.008

Mayer, K. H., Gangakhedkar, R., Sivasubramanian, M., Biello, K. B., Abuelezam, N., Mane, S., . . . Mimiaga, M. J. (2015). Differing identities but comparably high HIV and bacterial sexually transmitted disease burdens among married and unmarried men who have sex with men in Mumbai, India. *Sexually Transmitted Diseases*, *42*, 629–633.

Meyer, I. H. (2003). Prejudice, social stress, and mental health in lesbian, gay, and bisexual populations: Conceptual issues and research evidence. *Psychological Bulletin*, *129*, 674–697. http://dx.doi.org/10.1037/0033-2909.129.5.674

Mimiaga, M. J., Thomas, B., Mayer, K. H., Reisner, S. L., Menon, S., Swaminathan, S., . . . Safren, S. A. (2011). Alcohol use and HIV sexual risk among MSM in Chennai, India. *International Journal of STD & AIDS*, *22*, 121–125.

Ministry of Social Justice and Empowerment Expert Committee. (2014). *Transgender persons: Report of the Expert Committee on the Issues relating to Transgender Persons*. New Delhi: MSJE, Government of India.

Mitra, M. (2014, October 7). Two steps forward, one step back: India's u-turn on LGBTQ rights. *Brown Political Review*. Retrieved from http://www.brownpoliticalreview.org/2014/10/two-steps-forward-one-step-back-indias-u-turn-on-lgbtq-rights/

Munoz-Plaza, C., Quinn, S. C., & Rounds, K. A. (2002). Lesbian, gay, bisexual and transgender students: Perceived social support in the high school environment. *The High School Journal, 85*, 52–63.

Narrain, A., & Chandran, V. (2016). *Nothing to fix: Medicalisation of sexual orientation and gender identity*. New Delhi, India: Sage Yoda Press.

National AIDS Control Organisation. (2013). *HIV Sentinel Surveillance 2012–13: A technical brief*. New Delhi: National AIDS Control Organisation, Government of India.

National AIDS Control Organisation. (2015). *National Integrated Biological and Behavioural Surveillance (IBBS), India 2014–15*. New Delhi: NACO, Ministry of Health and Family Welfare, Government of India.

National Legal Services Authority v. Union of India, Writ Petition No. 400 of 2012 with Writ Petition No. 604 of 2013. Supreme Court of India Judgments, April 15, 2014.

Operario, D., & Nemoto, T. (2010). HIV in transgender communities: Syndemic dynamics and a need for multicomponent interventions. *Journal of Acquired Immune Deficiency Syndromes*, *55*(Suppl. 2), S91–S93. http://dx.doi.org/10.1097/QAI.0b013e3181fbc9ec

Pandya, A. (2011). Psycho-socio-cultural issues of men who have sex with men in Gujarat, India. *International Journal of Psychology and Behavioral Sciences*, *1*, 18–23. http://dx.doi.org/10.5923/j.ijpbs.20110101.03

Pattanaik, D. (2014). *Shikhandi and other stories they don't tell you*. New Delhi: Zubaan and Penguin India.

Phillips, A. E., Boily, M. C., Lowndes, C. M., Garnett, G. P., Gurav, K., Ramesh, B. M., . . . Alary, M. (2008). Sexual identity and its contribution to MSM risk behavior in Bangaluru (Bangalore), India: The results of a two-stage cluster sampling survey. *Journal of LGBT Health Research*, *4*, 111–126. http://dx.doi.org/10.1080/15574090902922975

Poongothai, S., Pradeepa, R., Ganesan, A., & Mohan, V. (2009). Prevalence of depression in a large urban South Indian population—The Chennai Urban Rural Epidemiology Study (CURES-70). *PLoS ONE*, *4*(9), e7185. http://dx.doi.org/10.1371/journal.pone.0007185

Prabhugate, P., Noronha, E., & Narang, A. (2014). Gender-based violence faced by hijras in public spaces in urban India. In L. Prabhu & S. Pilot (Eds.), *The fear that stalks: Gender-based violence in public spaces* (pp. 173–196). New Delhi, India: Zubaan.

Reddy, G. (2007). *With respect to sex: Negotiating hijra identity in South India.* Chicago, IL: University of Chicago Press.

Safren, S. A., Thomas, B. E., Mayer, K. H., Biello, K. B., Mani, J., Rajagandhi, V., . . . Mimiaga, M. J. (2014). A pilot RCT of an intervention to reduce HIV sexual risk and increase self-acceptance among MSM in Chennai, India. *AIDS and Behavior*, *18*, 1904–1912.

Safren, S. A., Thomas, B. E., Mimiaga, M. J., Chandrasekaran, V., Menon, S., Swaminathan, S., & Mayer, K. H. (2009). Depressive symptoms and human immuno-deficiency virus risk behavior among men who have sex with men in Chennai, India. *Psychology Health and Medicine*, *14*, 705–715. http://dx.doi.org/10.1080/13548500903334754

Shahani, P. (2008). *Gay Bombay: Globalization, love and (be)longing in contemporary India.* Thousand Oaks, CA: Sage. http://dx.doi.org/10.4135/9788132100140

Shaw, S. Y., Lorway, R. R., Deering, K. N., Avery, L., Mohan, H. L., Bhattacharjee, P., . . . Blanchard, J. F. (2012). Factors associated with sexual violence against men who have sex with men and transgendered individuals in Karnataka, India. *PLoS ONE*, *7*, e31705. http://dx.doi.org/10.1371/journal.pone.0031705

Singh, Y., Aher, A., Shaikh, S., Mehta, S., Robertson, J., & Chakrapani, V. (2014). Gender transition services for hijras and other male-to-female transgender people in India: Availability and barriers to access and use. *International Journal of Trans-genderism*, *15*, 1–15. http://dx.doi.org/10.1080/15532739.2014.890559

Sivasubramanian, M., Mimiaga, M. J., Mayer, K. H., Anand, V. R., Johnson, C. V., Prabhugate, P., & Safren, S. A. (2011). Suicidality, clinical depression, and anxiety disorders are highly prevalent in men who have sex with men in Mumbai, India: Findings from a community-recruited sample. *Psychology Health and Medicine*, *16*, 450–462. http://dx.doi.org/10.1080/13548506.2011.554645

Solomon, S. S., Mehta, S. H., Srikrishnan, A. K., Vasudevan, C. K., Mcfall, A. M., Balakrishnan, P., . . . Celentano, D. D. (2015). High HIV prevalence and incidence among MSM across 12 cities in India. *AIDS*, *29*, 723–731. http://dx.doi.org/10.1097/QAD.0000000000000602

Stief, M. (2017). The sexual orientation and gender presentation of hijra, kothi, and panthi in Mumbai, India. *Archives of Sexual Behavior*, *46*, 73–85. http://dx.doi.org/10.1007/s10508-016-0886-0

Tomori, C., McFall, A. M., Srikrishnan, A. K., Mehta, S. H., Solomon, S. S., Anand, S., . . . Celentano, D. D. (2016). Diverse rates of depression among men who have sex with men (MSM) across India: Insights from a multi-site mixed method study. *AIDS and Behavior*, *20*, 304–316. http://dx.doi.org/10.1007/s10461-015-1201-0

Tomori, C., Srikrishnan, A. K., Ridgeway, K., Solomon, S. S., Mehta, S. H., Solomon, S., & Celentano, D. D. (2016). Friends, sisters, and wives: Social support and social risks in peer relationships among men who have sex with men (MSM) in India. *AIDS Education and Prevention*, *28*, 153–164. http://dx.doi.org/10.1521/aeap.2016.28.2.153

Uttamchandan, R. (2016, February 7). *At Mumbai's gay pride march, parents come out to support their queer children.* Retrieved from https://scroll.in/roving/803163/a-mumbais-gay-pride-march-parents-come-out-to-support-their-queer-children

Vanita, R. (2005). *Love's rite: Same-sex marriage in India and the West.* New York, NY: Palgrave Macmillan.

Vanita, R., & Kidwai, S. (2006). *Same-sex love in India: Readings from literature and history.* New York, NY: Palgrave.

Vatsyayana. (1994). *The complete Kama Sutra: The first unabridged modern translation of the classic Indian text* (A. Daniélou, Trans.). Rochester, VT: Park Street Press. (Original work published ca. 400 B.C.E.)

VHS & C-SHaRP. (2015). *Getting a job and keeping it: Issues faced by Thirunangai (Transgender people) and Kothis in Tamil Nadu in getting and retaining employment—A rapid assessment using mixed methods.* Chennai, India: Tamil Nadu AIDS Initiative, Voluntary Health Services.

Yadav, D., Chakrapani, V., Goswami, P., Ramanathan, S., Ramakrishnan, L., George, B., . . . Paranjape, R. S. (2014). Association between alcohol use and HIV-related sexual risk behaviors among men who have sex with men (MSM): Findings from a multi-site bio-behavioral survey in India. *AIDS and Behavior, 18,* 1330–1338. http://dx.doi.org/10.1007/s10461-014-0699-x

8

Being Gay and Lesbian in Malaysia

Hemla Singaravelu and Wai Hsien Cheah

Homosexuality is criminalized in Malaysia because of the nation's Sharia laws and penal codes (Carroll & Mendos, 2017). Lesbian, gay, bisexual, and transgender (LGBT) Malaysians are considered deviants, and as such they live under a cloak of silence in fear of persecution. The government's hostile stance of not accepting LGBT rights (Marlow & Thanthong-Knight, 2018) coupled with the criminalization of homosexuality has discouraged Malaysian scholars from conducting research for fear of losing their faculty appointments (Williams, 2009). The nation's laws impact both Muslims and non-Muslims in ways that are described later in this chapter. The authors of this chapter are non-Muslims, ethnic minorities (Indian and Chinese), born and raised in Muslim majority Malaysia, and both immigrated to the United States for tertiary education in the 1980s and 1990s, respectively. As a result of the scarcity of literature on LGBT Malaysians, we provide a glimpse of what it means to be gay and lesbian in Malaysia, a country with a Muslim majority. This chapter starts with a personal narrative of our experiences, followed by sections related to the historical sociopolitical context of Malaysia, attitudes toward LGBT individuals, intersectionality of identities discourse, and a discussion on the resulting sociopolitical compromise. Although mental health professionals and services exist in Malaysia, it is uncertain if there are affirmative treatment and support services for the LGBT community. Hence, this chapter ends with recommendations for mental health practitioners in Malaysia and practitioners who are working with gay and lesbian Malaysians abroad.

http://dx.doi.org/10.1037/0000159-009
LGBTQ Mental Health: International Perspectives and Experiences, N. Nakamura and C. H. Logie (Editors)

To enhance the content of this chapter, excerpts of narratives based on a study that we conducted are included. Because of the difficulty recruiting bisexual and transgender individuals, this research as well as the chapter focuses primarily on gay and lesbian Malaysians. In addition, Malay (Muslims) participants were not recruited out of respect for their safety.

PERSONAL NARRATIVES

In an attempt to add a personal dimension to our chapter, we are providing a brief narrative of our coming out process as gay and lesbian Malaysians. Some of our stories are similar to the ones told by our research participants. However, unlike them, we are living in the United States, where homosexuality is not criminalized, even when true civil rights have not been attained for LGBT Americans. Our narratives and chapter highlight the complex psychological maneuvering required of gay and lesbian Malaysians that inhibits personal development and formation of relationships.

Hemla's Story

As a teenager I knew I was different from my family and friends. My first exposure to anyone LGBT was at age 13 while I was on a shopping trip with my mother. I saw my first cross-dresser, who smiled and strutted in the mall like a runway model. I looked at my mother smiling, and she smiled back without saying anything while other shoppers smiled and chuckled and pointed at the cross-dresser. At that time I did not know anything about gender identity or homosexuality, or cross-dressing, for that matter. To this day, I do not know if the cross-dresser was a drag performer or actually living as a woman. Homosexuality and transgenderism were not part of my family's or society's discourse; my discovery of homosexuality was through the *Medical Encyclopedia Britannica* set my father purchased for us. Upon reading the section on homosexuality, I secretly feared that I fit the description of a lesbian. It was when I came to the United States to study at a university that I discovered LGBT individuals and activism. Soon after, I met someone and formed a long-term same-sex relationship. I knew that if I wanted to continue with the relationship, I had to come out of the closet because she was out. Two years later, my partner and a close friend traveled with me to visit my family in Malaysia. They were introduced as my close friends, and even though the experience there was positive, I felt as if I was keeping a secret from them. I wanted my family to meet the woman I loved, but I was fearful of negative reactions if I revealed my relationship. A year after the trip home, I arduously wrote a "coming out" letter to my eldest sister. I wanted a family member to know that I was happy, not to worry about me, and indirectly convey to them to stop asking me to get married to a man. Although I was relieved for being out to my family, I had to deal with the strained family relationship for several years.

In spite of their not wanting me to talk about my relationship, they did not say anything negative when I shared details of my relationship. It felt as if they needed time to reconcile having a lesbian daughter and a sibling with maintaining a relationship with me. As time passed, my relationship with my family improved, and they seem more supportive and comfortable with my sexual orientation. Through the years, my energy and scholarship have been directed to educating others, including my family, about sexual orientation and gender identity.

Wai Hsien's Story

I came out as a gay man at the age of 34, after moving to St. Louis, Missouri, to start my new job, right after the completion of my doctoral degree in the United States. Although I knew I was somewhat different from my peers back then, I did not spend much time exploring my "true self" or dwelling on my sexual identity. I concentrated on completing my graduate coursework and finishing my dissertation research and doctoral degree. Needless to say, things changed after I met my significant other, Benjamin (now spouse). I learned more about myself with Benjamin's help and began to understand gay culture, gay community, and what it meant to be gay. A few years later, I took Benjamin home to visit my family in Kuala Lumpur, Malaysia. I introduced him as my good friend and never came out to any of my family members even though I was asked by my father privately. A year later, when I went home by myself, I concealed my sexual orientation once again even though I was asked a second time by my father. Until this day, I have yet to reveal my sexual orientation to my father, stepmother, and older siblings. Although my relationships with my family members have not changed, the question of whether I have made the correct decision in not coming out to them lingered for many years. Fortunately, I found my answer after conducting a research project with my coauthor, Hemla, to understand the lived experiences of gay and lesbian individuals in Malaysia. We examined the question of whether gay and lesbian individuals reveal their sexual orientations to others or conceal their same-sex attractions from others, and more specifically, under what conditions they reveal themselves and what barriers prevent them from doing so. Hence, I regard this as the starting point of my lesbian, gay, bisexual, transgender, and queer scholarship.

THE HISTORICAL, SOCIOPOLITICAL, CULTURAL CONTEXT OF MALAYSIA

The uniqueness of Malaysia lies in its multiethnic, multicultural, multireligious, albeit Muslim-ruled nation and its history of colonization by the British. Located in Southeast Asia and flanked by Singapore in the south, Thailand in the north, Indonesia in the west, and Borneo in the east, Malaysia (then Malaya) was strategically located for trade even before colonial rule. Traders from China and India would move freely along the Straits of Malacca and South China Sea, and many settled on the Malay Peninsula starting from the turn of the 1st century A.D. The settlements increased during the British occupation in Malaysia from 1874 to 1957 (Stockwell, 1976), when indentured laborers were brought by the British from India and China to work as tin miners, spice harvesters, and rubber tappers in plantations, whereas others came on their own for better work opportunities. Based on the most recent census data, the Department of Statistics (2011) in Malaysia estimates the Malaysia's total population at 31.7 million, with the following ethnic composition: 68.6% Bumiputeras (Malays and Indigenous peoples), 23.4% Chinese, 7.0% Indians, and 1.0% identified as other ethnicities. Shamsudin and Ghazali (2011) posited that a Malay is an individual who "professes the religion of Islam," "habitually speaks the Malay language," and "conforms to Malay customs" (p. 280). A Muslim is "a person who believes, follows, and upholds the teaching of Islam" (Cheah & Singaravelu, 2017, p. 403).

Although Islam is the official religion of Malaysia, non-Malays (e.g., Indians, Chinese) and non-Muslim citizens are constitutionally guaranteed their freedom of religion. An individual's religious status is indicated on his or her birth certificate (Cheah & Singaravelu, 2017). Individuals generally assume the religion of their parents; however, some non-Malays are allowed to switch religions. The religions and faiths practiced in Malaysia are broken down as follows: 61.3% Islam (all ethnic Malays); 19.8% Buddhism; 9.2% Christianity; 6.3% Hinduism; 1.3% Confucianism, Taoism, and tribal/folk/other traditional Chinese religion; 1.0% religion unknown; 0.7% no religion; and 0.4% other religion (Department of Statistics, 2011).

The diversity in Malaysia extends to the languages spoken, with Bahasa Malaysia (Melayu) as the official language of the country and English the second most commonly spoken language, inherited from the colonial era. Although the Malaysian Indians speak different dialects such as Tamil, Malayalam, Telugu, Punjabi, and Hindi, the main dialects spoken by the Malaysian Chinese include Cantonese, Hokkien, Hakka, Mandarin, and Hainanese (Library of Congress, Federal Research Division, 2006). Indigenous languages are also spoken by groups such as the Ibans and Kadazans in East Malaysia. For generations, Malaysians have experienced an integration of cultures and identities through interracial marriages and interactions among members from different ethnic groups, particularly in urban areas.

Politically, Malaysia has been governed by the Muslim majority and has mostly followed the colonial British parliamentary system with a prime minister and a constitutional monarch. The king is the nominal head of state, and the prime minister holds the authority to govern the country. The citizens of Malaysia are governed by both the Sharia laws of Islam and Secular Law (the Penal Code Act 574) inherited from colonial Britain. The population of Malaysia is made up of members from various ethnic groups, and the Sharia law applies only to the Muslim population in the country.

ATTITUDES TOWARD LGBT AND
GENDER-NONCONFORMING MALAYSIANS

LGBT, gender variant, or gender-nonconforming individuals and same-sex relationships are not accepted in Malaysia's social or political spheres (Baba, 2001). Lesbians, gay men, bisexual persons, and nonbinary and gender-nonconforming individuals are considered by many as deviants (Alagappar & Kaur, 2009). Their sexual practices and gender expressions are deemed immoral and illegal and are punishable by law (Shamsudin & Ghazali, 2011). The Sharia law for Muslims is enforced by (a) state religious figures, called *Muftis*, who serve as the interpreters of the laws; (b) the religious department; and (c) the Sharia court system. Even though non-Muslims are not governed by the Sharia law, there is a sense of vigilance in knowing that they are living in an Islamic country. The prominent components of the law that criminalizes same-sex practices and gender-variant individuals are *musahaqah* (meaning sexual relationships between women), *tasyabbuh* (meaning a man expressing/identifying with the female gender and vice versa), and *liwat* (meaning carnal intercourse or sex against the order of nature, which include same-sex sexual intercourse). If found guilty of violating these laws, and depending on the severity of the offense, a Muslim could be fined RM5,000 (Malaysian ringgit currency; US$1,250) and/or face imprisonment for 3 years with or without whipping. Furthermore, in Sections 377A and 377B of the Penal Code Act, carnal intercourse against the order of nature, including oral and anal sex, is prohibited for all individuals, and offenders are punishable with imprisonment up to 20 years and/or they may face whipping. According to Fuad Rahmat (2012), these laws regarding same-sex practices have been invoked only seven times in Malaysia since 1938. Four of these were against Mr. Anwar Ibrahim, the former deputy prime minister of Malaysia. Mr. Ibrahim was accused of having sex with two men in 1998, and again in 2012 with his political assistant (International Gay and Lesbian Human Rights Commission [IGLHRC], 2014), and was convicted. People have speculated that his imprisonment was politically motivated (Holmes, 2016).

Despite having independence from Britain for about 60 years, and with Britain having legalized same-sex marriage in 2013 and recognizing the rights of transgender individuals in changing their legal gender designation on their birth certificates, Malaysia continues to retain the previous colonial laws and views. Therefore, with both Penal Code Act 574 and Sharia Law in existence, no antidiscrimination laws have been established to protect the rights of LGBT and other gender-nonconforming individuals in Malaysia. In fact, Malaysia's negative stance toward same-sex practices and LGBT identities has intensified over the years following the dismissal of Mr. Anwar Ibrahim as the deputy prime minister (IGLHRC, 2014). The government's reluctance to accept "sexual orientation and gender identity issues as human rights issues" (IGLHRC, 2014, p. 9), the former prime minister Najib's proclamation that "human rights-ism goes against Muslim values" (Ong, 2014) and "LGBTs, liberalism, and pluralism as enemies of Islam" (Baharom, 2012), and the call made by numerous high-position government officials to curb the spread of LGBT visibility in schools (IGLHRC, 2014) were clear indicators of the government's hostile stance toward LGBT communities. The actions of these influential figures ultimately pushed public discourse of LGBT issues in a negative light, creating a "wave of fear for the LGBT community" (IGLHRC, 2014, p. 12). The cancellation of Seksualiti Merdeka in 2011, an annual sexuality rights festival held in Kuala Lumpur since 2008, and the cancellation of Pink Dot Penang 2014, an event scheduled to celebrate human rights and freedom of expression, were consequences of this negative discourse. These two events were misconstrued by many Islamic nongovernmental organizations as immoral events held to poison the minds of the younger generation (Mok, 2014). Individuals who choose to reveal their sexual orientation publicly also face public condemnations, harassment, and sometimes death threats. According to Lim (2014), death threats were received by Mr. Azwan Ismail (an ethnic Malay man) after he came out in an online video presentation in 2010, mimicking the It Gets Better Project created to inspire hope for LGBT youths facing harassment worldwide.

The mass media in Malaysia have never been kind to the LGBT community. In a systematic content analysis study conducted to understand how the print media in Malaysia portray sexual orientation and gender identity issues, Alagappar and Kaur (2009) revealed that 74% of the articles they analyzed framed same-sex relationships in a negative manner. The news stories often portray LGBT persons as having "an illness and a threat to the nation" (p. 42). Words that were consistently found in relation to the topic of homosexuality include "immoral act," "illegal," "not halal" (not permissible in traditional Islamic law), "criminal offence," and "harsh punishment." Prominent politicians and religious leaders were often quoted as expert sources on the topic of sexual orientation, while the voices of LGBT individuals and communities were silenced and not presented. These findings were not at all surprising considering that "the State's ruling coalition owns and controls most of the mainstream media, making it easy for the government to propagate anti-homosexual and transgender messages to the public" (IGLHRC, 2014, p. 12). Furthermore, when teenagers write to the editors of the local newspapers and magazines seeking advice on how to deal with their same-sex attractions, they are often told "not to pursue their sexual orientation for the simple reason that it is unnatural and considered abnormal behavior" (Baba, 2001, p. 148). The persecution of LGBT individuals, especially those who are visibly gender-nonconforming (feminine men, masculine women, and transgender persons), by legal and religious authorities, family members, friends, and strangers had occurred prior to the dismissal of Mr. Ibrahim as the deputy prime minister of Malaysia in 1998. The resurgence of Islam, which occurred during the 1980s (Baba, 2001), has been identified as the starting point of the many instances of persecution of LGBT individuals in Malaysia. Evidence of targeted violence and discrimination experienced by gay men, lesbians, bisexual persons, and transgender individuals can be found in the narratives shared by the participants of an empirical study conducted in Malaysia (between November 2010 and November 2011) by a team of researchers commissioned by IGLHRC. For a detailed description of the research findings, see IGLHRC (2014).

INTERSECTIONALITY OF IDENTITIES, DISCOURSE, AND THE SOCIOPOLITICAL COMPROMISE

With the aforementioned societal barriers and overt oppression faced by gays and lesbians in Malaysia, the concept of coming out and attending to their psychological well-being as described by the sexual identity development models (Cass, 1979; Troiden, 1989) is not typically on the minds of gay and lesbian Malaysians. Western-based conventional identity development models are useful in understanding certain development tasks that individuals may encounter. However, these models are inadequate for understanding how multiple identities (Fukuyama & Ferguson, 2000; Israel & Selvidge, 2003) and the intersectionality of these identities are negotiated, particularly in the Malaysian context. The formation of a Malaysian identity, and particularly gay or lesbian identity, is highly influenced by the collectivistic orientation (Triandis, 1995), the large power distance value pattern (Hofstede, 2001), and cultural expectations of the society. The definition of responsibility and how Malaysians make decisions about themselves and others is similarly dependent on the collectivistic and power distance dynamic, cultural expectations, and resulting communication styles.

Collectivistic values such as respect and reverence for elders; family loyalty and obligation; self-discipline; and morality, shame, order, and familial and gender hierarchy are typically followed in Malaysia. Given the criminalization of same-sex practices by the Penal Code 574, the Sharia law, and the collective family dynamic and attitudes toward same-sex practices, it is common for gay and lesbian Malaysians to either live under a cloak of silence or be very selective in the disclosure of their sexual orientation to others.

COMING OUT RESEARCH DATA ON MALAYSIAN GAYS AND LESBIANS

In our exploratory study (Cheah & Singaravelu, 2017), 10 gay men and seven lesbians (all self-identified) were interviewed about their coming out process and lived experiences in Malaysia. The sample comprised mainly Malaysian Chinese and a few Malaysian Indians. Six of the participants identified as nonreligious, four as Agnostic, four as Christians, and three as Buddhist. All participants reported that they were comfortable with their respective sexual orientation. In spite of using the labels *gay*, *lesbian*, and *queer*, a majority of them preferred the descriptor of *people like us* (PLU). The data from the study suggest that friends were the most frequently cited individuals whom the participants came out to in their initial disclosure. This was followed by siblings and then parents. Coming out to friends allowed the participants to maintain their friendships and to enhance their closeness (Bhugra, 1997). Honesty, loyalty, and openness are typical attributes valued by collectivistic societies; hence, it was no surprise when a 33-year-old gay man and small-business owner made the following comment:

> Because I want to make lifelong friends, and I have known them for a long time, from primary school to secondary school and now. We are still good, and we will keep in touch. After secondary school, before university, I told them all because I have confirmed that I am a gay man. I just told them that I am gay. I hope you all will not mind. I told them because I did not want our topic of discussion to be awkward. Straight people and gay people talk about different things when it comes to sexual matters. So, I do not want them to ask me whether I have a girlfriend and how is my sex life. (Participant 8)

According to Narui (2011), coming out to a sibling is much easier than to a parent because the siblings were raised "under the same discursive regime," and they developed "a mutual understanding of how sexual orientation is viewed in their household" (p. 1221). Siblings with a close relationship can serve as the pillar of support for the gay sibling during his or her coming out process to the parents or can help to keep the gay sibling's sexual orientation from the parents. In fact, the protective experience was highlighted by a 25-year-old Malaysian Indian lesbian lawyer:

> My sister especially has been very accepting. . . . She has been a pillar of strength because my mom actually confided in her and said, "Oy, has your sister told you anything. Is she gay?" My sister just said, "Oh! No, she hasn't told me anything. And I don't think you should ask her. You should just leave her alone. Maybe she is just comfortable being like that, the way she is. . . ." So my mom hasn't asked me anything yet, yet for now. (Participant 14)

Another participant came out to his older sister before telling their parents. He indicated that his older sister served as his mediator and laid the foundation for his disclosure to his parents:

> . . . After I told my sister, and . . . told her about my situation, she helped me, to become the mediator . . . you know talked to my mom a bit you know, . . . helped me to manage my situation better. The second person who knows is my mom herself of course. I have to come out to her after my sister did all the ground work of you know, paving the way in for me. I had to directly tell my mom because I have to move in . . . with J. I also have to tell my mom why I am not staying with them or why I am disappearing and all that. . . . Few months after that I had to come out to my dad directly because my dad saw my mom being very sad and crying all the time. So my dad sensed it. He asked my mom, my mom told him, . . . I came out to her, and so my dad knew from there. So three members of my family know. The sister first, then my mom, then my dad. There is only four of us in the family so particularly everybody knows in the family now. (Participant 17)

Coming out to Malaysian parents can be a challenge because they are usually heterosexual, they possibly have no direct contact with any gay or lesbian individuals, and their worldviews may be influenced by the negative public discourse and damaging portrayals of LGBT individuals in the Malaysian media. As such, Malaysian parents' lack of understanding regarding same-sex attraction can serve as a barrier to acceptance. Moreover, Malaysia is a large power-distance country, and parents are to be obeyed and respected (Ting-Toomey & Chung, 2012). *Power distance* is the level of acceptance and expectation of an unequal distribution of power in collectivistic hierarchical family systems, institutions, and societies such as Malaysia. Thus, it is common for gay and lesbian Malaysians to hide their same-sex attractions from their parents because "the parent–child relationship is more distant than the sibling relationships or friendships" (Wong & Tang, 2004, p. 155). According to Tan (2011), disclosing one's sexual orientation or sexual identity may threaten familial ties and cause shame and grief to the family. Chow and Cheng (2010) posited that whereas Chinese daughters are expected to perform their familial roles and bear children for their husbands, sons are expected to marry and produce sons of their own for the purpose of maintaining the family heritage and family line. Therefore, having a gay son is equivalent to the loss of a "real son," hence the discontinuity of the family line (Wong & Tang, 2004). These cultural expectations make disclosure a challenge for many gay and lesbian individuals of Chinese descent in Malaysia.

In fact, most would choose concealment over disclosure because concealment is enacted for the self and other's protection. Several of the study participants indicated that they did not want to ruin the parent–child relationship, hurt their parents' feelings, and be perceived by their parents as the *unfillial* (bad or horrible) son or daughter of the family. The importance of being able to maintain the parent–child relationship was clearly explained by Participant 8 once again, who described the following:

> I don't think the time is right yet because sometimes when your parents reached a certain age, they may not be as accepting when you come out to them. They not only will not accept, but at the same time, they will also feel very upset. Yes, if I come out and say, I am gay, I am not considering how they may feel. This is what I am trying to prevent. Furthermore, they may not even understand what gay is. They may think a gay person should show signs of a sissy, but you are not. Hence they may ask why are you gay? I don't want to hurt their feelings. If they are not able to understand, why would I want to go tell them? On the other hand, they may have already known, but they do not want to verbalize it. I personally think Malaysian parents can be open-minded, and not necessary conservative in their thinking. My significant other will stay over-night at our house. He comes often, and when they ask "who is this person?" I will just tell them that he is my good friend-loh [*loh* is slang used to emphasize the preceding word] at the beginning. You see, a good friend will come once or twice, but if a good friend comes frequently, they will suspect. Ultimately, they will not ask the question anymore, but accept the person. And sometimes, when my good friend didn't show up at the house for a period of time, my parents will ask me where

is your good friend? How come he did not come visit? So you know they know. I don't think they want you to come out and verbalize your sexual identity to them directly.

Taking a significant other home to meet the family is not a new phenomenon. Gay men in many Chinese societies (e.g., Singapore, China, Taiwan, Hong Kong) integrate their sexual identities into the familial context (Chou, 2000; Tan, 2011). Taking a "good friend" home, coupled with an increased frequency over time, allows the romantic couple to show their respective family members that their friendship is beyond platonic. The idea of "coming home" serves two purposes: It gives the couple the opportunity to develop, and perhaps enhance, the relationship with both sets of parents, and it allows the couple to show family members the nature of their relationship in family-kinship terms. Similarly, we (the authors) brought our partners home and introduced them as friends to our families.

Although the motives for disclosure and concealment did vary from individual to individual, the findings from our exploratory study do indicate that (a) having a relationship with others and (b) safety appeared to be the two most common reasons for why disclosure and concealment were enacted by their participants (Cheah & Singaravelu, 2017). The findings further suggest that the gay and lesbian individuals in Malaysia must constantly "negotiate their coming out process in a way that is best suited to integrate their individual needs of the culture and family" (Mosher, 2001, p. 168).

AVOIDANCE, INDIRECT VERBAL STYLES, AND HIGH-CONTEXT INTERACTION PATTERNS

According to Ting-Toomey and Chung (2012), *high-context communication* is defined as a form of interaction pattern that emphasizes "how intention or meaning can best be conveyed through the embedded contexts (e.g., social roles or positions, relationship types, intergroup history) and the nonverbal channels (e.g., pauses, silence, tone of voice) of the verbal message" (p. 123). In the high-context communication system, the listeners are expected to "read between the lines" and interpret the nonverbal subtleties that are conveyed along with the verbal message. Given that the topic of sex (including sexuality) is still considered by many Asians as a taboo and sensitive subject (Poon & Ho, 2008), and that open disclosure of one's sexual orientation may be seen as a threat (Greene, 1997), gay men and lesbians in Malaysia are also much more likely to conceal their sexual identities and avoid discussing the topic altogether. One of the participants in our research study (Cheah & Singaravelu, 2017) indicated that he had taken his then boyfriend home many times, but somehow he had never come out to any of his family members. He said, in a way, his mom knows that he is gay, but they never discuss his sexual orientation openly.

A similar sentiment was also expressed by another participant. He stated that "family is a bit more sensitive. I did not and have never revealed directly.

I think . . . being the Asian family is like don't ask and don't tell." Wai Hsien Cheah certainly did all of these things, and Hemla Singaravelu, having revealed her sexual orientation to her family, was later told by her family, "We don't talk about these things in Malaysia." It was certainly easier to avoid talking about the relationship while being oceans apart as well.

As for those who did decide to discuss the issue, they were much more likely to use the indirect verbal style of talk. The indirect verbal style of talk refers to the use of "verbal statements that tend to soften the speaker's actual intentions and are carried out with a tentative, indirect tone" (Ting-Toomey & Chung, 2012, p. 380). The conversation that one of the lesbian participants had with her older sister was a reflection of this particular style of talk. She said,

> I think my sister is the one with the highest level of suspicion because when I talk to her, she might give me some hints that she knew of my sexual orientation. She would indicate things like try not to be a PLU or lesbian or something like this. I have never told her that this is who I am. She would sometimes ask how I feel about PLU or lesbian people. I suspect she was testing me. (Participant 15)

Wai Hsien Cheah has used the indirect verbal style of talk as well. Rather than telling his family members that he is in fact gay, he told his family members that he has no intention of getting married and does not plan on having children in the future. He verbalized his intent repeatedly on his subsequent trips home to Malaysia, and his father and stepmother no longer ask him about girlfriends, marriage, and children.

The Negotiation of Multiple Identities and Compromise

In a multiethnic and multicultural country such as Malaysia, gay men and lesbian Malaysians could identify as Indian Malaysian or Chinese Malaysian or Malay Malaysian; and a Hindu or Buddhist/Taoist or a Muslim or a Christian; and a woman or a man; and a father or mother, and a daughter or son, and as a professional—in addition to identifying as a member of a politically oppressed group. The intersection of these multiple identities is created by the individual's unique experiences and environmental discourse within each of the social identities. As described by Alvarado and Hurtado (2012), "no one social identity can be understood without examining how it interacts with each of the social identities" (p. 4). Individuals are tasked with managing their identities and continually negotiating their roles, their speech, their behavior, and ultimately whether it is safe to reveal their sexual orientation in a manner that is appropriate to their culture and family.

The data from our exploratory study revealed valuable insights into the lives and coming out process of our study participants. Nevertheless, our findings may not be applicable to other gay and lesbian Malaysians because of the small sample. Because our participants comprised mainly Malaysian Chinese and a few Malaysian Indians, our findings may not completely mirror the experiences of other gay and lesbian Malaysians, particularly the Malay

Malaysians. Our findings, however, suggest basic guidelines that mental health practitioners need to be aware of when working with gay men and lesbian Malaysians.

RECOMMENDATIONS FOR MENTAL HEALTH PRACTITIONERS

Even though it is uncommon for Malaysians to seek out mental health services, the number of mental health practitioners (counselors and psychologists) has increased in recent years. With the exception of the PT Foundation that publicly provides support/counseling services for the LGBT community, to date, other agencies and private practitioners have not advertised services for gay and lesbian Malaysians. Consequently, it is unknown whether LGBT affirmative services for gay and lesbians are available. In light of the nation's laws, it is imperative that mental health practitioners in Malaysia are aware of their own attitudes and biases toward LGBT Malaysians. Formally trained mental health practitioners must reconcile national attitudes toward LGBT Malaysians with their professional obligation to ethically provide services for LGBT clients. Practitioners must be knowledgeable of the distinction between sexual orientation and gender/transgender identity and understand that they are not the same or interchangeable. Homosexuality and same-sex practice are not mental disorders; sexual orientation is a continuum, and individuals can be anywhere on it. Although this chapter mainly focused on gay men and lesbians, it is important for practitioners to note that biological sex and gender are also continuums and transgender individuals typically do not identify with their assigned sex; hence, they may express themselves as gender non-conforming or nonbinary.

Further training is necessary for Malaysian practitioners and non-Malaysian practitioners working with LGBT Malaysians abroad to improve their competencies in working with this population. Non-Malaysian mental health practitioners must make a concerted effort to know the sociopolitical structure of the country, including knowing the laws of the land as they pertain to LGBT persons and the society's attitudes toward of sexual diversity and gender variance. The preceding information allows for further discussion with the clients on how to be safe in a nonaccepting environment. Both Malaysian and non-Malaysian practitioners must facilitate this discussion with their clients to create critical consciousness of their cultural positioning and the sociopolitical context of their concerns.

Malaysian and non-Malaysian mental health practitioners must use the nuanced dynamic of the country's collectivistic value pattern, high-contact communication, high-context family, and societal system, particularly as they relate to clients' gay and lesbian identities. Practitioners who are more familiar with the individualistic dynamic and style of communication may find it challenging to work with clients from a collectivistic culture. The role of the practitioner here would be to practice "perspective taking" and to be mindful of the cultural worldview of the clients. Without cultural empathy, counseling such clients will be a struggle, and crucial nuances in clients' stories could be missed.

Practitioners must tease out clients' multiple identities (e.g., Malaysian, sexual orientation, gender, Malay/Chinese/Indian) and explore how these identities and roles are played out in their daily lives, including how the roles overlap and the level of integration. Thus, the focus on counseling includes helping the clients attend to psychological distress associated with the concealment of their sexual orientation and the daily management of their multiple identities.

In spite of the existence of well-developed sexual identity development models, mental health practitioners should be cautious about the use of the models when conceptualizing their clients. As mentioned, the models do not attend to the unique developmental tasks of gay and lesbian Malaysians addressed in this chapter. Practitioners must explore the coming out process from a culture-centered perspective integrating the high-context communication style. Furthermore, practitioners should help clients to identify their multiple identities and negotiate the compromises that need to be made as clients navigate through their sociopolitical environment. Malaysian clients themselves need to be aware that their LGBT identities are not a mental disorder and that there are ways to create a support system for themselves and others like them.

REFERENCES

Alagappar, P. N., & Kaur, K. (2009). The representation of homosexuality—A content analysis in a Malaysian newspaper. *Language in India*, 9, 24–47.

Alvarado, A., & Hurtado, S. (2012, November). *Salience at the intersection: Latina/o identities across different campus contexts.* Paper presented at the 2012 Annual Conference of the Association for Studies in Higher Education, Las Vegas, NV.

Baba, I. (2001). Gay and lesbian couples in Malaysia. *Journal of Homosexuality*, 40, 143–163. http://dx.doi.org/10.1300/J082v40n03_08

Baharom, H. (2012, July 19). *Najib: LGBTs, liberalism, pluralism are enemies of Islam.* Retrieved from https://www.malaysia-today.net/2012/07/19/najib-lgbts-liberalism-pluralism-are-enemies-of-islam/

Bhugra, D. (1997). Coming out by South Asian gay men in the United Kingdom. *Archives of Sexual Behavior*, 26, 547–557. http://dx.doi.org/10.1023/A:1024512023379

Carroll, A., & Mendos, L. R. (2017). *State sponsored homophobia: A world survey of sexual orientation laws: Criminalisation, protection and recognition.* Geneva, Switzerland: ILGA.

Cass, V. C. (1979). Homosexual identity formation: A theoretical model. *Journal of Homosexuality*, 4, 219–235. http://dx.doi.org/10.1300/J082v04n03_01

Cheah, W. H., & Singaravelu, H. (2017). The coming-out process of gay and lesbian individuals from Islamic Malaysia: Communication strategies and motivations. *Journal of Intercultural Communication Research*, 46, 401–423. http://dx.doi.org/10.1080/17475759.2017.1362460

Chou, W.-S. (2000). *Tongzhi: Politics of same-sex eroticism in Chinese societies.* New York, NY: Routledge.

Chow, P. K., & Cheng, S. T. (2010). Shame, internalized heterosexism, lesbian identity, and coming out to others: A comparative study of lesbians in mainland China and

Hong Kong. *Journal of Counseling Psychology, 57,* 92–104. http://dx.doi.org/10.1037/a0017930

Department of Statistics. (2011). Population distribution and basic demographic characteristics 2010. Retrieved from https://www.dosm.gov.my/v1/index.php?r=column/ctheme&menu_id=L0pheU43NWJwRWVSZklWdzQ4TlhUUT09&bul_id=MDMxdHZjWTk1SjFzTzNkRXYzcVZjdz09

Fuad Rahmat, A. (2012, April 15). A review of 'homosexuality, right or crime'? Retrieved from https://irfront.net/post/articles/articles-english/a-review-of-homosexuality-right-or-crime/

Fukuyama, M. A., & Ferguson, D. (2000). Lesbian, gay, and bisexual people of color: Understanding cultural complexity and managing multiple oppressions. In R. M. Perez, K. A. DeBord, & K. J. Bieschke (Eds.), *Handbook of counseling and psychotherapy with lesbian, gay, and bisexual clients* (pp. 81–105). Washington, DC: American Psychological Association. http://dx.doi.org/10.1037/10339-004

Greene, B. (1997). Ethnic minority lesbians and gay men: Mental health and treatment issues. In B. Greene (Ed.), *Ethnic and cultural diversity among lesbians and gay men* (pp. 216–239). Thousand Oaks, CA: Sage.

Hofstede, G. (2001). *Culture's consequences: Comparing values, behaviors, institutions, and organizations across nations* (2nd ed.). Thousand Oaks, CA: Sage.

Holmes, O. (2016, December 13). Anwar Ibrahim: Malaysian court upholds jailing of key rival to PM. *The Guardian.* Retrieved from https://www.theguardian.com/

Israel, T., & Selvidge, M. M. (2003). Contributions of multicultural counseling to counselor competence with lesbian, gay, and bisexual clients. *Journal of Multicultural Counseling and Development, 31,* 84–98. http://dx.doi.org/10.1002/j.2161-1912.2003.tb00535.x

International Gay and Lesbian Human Rights Commission. (2014). *On the record: Violence against lesbians, bisexual women and transgender persons in Malaysia.* Retrieved from https://www.outrightinternational.org/sites/default/files/MalaysiaCC_0.pdf

Library of Congress, Federal Research Division. (2006, September). *Country profile: Malaysia.* Retrieved from https://www.loc.gov/rr/frd/cs/profiles/Malaysia.pdf

Lim, L. M. (2014, July 3). *Still in the closet: Life isn't easy for Malaysian gays. And it may actually be getting worse.* Retrieved from http://www.foreignpolicy.com/articles/2014/07/02/still_in_the_closet

Marlow, I., & Thanthong-Knight, R. (2018, October 25). *Malaysia's Mahathir says Asia won't follow West on LGBT rights.* Retrieved from https://www.bloomberg.com/news/articles/2018-10-25/malaysia-s-mahathir-says-asia-won-t-follow-west-on-lgbt-rights

Mok, O. (2014, March 14). *Penang organiser calls off Pink Dot over Muslim fire.* Retrieved from https://www.malaymail.com/news/malaysia/2014/03/14/penang-organiser-calls-off-pink-dot-over-muslim-fire/635057

Mosher, C. M. (2001). The social implications of sexual identity formation and the coming out process: A review of the theoretical and empirical literature. *The Family Journal, 9,* 164–173. http://dx.doi.org/10.1177/1066480701092011

Narui, M. (2011). Understanding Asian/American gay, lesbian, and bisexual experiences from a poststructural perspective. *Journal of Homosexuality, 58,* 1211–1234. http://dx.doi.org/10.1080/00918369.2011.605734

Ong, H. S. (2014, May 13). *Najib: 'Human rights-ism' goes against Muslim values.* Retrieved from http://www.thestar.com.my/News/Nation/2014/05/13/Najib-human-rightsism-against-muslim-values/

Poon, M. K., & Ho, P. T. (2008). Negotiating social stigma among gay Asian men. *Sexualities, 11,* 245–268. http://dx.doi.org/10.1177/1363460707085472

Shamsudin, Z., & Ghazali, K. (2011). A discursive construction of homosexual males in a Muslim-dominant community. *Multilingua, 30,* 279–304. http://dx.doi.org/10.1515/mult.2011.013

Stockwell, A. J. (1976). The historiography of Malaysia: Recent writings in English on the history of the area since 1874. *The Journal of Imperial and Commonwealth History, 5*, 82–110. http://dx.doi.org/10.1080/03086537608582474

Tan, C. K. K. (2011). Go home, gay boy! Or, why do Singaporean gay men prefer to "go home" and not "come out"? *Journal of Homosexuality, 58*, 865–882. http://dx.doi.org/10.1080/00918369.2011.581930

Ting-Toomey, S., & Chung, L. (2012). *Understanding intercultural communication* (2nd ed.). New York, NY: Oxford University Press.

Triandis, H. C. (1995). *Individualism and collectivism*. Boulder, CO: Westview.

Troiden, R. R. (1989). The formation of homosexual identities. *Journal of Homosexuality, 17*, 43–74. http://dx.doi.org/10.1300/J082v17n01_02

Williams, W. L. (2009). Strategies for challenging homophobia in Islamic Malaysia and secular China. *Nebula, 6*, 1–20.

Wong, C. Y., & Tang, C. S. (2004). Coming out experiences and psychological distress of Chinese homosexual men in Hong Kong. *Archives of Sexual Behavior, 33*, 149–157. http://dx.doi.org/10.1023/B:ASEB.0000014329.00994.b6

Whose Paradise?

An Intersectional Perspective on Mental Health and Gender/Sexual Diversity in Thailand

Timo T. Ojanen, Peter A. Newman, Rattanakorn Ratanashevorn,
Jan W. de Lind van Wijngaarden, and Suchon Tepjan

CASE STUDY 1: CHAI

Chai[1] was born in a city in Northern Thailand. IIis aunt and uncle, both university professors, have raised him since he was 10 years old. As a teenager, Chai became aware that he was attracted to other men. He behaved in a slightly more feminine manner than his classmates, and his uncle's colleagues teased his uncle about this. Believing in a link between hormones and sexual orientation, his aunt sent him to an endocrinologist to see whether Chai lacked testosterone. She then sent him to a psychologist, hoping that treatment could make Chai heterosexual. Finally, his desperate guardians enlisted three traditional healers, who explained that Chai was born gay in this life because in previous lives he had committed sexual misconduct against women. On a carefully chosen day, a traditional healer had the family burn Chai's clothes in a rice field and conducted rituals over Chai's naked body to expel a female spirit—indicative of how Thai popular culture approaches gender and sexuality as a single dimension and may invoke spiritual beliefs to explain homosexuality.

[1]The names and identities of the individuals in the case studies have been altered, and the narratives extensively redacted, to preserve their confidentiality.

Dr. Newman was supported in part by the Canada Research Chairs program (Canada Research Chair in Health & Social Justice) and the Canada Foundation for Innovation. We thank Dr. James Burford for proofreading and commenting on a draft of this chapter.

http://dx.doi.org/10.1037/0000159-010
LGBTQ Mental Health: International Perspectives and Experiences, N. Nakamura and C. H. Logie (Editors)

These humiliating experiences made Chai depressed. When he started having suicidal thoughts, his friends sought mental health care for him. He saw a psychologist for several months, was diagnosed with depression, and took medication. Chai's situation improved. His 9 months studying in the United States was a turning point. He temporarily cut ties with his aunt and uncle, gaining new self-confidence and friends. Chai is thriving now as a respected academic, doing the lesbian, gay, bisexual, transgender, intersex, and queer (LGBTIQ)[2] research he had dreamed of, far from his hometown and family.

CASE STUDY 2: MALEEWAN

Maleewan is a transgender woman in her early 30s from a Buddhist, Southern Thai middle-class family. After high school, she chose to attend university far away from home. She hoped to establish an independent life, free from the devaluation by her disapproving parents, who expected her to behave like a man. While at university, Maleewan found out she had HIV. She could not tell her parents, and she thought of ending her life. With support and intervention from her professors and trusted friends, Maleewan got over the initial shock and started antiretroviral therapy. Dealing with this trauma, she decided to see a psychiatrist, who diagnosed her with depression and prescribed antidepressants. However, she felt that the psychiatrist was not very helpful. She then approached a counselor specializing in gay and transgender clients, who was able to discuss HIV and sexuality in a non-judgmental way.

Maleewan's parents still expect her to downplay her femininity. She is continuing her studies, trying to become a lecturer. She feels her master's degree program is unsupportive, and she continues to struggle with academic and relationship issues. Maleewan can sleep only a few hours per night, often wakes up screaming, and has a poor appetite and memory. She is most concerned about her worsening physical health. She continually experiences mood swings and suicidal thoughts. Maleewan uses sex and crystal methamphetamine to temporarily escape her emotional problems. Currently she is seeing another psychiatrist, who is more supportive and provides her with greater opportunities to discuss her challenges.

---

[2]We use LGBTIQ as an international, inclusive acronym. It is problematic, as it does not directly correspond to Thai identity categories. Thailand has multiple identity labels corresponding to lesbian, gay, bisexual, and transgender identities, and some intersex individuals identify as intersex. The term *queer* is mostly used as an umbrella term in academic works using queer theory as a theoretical lens (e.g., Duangwises et al., 2014); few Thais use it as a self-assigned identity label.

INTRODUCTION

Thailand is often represented as a "gay paradise" (Jackson, 1999). The Tourism Authority of Thailand (n.d.) exploits this representation in a website targeting mainly gay and lesbian foreign tourists. As our case examples indicate, this representation is not an accurate portrayal of the lived experiences of many Thai LGBTIQ individuals. In this chapter, we discuss this paradox between the touristic image of Thailand as carefree and LGBTIQ affirming and the sometimes oppressive realities of LGBTIQ people who live in the country.

We first discuss the cultural and historical context of Thailand and the emergence of its numerous LGBTIQ identities. We then describe the Thai context of mental health and LGBTIQ issues, including the stigma associated with each of these. We explore conceptualizations of sexual orientation and gender identity, mental health, and cultural values that differ from those of many contexts in the Global North. Next, we describe common mental health problems and their multiple antecedents among LGBTIQ individuals in the Thai context. Finally, we present our perspectives on implications for improving LGBTIQ mental health in Thailand.

THAILAND: HISTORICAL AND CULTURAL CONTEXT

Thailand has approximately 66 million inhabitants. The official language is Central Thai, a second language for most of its speakers; the Northeast, North, and South are dominated by distinct regional languages, with 72 languages (50 are indigenous) spoken altogether in the country (Lewis, Simons, & Fennig, 2016). Politically, Thailand is a constitutional monarchy and has featured alternating civilian/democratic and military/autocratic governments since the end of absolute monarchy in 1932 (Bremmer, 2016).

Thailand takes pride in not having been formally colonized, but aspects of Indian, Chinese, and Western cultures, among others, have been adopted or adapted into Thai culture (Harrison & Jackson, 2010). One of the key Indic influences has been religion. Officially, 95% of Thais are registered as Theravada Buddhists, and the remaining 5% are mostly Muslims (4%) or Christians (National Statistical Office of Thailand, 2015). However, Thai Buddhism itself is often syncretic or hybridized with Hindu and animist beliefs (Kitiarsa, 2005).

EMERGENCE AND EVOLUTION OF THAI LGBTIQ IDENTITIES

Many countries in South and Southeast Asia have cultures that recognize more than two genders, often including at least one transgender identity (Winter, 2012). Buddhist scriptures record that in the time of the Buddha (ca. 2,500 years ago), it was thought that there were four sexes or genders, with many subtypes (Likhitpreechakul, 2012). In Thailand, the word *kathoey* historically referred to people of intermediate sex or gender; now it refers to transgender women (Chonwilai, 2012). It is debatable whether a distinct *kathoey* identity has been recognized for centuries or emerged only in the past century (Jackson, 2003). Thai documents prior to the past century described same-sex relations and behaviors but not identities based on being same-sex attracted or transgender (Jackson, 2003).

According to Jackson (2003), a specific *kathoey* identity emerged in the 1950s, from which more masculine *gay* identities gradually diverged from the 1960s onward; by the 1980s, masculine *tom* and feminine *dee* identities emerged among same-sex-attracted females. These identities are understood in everyday Thai culture as distinct gender categories (*phet*), leaving concepts like sexual orientation or gender identity redundant, because the attributes they describe are already contained within fixed categorical identities (Jackson, 2003). Although various Thai translations exist for the terms *gender, sexual orientation,* and *gender identity,* they are mostly known or used by academics and activists, not in everyday discourse (Ojanen, 2009).

The emergence of further identities and their subtypes continues; new identity terms are coined or adopted when existing terms appear inaccurate or stigmatizing (Ojanen, 2009). A study on bullying (Mahidol University, Plan International Thailand & UNESCO, 2014, p. 34) provided 14 response options for participants' *phet,* including "man" or "woman"; 11 options describing various Thai LGBTIQ identities[3]; and "other." Among 2,070 secondary students, 11.4% (*n* = 235) chose one of the 11 LGBTIQ options in the computerized survey. Eleven (0.5%) participants chose "other," underscoring the diversity of Thai gender and sexuality terms. *Phet* definitions may be relatively fixed, but these identity labels can be appropriated temporarily or situationally and cannot be seen as static or permanent attributes of an individual, who may move between different *phet* over a lifetime (de Lind van Wijngaarden & Ojanen, 2015).

Thailand has been described as tolerant but unaccepting of transgenderism and homosexuality (Jackson, 1999). This can be understood as a willingness to acknowledge and accept the diversity of sexuality and gender identities and expressions, but only in some situations and social contexts. Characteristic of a high-context (Adair & Brett, 2005) and collectivist culture (Triandis, 1988), acceptance versus nonacceptance is not a fixed attitude but depends on what is considered appropriate for a given situation (Jackson, 2003).

The Thai context challenges some fundamental assumptions of positive LGBTIQ youth development typically associated with a Global North perspective. Perhaps foremost among these is that coming out is a universal

---

[3]These options were *kathoei* (transgender woman), *sao praphet song* (transgender woman), *phu ying kham phet* (transgender woman), *gay* (gay male), *chai rak chai* (man who loves men), *tom* (masculine lesbian), *phu chai kham phet/transman* (transgender man), *dee* (feminine lesbian with preference for toms), *les* (feminine lesbian), *ying rak ying* (woman who loves women), and *bi* (bisexual of either sex).

prerequisite of psychological well-being among same-sex-attracted youth. In a qualitative longitudinal study of young same-sex-attracted men and transgender women, largely from rural Thailand, many participants found the concept of coming out to be unintelligible or even stupid; maintaining harmony in familial relationships and not damaging the family's image were more salient goals (de Lind van Wijngaarden & Ojanen, 2015). The family was not seen as a proper context for asserting their identity. In Thai culture, controlling and deferring one's personal emotions for the sake of social harmony is a highly valued goal (Mulder, 1997). The more formal the context, the more likely the rejection of openly LGBTIQ individuals (Jackson, 2003). Visibly non-normative gender presentation appears to be the key trigger of discrimination in contexts like employment (Ojanen et al., 2018), education (Suriyasarn, 2014), and families (de Lind van Wijngaarden & Ojanen, 2015).

As in many other cultures, the social status and treatment of LGBTIQ persons are related to class, ethnicity, education, and HIV status (Ojanen, Ratanashevorn, & Boonkerd, 2016). The particular alignments of such intersectional characteristics may challenge some preconceptions. In a high-context, collectivist culture, higher socioeconomic status and educational attainment are not necessarily aligned with lesser stigmatization or marginalization; rather, these attributes may be sources of vulnerability because high-status families and individuals may feel the need to protect their public image more carefully than others (Ojanen et al., 2018). Chai's narrative suggests that his well-educated guardians were particularly concerned about the family losing face through their nephew being visibly gay. Chai's parents may also have felt more trust and confidence in accessing modern medicine and psychology as intervention modalities than less educated or less wealthy parents. Yet Chai's access to higher education and foreign travel afforded him an outlet for support and growth, which a youth from a poorer family might not have. Maleewan, likewise, benefited from her class background in being able to access higher education, but not being able to conceal her difference from mainstream gender norms might result in intense pressure to conform, from both her family and her university.

CONCEPTUALIZATIONS OF MENTAL HEALTH IN THAILAND

An illuminating ethnographic study addressed coexisting models for understanding mental health and illness in contemporary Thailand: the modern medical model, Buddhist notions of karma (*kam*) and merit (*bun*), and animist notions of *khwan* and spirit possession (Burnard, Naiyapatana, & Lloyd, 2006). Possession by spirits or ghosts is a prevalent local explanation for mental illness; another is that a khwan, a life spirit, can be lost, especially through a traumatic event (Burnard et al., 2006). If a khwan is lost, it is believed that the individual may become mentally or physically ill, and ceremonies may be arranged for calling the lost *khwan* back (Engel & Engel, 2010). These ideologies are adopted and adapted in various combinations by health care practitioners, religious practitioners, and laypeople.

The concept of karma may contribute to the stigmatization faced by LGBTIQ persons and those with mental health problems; both may be interpreted as the consequence of unmeritorious activities in past lifetimes, and therefore as justified and unavoidable (Burnard et al., 2006; United Nations Development Program & United States Agency for International Development, 2014). The concept of merit refers to the accumulation of good deeds, expected to result in better life circumstances in the present or future incarnations (Burnard et al., 2006). Those who experience problems related to mental health or to being LGBTIQ may attempt to resolve these by merit making—making donations to a temple or by ordaining as monks (Burnard et al., 2006). Sons in Thai Buddhist families are typically expected to ordain as monks for a period of time to pay back a debt of gratitude to their parents by dedicating the resulting merit to them. Parents may force a feminine or gay son into monkhood, hoping that ordination will make him normatively masculine; women, including visibly transgender women, are not allowed to join the monkhood and thus cannot pay their debt of gratitude to their parents in this way, so they may be expected to pay it back by taking care of their parents indefinitely (United Nations Development Program & United States Agency for International Development, 2014).

INDIGENOUS AND MODERN MEDICAL OPTIONS FOR ADDRESSING MENTAL HEALTH ISSUES

Next we describe both indigenous and modern medical approaches to addressing mental illness. Fortune tellers (*mo du*), spirit mediums (*rang song*), and shamans (*mo phi*, literally "ghost doctors") are often consulted when personal problems are experienced (Kitiarsa, 2012). As the case study of Chai indicates, even highly educated Thais may believe in the influence of bad karma, lack of merit, lost khwan, or spirit possession on mental health. It is less stigmatizing to consult a fortune-teller or a spirit medium than a mental health care professional, as consulting the latter implies to outsiders the presence of a mental health problem (Ojanen, 2009, 2010). Spiritual practitioners may thus be more culturally acceptable, more accessible, and available in greater numbers to provide a listening ear to those in need than mental health professionals. As Chai's case suggests, more educated Thais might choose to solve mental health problems first through modern medicine, and if it fails, through other means. For less educated Thais, the reverse might be true. When health care practitioners' and clients' beliefs differ, it might impede mutual understanding and trust, unless the situation is handled sensitively.

The availability of openly gay or transgender spirit mediums in Thailand, in contrast to psychologists or psychiatrists, for whom it can be risky or difficult to be openly gay (Ojanen et al., 2016; Suriyasarn, 2014), may make spirit mediums an attractive choice for LGBTIQ individuals experiencing various problems. Spirit mediumship also provides some LGBTIQ individuals an acceptable context for expressing gender atypical behaviors (when channeling a spirit of another gender) and gaining social acceptance and prestige. Fortune-tellers, spirit mediums, and other indigenous practitioners likely outnumber mental health practitioners; the number of practicing psychiatrists, psychologists, and social workers has been estimated at only a few hundred each for a population of 66 million (World Health Organization [WHO], 2011).

Because of understaffing, psychiatrists in state hospitals are usually able to spend only a few minutes per patient to establish a diagnosis and prescribe medication, providing few opportunities for talk therapy (Ojanen, 2010). Psychiatrists in private hospitals have more time per patient, but fees may be too high for low-income patients (Ojanen, 2010). The role of clinical psychologists has traditionally been to act as a "technician who would take orders from psychiatrists, administer tests, and write reports" (Tapanya, 2001, p. 70), implying that in many contexts, neither psychiatrists nor psychologists provide much counseling (Ojanen, 2010). Generalist physicians account for most of mental health care provision in public primary care facilities; many of them lack skills and interest in mental health (Lotrakul & Saipanish, 2006) and may not have received recent training in psychiatric issues (WHO, 2011).

LGBTIQ MENTAL HEALTH ISSUES IN THAILAND

Scholarship has suggested that the minority stress perspective (Meyer, 2003) is useful for understanding mental health issues among Thai LGBTIQ people. For example, Yadegarfard, Meinhold-Bergmann, and Ho (2014) reported that the prevalence of depression, suicidal thinking, and sexual risk behaviors was significantly higher among those transgender women ($n = 129$) who experienced more loneliness, family rejection, and social isolation. Among adult lesbian women in the Northeast ($n = 339$), those who were exposed to heterosexist verbal abuse had a higher prevalence of depression (Sumonthip Boonkerd, 2014).[4] In a study of secondary school students ($n = 2,070$), those who experienced homophobic or transphobic school bullying had significantly higher rates of depression and suicide attempts: Students bullied for gender- and sexuality-related reasons were 5 times more likely to try killing themselves than students who were not bullied (Mahidol University et al., 2014).

Evidence also indicates high rates of substance abuse among some Thai LGBTIQ groups. In a 2005 study among 474 transgender women recruited

---

[4]Thai-language publications are cited by the first name and surname of the author, and alphabetized by the first name, in keeping with Thai academic customs. Thai-language titles have been translated by the authors of this chapter unless an English-language title was indicated in the cited work. Thai titles of cited works are not provided in the interest of space but are available upon request from the corresponding author.

from Bangkok, Phuket, and Chiang Mai, 42.6% reported drug use (methamphetamine, ketamine, ecstasy, or sleeping pills) in the past 3 months (Guadamuz et al., 2011). A study in Chiang Mai comparing lesbian and bisexual women (*n* = 37) with heterosexual women (*n* = 84), all recruited from drinking venues, found statistically significant differences in harmful alcohol use (57% of lesbian and bisexual women vs. 31% of heterosexual women) and ever having used methamphetamine (32% of lesbian/bisexual vs. 13% of heterosexual women; Patel et al., 2013).

Tablet-form methamphetamine (*ya ba*, "crazy drug") has been designated the primary drug of concern in Thailand, accounting for 84% of all individuals receiving treatment for drug abuse (United Nations Office on Drugs and Crime, 2015). Among young men who have sex with men (MSM), crystal (locally known as *ice*) rather than tablet-form methamphetamine has a desirable public image as "cool, pure, clean and *hiso* (high society)" (Guadamuz & Boonmongkon, 2013, p. S229). It is considered useful for skin whitening and weight control; because of its high price, younger men may trade sex in exchange for it (Guadamuz & Boonmongkon, 2013). In a recent study of 499 MSM who presented for an HIV test in Bangkok, 11% reported drug use in the past 3 months, with 4% indicating regular methamphetamine use; 38% were assessed as alcoholic and 64% as depressed (Sapsirisavat et al., 2016).

Transgender individuals face additional risks to health and well-being from the unsupervised use of hormones. Among Thai transgender people, hormones are obtained mainly over the counter from pharmacies (Guadamuz et al., 2011) or through friends (Gooren, Sungkaew, Giltay, & Guadamuz, 2015). Unsupervised use may be associated with overdosing and greater side effects, such as mood swings and kidney disease. Given the intense pressure transgender women face to look beautiful and the inconvenience and expense of accessing medically supervised hormone treatment, unsupervised use of hormones and other chemicals (e.g., injectable glutathione for skin whitening) may be considered socially reasonable but is associated with health risks (Poompruek, Boonmongkon, & Guadamuz, 2014).

Finally, HIV stigma directly impacts the mental health of people living with HIV in Thailand by intensifying self-blame and shame; reducing opportunities for social and familial support; and engendering and justifying discrimination in health care, employment, and other domains (Li, Lee, Thammawijaya, Jiraphongsa, & Rotheram-Borus, 2009). Given the vast and sustained disparities in HIV incidence and prevalence among MSM and transgender women in Thailand, HIV-related stigma also exacts a negative toll on the physical and mental health of these populations more broadly (Logie, Newman, Weaver, Roungkraphon, & Tepjan, 2016). In Thailand, as elsewhere, HIV stigma and sexual stigma are associated with increased risk for HIV transmission among MSM and transgender women. Intersectional stigma operates through multiple pathways to increase HIV risk, such as minority stress and syndemic production, including depression and substance use, as well as negative judgments and discrimination in health care settings (Chakrapani, Kaur, Newman, Mittal, &

Kumar, 2018; Newman, Lee, Roungprakhon, & Tepjan, 2012). HIV and sexual stigma are associated with lower rates of HIV testing—crucial to early diagnosis and treatment, and thereby reduced HIV transmission—and create barriers in uptake and adherence to HIV prevention technologies among MSM and transgender women in Thailand (Logie et al., 2016; Newman, Roungprakhon, & Tepjan, 2013).

LGBTIQ COMMUNITY EMPOWERMENT AND ADVOCACY

Thai LGBTIQ organizations' efforts on mental health issues have focused mostly on depathologization and direct service provision in the form of para-professional online and telephone counseling. In 2001, a lesbian organization, Anjaree, requested a letter from the Department of Mental Health to affirm that homosexuality is not a mental illness; the department complied, issuing a letter simply stating that the *International Statistical Classification of Diseases and Related Health Problems* (10th ed.; ICD-10) disease classification (WHO, 2007) used by Thailand does not list homosexuality as a mental illness (Ojanen et al., 2016). More recently, the Foundation of Thai Transgender Alliance for Human Rights has campaigned for delisting transsexualism as a mental illness in the ICD-10.[5]

Provision of counseling by Thai LGBTIQ groups, mostly online and by telephone, has been more targeted at HIV and sexual health rather than psycho-social issues, but it has played an important role by offering a listening ear to those reluctant to use formal mental health services (Ojanen, 2009, 2015). These services have gradually diversified. For example, Rainbow Sky Association of Thailand (https://www.rsat.info), Thailand's largest LGBTIQ organization, as of 2017 operated a sexual health and HIV testing clinic at its main office in Bangkok and had a dedicated transgender staff member for registering complaints of discrimination and helping clients to access justice, in addition to operating its *Sai Sabai Jai* (Peace of Mind Line) helpline. Other activities arranged by LGBTIQ groups may also indirectly benefit LGBTIQ mental health by improving the social climate and by providing informal peer support.

Overall, there has not been much advocacy in Thailand to demand appropriate mental health services for LGBTIQ individuals. However, in 2014, the Bangkok-based advocacy group Asia Pacific Coalition on Male Sexual Health, or APCOM, called for governments in the region to attend to LGBTIQ mental health (Hynes, 2014). To our knowledge, training programs preparing psychologists and psychiatrists usually involve little if any training on LGBTIQ issues. Including such training components from an affirmative point of view would be essential.

---

[5]Photographs and a description of their campaign activities are shown on their Facebook page (https://www.facebook.com/pg/thaitga/photos/?tab=album&album_id=775719119162976).

LGBTIQ-AFFIRMATIVE MENTAL HEALTH CARE

Mental health issues are somewhat neglected in Thailand, as just described. Mental health disparities experienced by LGBTIQ people due to stigma and minority stress have received even less attention. To illustrate what service providers can do in a context that lacks formal definitions for LGBTIQ competencies and has low mental health capacity, we describe three public sector clinics that have strived to provide appropriate care for LGBTIQ clients.

- The Gender Variation Clinic (http://www.teenrama.com) in Ramathibodi Hospital (a teaching hospital of Mahidol University) is a specialized service for LGBTIQ and questioning adolescents with psychosocial adjustment and medical issues, as well as for their parents. Focus areas include helping parents accept the identity of their child and providing transgender youth with medically supervised hormone treatment. The clinic also arranges seminars and conducts research on LGBTIQ mental health issues (Ojanen et al., 2016).

- The Thai Red Cross Tangerine Community Health Center (http://www. facebook.com/TangerineCenter) is the first transgender-specific health center in Asia, operated by gender-sensitive medical professionals, including transgender staff. Its focus areas include using hormones safely, preventing HIV and sexually transmitted infections, and addressing the stigma and discrimination faced by transgender people. The clinic aims to serve as a model for the region in expanding transgender people's access to competent health care and promoting their rights.

- Chulalongkorn University, a prestigious state university in Central Bangkok, operates two counseling centers: the Chula Student Wellness Center (http://wellness.chula.ac.th) for university students and staff, and the Center for Psychological Wellness (https://www.facebook.com/WellnessPsyCU) for the general public. Both centers use a client-centered and holistic approach that affirms LGBTIQ identities. The student clinic offers mental health services, as well as other programs and activities, such as a small LGBTIQ-themed film festival. Given the stigma around mental health issues in Thailand, these other activities aim to familiarize students with clinic staff, build trust, and increase comfort in accessing counseling or mental health treatment.

CONCLUSION AND IMPLICATIONS

The mental health of LGBTIQ people in Thailand is threatened by intersectional stigma and minority stress caused by actual and anticipated discrimination, ostracism, and violence. As occurs elsewhere, Thai LGBTIQ individuals are most vulnerable when (a) their difference from the societal mainstream is most visible (e.g., they are transgender or visibly gender nonconforming and less able to pass selectively under the radar); (b) they are in a social setting (e.g., workplace, educational institution) that expects them to fit in rather than be different (particularly in formal contexts); (c) they occupy intersectional identities or social statuses (e.g., ethnic or religious minority, living in poverty, living with HIV) that compound their vulnerability; and (d) they have limited access to social, financial, and medical support (more common if they are isolated or live on a low income).

Thailand now has a law (the 2015 Gender Equality Act; Human Rights Watch, 2015) banning discrimination on the basis of gender and gender expression. However, there is no same-sex marriage legislation or gender-recognition law for transgender individuals. As of 2019, the military government was considering a civil partnership bill that would provide limited rights to same-sex couples. Basic education students and civil servants are mostly expected by their institutions to dress, behave, and have hairstyles matching stereotypical gender roles associated with their birth sex (Mahidol University et al., 2014). Secondary school health education textbooks and the 2008 national core curriculum (on which textbooks are based) teach that being attracted to the same sex, being transgender, and masturbating too frequently are forms of sexual deviation (among others) and are to be avoided (Wijit Wongwareethip, 2016). Following a complaint under the Gender Equality Act in 2018, the Ministry of Education established working groups to identify contents that would need to be revised in new versions of the textbooks.

Unjust laws and regulations cause direct discrimination; in conjunction with outmoded school curricula and lack of training in LGBTIQ-specific competencies for mental health care providers, these produce a social climate in which being visibly LGBTIQ means being a less valuable person. Increasing evidence demonstrates associations between legal and policy statutes and the mental health of LGBTIQ persons. For example, a recent U.S. study demonstrated a significant reduction in suicide attempts among sexual minority high school students after implementation of same-sex marriage policies in their states relative to sexual minority students in states without such policies (Raifman, Moscoe, Austin, & McConnell, 2017). The specific policies and laws that may be most important and effective in Thailand for promoting LGBTIQ health may differ from those in the United States. However, convincing evidence of the positive impact of LGBTIQ-affirmative laws and policies on the mental health of LGBTIQ individuals supports such structural interventions as a powerful and far-reaching mechanism to promote the health and human rights of LGBTIQ individuals.

Access to LGBTIQ-competent care is also essential. Although Thailand still lacks locally grounded definitions of LGBTIQ competencies, care intended to be LGBTIQ affirmative can be provided in diverse contexts, as our examples indicate. Often, it is not delivered through formal mental health facilities but through community organizations, university clinics, online services, and facilities of other medical specialties (e.g., HIV care, adolescent health). Key research and advocacy areas that need further attention include defining and training LGBTIQ competencies for health care providers in the Thai context, addressing relevant cultural notions and involving spiritual practitioners in providing care for LGBTIQ individuals, addressing mental health stigma, establishing relevant services also outside of Bangkok, and depathologizing transgender identities while increasing access to transgender health care. Attending to these issues will help to ensure that Thai LGBTIQ individuals and their family members have appropriate and acceptable forms of help available when and where they need it, as well as empower them in asserting their fundamental rights as members of Thai society.

REFERENCES

Adair, W. L., & Brett, J. M. (2005). The negotiation dance: Time, culture and behavioral sequences in negotiation. *Organization Science, 16*, 33–51. http://dx.doi.org/10.1287/orsc.1040.0102

Bremmer, I. (2016, August 12). Here's what you need to know about Thailand's new constitution. *Time Magazine*. Retrieved from http://time.com/4448655/thailand-constitutional-referendum/

Burnard, P., Naiyapatana, W., & Lloyd, G. (2006). Views of mental illness and mental health care in Thailand: A report of an ethnographic study. *Journal of Psychiatric and Mental Health Nursing, 13*, 742–749. http://dx.doi.org/10.1111/j.1365-2850.2006.01028.x

Chakrapani, V., Kaur, M., Newman, P. A., Mittal, S., & Kumar, R. (2018). Syndemics and HIV-related sexual risk among men who have sex with men in India: Influences of stigma and resilience. *Culture, Health & Sexuality, 21*, 416–431.

Chonwilai, S. (2012). Kathoey: Male-to-female transgenders or transsexuals. In P. Boonmongkon & P. A. Jackson (Eds.), *Thai sex talk: The language of sex and sexuality in Thailand* (pp. 109–117). Chiang Mai, Thailand: Mekong Press.

de Lind van Wijngaarden, J. W., & Ojanen, T. T. (2015). Identity management and sense of belonging to gay community among young rural Thai same-sex attracted men: Implications for HIV prevention and treatment. *Culture, Health & Sexuality, 18*, 377–390. http://dx.doi.org/10.1080/13691058.2015.1087595

Duangwises, N., Iamsilpa, R., Topananan, S., Boonmongkon, P., Ojanen, T. T., & Guadamuz, T. E. (2014). BlackBerry smartphones and sexuality among queer university students in Bangkok. In P. Boonmongkon & T. T. Ojanen (Eds.), *Mobile sexualities: Transformations of gender and sexuality in Southeast Asia* (pp. 281–356). Nakhon Pathom, Thailand: Southeast Asian Consortium on Gender, Sexuality, and Health.

Engel, D., & Engel, J. S. (2010). *Tort, custom and karma: Globalization and legal consciousness in Thailand*. Stanford, CA: Stanford Law Books.

Gooren, L. J., Sungkaew, T., Giltay, E. J., & Guadamuz, T. E. (2015). Cross-sex hormone use, functional health and mental well-being among transgender men (*Toms*) and transgender women (*Kathoeys*) in Thailand. *Culture, Health & Sexuality, 17*, 92–103. http://dx.doi.org/10.1080/13691058.2014.950982

Guadamuz, T. E., & Boonmongkon, P. (2013). Ice (crystal meth) use among young men who have sex with men in Thailand: Power, transactions and sexual networks. *Culture, Health & Sexuality, 15*(Suppl. 2), S229–230.

Guadamuz, T. E., Wimonsate, W., Varangrat, A., Phanuphak, P., Jommaroeng, R., McNicholl, J. M., . . . van Griensven, F. (2011). HIV prevalence, risk behavior, hormone use and surgical history among transgender persons in Thailand. *AIDS and Behavior, 15*, 650–658. http://dx.doi.org/10.1007/s10461-010-9850-5

Harrison, R. V., & Jackson, P. A. (Eds.). (2010). *The ambiguous allure of the West: Traces of the colonial in Thailand*. Chiang Mai, Thailand: Silkworm Books. http://dx.doi.org/10.5790/hongkong/9789622091214.001.0001

Human Rights Watch. (2015). Thailand Gender Equality Act. Retrieved from https://www.hrw.org/news/2015/09/21/thailand-gender-equality-act

Hynes, C. (2014, October 19). APAC needs to step up mental health services for gay and transgender people. *Asian Correspondent*. Retrieved from https://asiancorrespondent.com/2014/10/apac-needs-to-step-up-mental-health-services-for-gay-and-transgender-people/

Jackson, P. A. (1999). Tolerant but unaccepting: The myth of a Thai "gay paradise." In P. A. Jackson & N. M. Cook (Eds.), *Genders and sexualities in modern Thailand* (pp. 226–242). Chiang Mai, Thailand: Silkworm Books.

Jackson, P. A. (2003). Performative genders, perverse desires: A bio-history of Thailand's same-sex and transgender cultures. *Intersections: Gender, History and Culture in the Asian Context, 9*. Retrieved from http://intersections.anu.edu.au/issue9/jackson.html

Kitiarsa, P. (2005). Beyond syncretism: Hybridization of popular religion in contemporary Thailand. *Journal of Southeast Asian Studies, 36*, 461–487. http://dx.doi.org/10.1017/S0022463405000251

Kitiarsa, P. (2012). *Monks, mediums and amulets: Thai popular Buddhism today*. Chiang Mai, Thailand: Silkworm Books.

Lewis, M. P., Simons, G. F., & Fennig, C. D. (Eds.). (2016). *Ethnologue: Languages of the world* (19th ed.). Dallas, TX: SIL International. Retrieved from https://www.ethnologue.com/country/TH/

Li, L., Lee, S.-J., Thammawijaya, P., Jiraphongsa, C., & Rotheram-Borus, M. J. (2009). Stigma, social support, and depression among people living with HIV in Thailand. *AIDS Care, 21*, 1007–1013. http://dx.doi.org/10.1080/09540120802614358

Likhitpreechakul, P. (2012). Semen, Viagra and Pandaka: Ancient endocrinology and modern day discrimination. *Journal of the Oxford Centre for Buddhist Studies, 3*, 91–127. Retrieved from http://jocbs.org/index.php/jocbs/article/download/28/30

Logie, C. H., Newman, P. A., Weaver, J., Roungkraphon, S., & Tepjan, S. (2016). HIV-related stigma and HIV prevention uptake among young men who have sex with men and transgender women in Thailand. *AIDS Patient Care and STDs, 30*, 92–100. http://dx.doi.org/10.1089/apc.2015.0197

Lotrakul, M., & Saipanish, R. (2006). Psychiatric services in primary care settings: A survey of general practitioners in Thailand. *BMC Family Practice, 7*, 48. http://dx.doi.org/10.1186/1471-2296-7-48

Mahidol University, Plan International Thailand, & UNESCO. (2014). *Bullying targeting secondary school students who are or are perceived to be transgender or same-sex attracted: Types, prevalence, impact, motivation and preventive measures in 5 provinces of Thailand*. Bangkok, Thailand: UNESCO.

Meyer, I. H. (2003). Prejudice, social stress, and mental health in lesbian, gay, and bisexual populations: Conceptual issues and research evidence. *Psychological Bulletin, 129*, 674–697. http://dx.doi.org/10.1037/0033-2909.129.5.674

Mulder, N. (1997). *Thai images: The culture of the public world*. Chiang Mai, Thailand: Silkworm Books.

National Statistical Office of Thailand. (2015). *Statistical year book—Thailand 2015*. Retrieved from http://service.nso.go.th/nso/nsopublish/pubs/e-book/esyb58/index.html#223/z

Newman, P. A., Lee, S.-J., Roungprakhon, S., & Tepjan, S. (2012). Demographic and behavioral correlates of HIV risk among men and transgender women recruited from gay entertainment venues and community-based organizations in Thailand: Implications for HIV prevention. *Prevention Science, 13*, 483–492. http://dx.doi.org/10.1007/s11121-012-0275-4

Newman, P. A., Roungprakhon, S., & Tepjan, S. (2013). A social ecology of rectal microbicide acceptability among young men who have sex with men and transgender women in Thailand. *Journal of the International AIDS Society, 16*, 18476. http://dx.doi.org/10.7448/IAS.16.1.18476

Ojanen, T. T. (2009). Sexual/gender minorities in Thailand: Identities, challenges, and voluntary-sector counseling. *Sexuality Research and Social Policy, 6*(2), 4–34. http://dx.doi.org/10.1525/srsp.2009.6.2.4

Ojanen, T. T. (2010). *Mental health services and sexual/gender minority clients in Bangkok, Thailand: Views by service users and service providers.* Unpublished master's thesis, Assumption University, Bangkok, Thailand.

Ojanen, T. T. (2015). Online counseling services for LGBTI people in Thailand: Rationale, realisation, and research. In *15th BUU & AMSAR 2015 International Conference: Communication perspective: Social connection in the age of digital technology practice* (pp. 14–24). Bang Saen, Thailand: Burapha University & ASEAN Media and Communication Studies and Research Center, University of the Thai Chamber of Commerce. Retrieved from http://www.amsarthailand.utcc.ac.th/images/Proceeding_100715.pdf

Ojanen, T. T., Burford, J., Juntrasook, A., Kongsup, A., Assatarakul, T., & Chaiyajit, N. (2018). Intersections of LGBTI exclusion and discrimination in Thailand: The role of socio-economic status. *Sexuality Research and Social Policy.* Advance online publication. http://dx.doi.org/10.1007/s13178-018-0361-x

Ojanen, T. T., Ratanashevorn, R., & Boonkerd, S. (2016). Gaps in responses to LGBT issues in Thailand: Mental health research, services, and policies. *Psychology of Sexualities Review, 7*, 41–59.

Patel, S. A., Bangorn, S., Aramrattana, A., Limaye, R., Celentano, D. D., Lee, J., & Sherman, S. G. (2013). Elevated alcohol and sexual risk behaviors among young Thai lesbian/bisexual women. *Drug and Alcohol Dependence, 127*, 53–58. http://dx.doi.org/10.1016/j.drugalcdep.2012.06.010

Poompruek, P., Boonmongkon, P., & Guadamuz, T. E. (2014). 'For me . . . it's a miracle': Injecting beauty among *kathoeis* in a provincial Thai city. *International Journal of Drug Policy, 25*, 798–803. http://dx.doi.org/10.1016/j.drugpo.2014.06.015

Raifman, J., Moscoe, E., Austin, S. B., & McConnell, M. (2017). Difference-in-differences analysis of the association between state same-sex marriage policies and adolescent suicide attempts. *JAMA Pediatrics, 171*, 350–356. http://dx.doi.org/10.1001/jamapediatrics.2016.4529

Sapsirisavat, V., Phanuphak, N., Keadpudsa, S., Egan, J. E., Pussadee, K., Klaytong, P., . . . Stall, R. (2016). Psychosocial and behavioral characteristics of high-risk men who have sex with men (MSM) of unknown HIV positive serostatus in Bangkok, Thailand. *AIDS and Behavior, 20*(Suppl. 3), 386–397. http://dx.doi.org/10.1007/s10461-016-1519-2

Sumonthip Boonkerd. (2014). *Prevalence of depression among lesbians in North-east Thailand.* Unpublished master's thesis, Khon Kaen University, Khon Kaen, Thailand.

Suriyasarn, B. (2014). *Gender identity and sexual orientation: Promoting rights, diversity and equality in the world of work (PRIDE) project Thailand.* Bangkok, Thailand: International Labor Organization.

Tapanya, S. (2001). Psychology in medical settings in Thailand. *Journal of Clinical Psychology in Medical Settings, 8*, 69–72. http://dx.doi.org/10.1023/A:1011332024189

Tourism Authority of Thailand. (n.d.) *GoThai.beFree* [website]. Retrieved from http://gothaibefree.com/

Triandis, H. C. (1988). Collectivism v. individualism: A reconceptualization of a basic concept in cross-cultural social psychology. In G. K. Verma & C. Bagley (Eds.), *Cross-cultural studies of personality, attitudes and cognition* (pp. 60–95). London, England: Macmillan. http://dx.doi.org/10.1007/978-1-349-08120-2_3

United Nations Development Program, & United States Agency for International Development. (2014). *Being LGBT in Asia: Thailand country report.* Bangkok, Thailand: United Nations Development Program.

United Nations Office on Drugs and Crime. (2015). *The challenge of synthetic drugs in East and South-East Asia and Oceania: Trends and patterns of amphetamine-type stimulants.* Retrieved from https://www.unodc.org/documents/southeastasiaandpacific/ Publications/2015/drugs/ATS_2015_Report_web.pdf

Wijit Wongwareethip. (2016). *Sexual/gender diversity in Thai textbooks: Analysis of lower secondary health education textbooks.* Bangkok, Thailand: FOR-SOGI.

Winter, S. (2012). *Lost in transition: Transgender people, rights and HIV vulnerability in the Asia-Pacific region.* Retrieved from http://www.undp.org/content/dam/undp/library/ hivaids/UNDP_HIV_Transgender_report_Lost_in_Transition_May_2012.pdf

World Health Organization. (2007). *International statistical classification of diseases and related health problems* (10th rev.). Geneva, Switzerland: Author.

World Health Organization. (2011). *Mental Health Atlas 2011: Thailand.* Retrieved from http://www.who.int/mental_health/evidence/atlas/profiles/tha_mh_profile.pdf

Yadegarfard, M., Meinhold-Bergmann, M. E., & Ho, R. (2014). Family rejection, social isolation, and loneliness as predictors of negative health outcomes (depression, suicidal ideation, and sexual risk behaviour) among Thai male-to-female transgender adolescents. *Journal of LGBT Youth, 11*, 347–363. http://dx.doi.org/10.1080/ 19361653.2014.910483

10

Mental Health Needs of Transgender Women, Gay Men, and Other Men Who Have Sex With Men Across Sub-Saharan Africa

Carolyn Brown, Keletso Makofane, Kevin Rebe,
L. Leigh Ann van der Merwe, Bhekie Sithole, Daouda Diouf,
Kevin Kapila, Carrie Lyons, Tonia Poteat, Shauna Stahlman,
and Stefan Baral

The communities of gay men and other men who have sex with men and transgender women continue to be underserved in terms of basic health services, and this is especially the case as it relates to mental health needs across sub-Saharan Africa. In this context, individuals continue to serve their communities while studying their needs to continually improve the quality of those services. Without these individuals there would be little knowledge to synthesize in a chapter such as this. Consequently, we thank them for this work given the clear personal and professional risks and limited rewards. We give special thanks to Tani K, John Kashiha, Karishma Kwofie, Marvellous Moffat, Samuel Matsikure, Augustus Mokabedi, Renugan Raidoo, Phyllis Sullivan, and Jeffrey Walimbwa Wambaya for their contributions to this chapter.

> 1999 was a painful year for me. I lost many family members that year, including my only role model and cousin who at the time was called a gay man. In my heart, I always respected her as a trans woman. She was married to a man in the village and contracted HIV and died of related complications on 14 October 1999. Whenever I was reprimanded for my feminine ways, the grown folks

Carolyn Brown and Keletso Makofane contributed equally to this chapter.

http://dx.doi.org/10.1037/0000159-011
LGBTQ Mental Health: International Perspectives and Experiences, N. Nakamura and
C. H. Logie (Editors)

would ask me, "Do you wanna be like Louis?" Something in me wanted to scream "YES, YES, YES!" That is how I saw my own life. She was one of the few people with whom I shared a strong bond and struggle. I have never known anyone more resilient than her. In 2010, after many years of difficulty, I founded an organization focused exclusively on the struggles of trans women, sex work, access to gender affirming care, poor physical and mental health, family and intimate partner violence, and HIV. Trans women across sub-Saharan Africa go through unimaginable challenges, but I built this foundation to enable trans women to work from a place where they are valued as human beings first, and embrace who they are. Trans women need to be made to understand that they are valued and loved. Self-love is the point of departure for all this work! My work has brought me to the understanding that just because the world has given up on us, and even we ourselves have given up at times, we must still take good care of ourselves and others. (L. Leigh Ann van der Merwe, Activist and Founder of S.H.E, Social, Health, and Empowerment Feminist Collective of Transgender Women of Africa)

INTRODUCTION AND CONTEXT TO LESBIAN, GAY, BISEXUAL, AND TRANSGENDER HISTORICAL PERSPECTIVES ACROSS SUB-SAHARAN AFRICA

In this chapter, our goal is to give an overview of mental health among gay men, other men who have sex with men (MSM), and trans women in countries across sub-Saharan Africa. Our task is complicated by the fact that the concepts of sexual orientation and gender identity are historically contingent and do not fully capture the multiplicity of ways that people identify, behave, or organize their lives. Across sub-Saharan Africa, a binary conceptualization of sexuality has not always been the hegemonic way of understanding human sexuality. Examples abound from across the continent of historical same-sex intimacies, sexual practices, and identities that do not neatly map onto the identity categories of lesbian, gay, bisexual, or transgender (LGBT). These examples range from the erotic relationships between Sotho women called *setsoalle* to the intimate relationships between feminine *Oubis* and masculine *Yauss* Wolof men in Senegal and more broadly across Western Africa. Among Ndebele and Ngoni warriors in southeast-central Africa, sexuality took on a spiritual dimension when they prepared for battle by engaging in male–male sex as a powerful protective medicine (Epprecht, 2008). Finally, the task is further complicated by the sheer diversity of the approximately 800 million people in the 49 countries of Africa, who speak more than 1,000 languages.

Just as there are multiple same-sex practices in this region, there are multiple homoprejudices and homophobias. Expressions of violence and prejudice against LGBT people emerge out of histories, political dynamics, and discourses that are specific to the cities, states, and regions in which they occur (Thoreson, 2014). Writing about mental health across this expanse requires generalizations, and these are useful only when carefully constructed, with recognition of the limitations. The study of mental health in any particular town or grouping in sub-Saharan Africa requires an understanding of the specific cultures in which mental health is produced and a sensitivity to the fact that the categories of *gay* and *transgender* might not fully describe the lives of people who have sex with people of the same gender or for whom gender identity and expression are different from the expectations associated with the sex they were assigned at birth.

In contrast to the invisibility and erasure of these historical forms of sexual expression, ancient African traditional medical practice is thriving across the region. Traditional healers are practitioners of traditional medicine, which is defined by the World Health Organization (WHO; 2017) as "the knowledge, skills and practises based on the theories, beliefs and experiences indigenous to different cultures, used in the maintenance of health and in the prevention, diagnosis, improvement or treatment of physical and mental illness" (para. 1). Traditional medicine is sometimes also termed as alternative or complementary medicine, and the most common form is herbal treatments. The WHO estimates that about 70% to 80% of people across the African continent depended on traditional medicines for their health care needs (WHO, 2017). For instance, in a sample of African countries the ratio of medical doctors to the population ranged from 1:1,000 to 1:7,000, but the ratio of traditional health practitioners ranged from 1:100 to 1:1,200 (Chatora, 2003). Traditional healers have a long history of attending to mental health issues in their communities. Their popularity stems not only from the widespread availability of their services but also from the wider acceptance of their explanatory models for mental health among the people they serve, which rely on spiritualism and divination (Akyeampong, Hill, & Kleinman, 2015).

There is a relatively short history of professional indigenous mental health research and service delivery in sub-Saharan Africa. The first formally trained African psychiatrists started practicing in Africa in the 1960s, developing innovative approaches that were grounded in local cultures (Akyeampong et al., 2015). Early psychological (Bulhan, 1981) and psychiatric (Akyeampong et al., 2015) research was dominated by scholars from Europe and North America and aided "colonial governments to understand, govern, and control their subjects" (Akyeampong et al., 2015, p. 3). Because of these, and various other reasons, the field of mental health across sub-Saharan Africa continues to be strongly influenced by developments in Europe and the United States of America (Akyeampong et al., 2015). Over the first half of the 20th century, the Western medical community reached a consensus on the classification of same-sex attraction as a mental illness, which was met with bold activism from LGBT persons and their allies highlighting the lack of evidence to justify this classification; as of 1973, homosexuality was removed from the American Psychiatric Association's manual of mental disorders (Bayer, 1981; Drescher & Merlino, 2007).

Historically, the health needs of LGBT people in sub-Saharan Africa have not been addressed by governments. On the contrary, governments have neglected or exacerbated ill health among this group. In response, LGBT people across the region have formed voluntary associations to provide for their own community needs and to advocate for improved treatment by governments. Community associations established to promote the rights of LGBT populations across the African continent began as early as the 1960s in South Africa (Epprecht, 2012). Since the 1990s, LGBT associations have pro-liferated across sub-Saharan Africa with the support of international donor funding. Reflecting the complex political environments in which they exist, they have taken on different forms and waged different struggles over time. Common concerns across these organizations have included breaking the taboo of same-sex sexuality and reducing stigma; protecting LGBT people from violence by state and nonstate actors; and addressing the health needs of LGBT people with a focus on HIV prevention, treatment, and care. With increasing focus on HIV among cisgender MSM and transgender women in the international donor community, many LGBT community organizations are implementing HIV programs specifically supporting these men and women.

Over the 2000s, LGBT organizing has faced tremendous backlash (Epprecht, 2012). A number of proposed and instated bills, particularly in countries such as Uganda, Nigeria, Malawi, and Burundi, have sought to further limit the already constrained rights of sexual and gender minorities across the continent. In contrast to countries that have deepened discriminatory laws targeting LGBT people and same-sex practices, others have taken progressive steps. Since the 1990s, same-sex sexual practices have been decriminalized in the Seychelles, South Africa, Cape Verde, Lesotho, Mozambique, and Angola. Aside from decriminalization, there have been a range of positive developments in the law, including the prohibition of discrimination in employment in several countries (Carroll & Itaborahy, 2015), the affirmation of freedom of associa-tion for LGBT people by courts in Kenya and Botswana, and legal gender change recognized as a constitutional right in Botswana (Benza, 2014; Human Rights Watch, 2015; Southern Africa Litigation Centre, 2017). South Africa was the first in sub-Saharan Africa to adopt nondiscrimination legislation to protect sexual and gender minorities in 1996 (Epprecht, 2012) and in November 2006 became only the fifth country globally to legalize same-sex marriage. However, progressive laws such as these do not always translate into changes in the lived experiences of LGBT populations nationwide, with considerable variation between regions and within cities (Lane, Mogale, Struthers, McIntyre, & Kegeles, 2008). Moreover, even with progressive steps taken on the part of the South African government, very little has been done to further investigate and act on the intersectionalities of oppression such as race, class, access to education, and economic empowerment. The classic example is the affirmation of human rights in the South African constitution versus the 20-plus-year wait-ing list for publicly funded gender-affirming surgeries for transgender people in South Africa (Wilson, Marais, de Villiers, Addinall, & Campbell, 2014).

Evaluating health among LGBT populations across sub-Saharan Africa is a dynamic process that has varied historically, has been subject to changing health outcome priorities and funding structures, and is subject to changing political climates. Much of the health research conducted among LGBT populations in sub-Saharan Africa has been among MSM in relation to HIV infection. However, LGBT persons living throughout the region are at higher risk for a variety of health outcomes, including negative mental health outcomes resulting from experiences of discrimination, harassment, and public policies prohibiting same-sex practices. Moreover, these events, as with any attack on a community, affect the mental health and social capital of all members of the community.

PERSPECTIVES AND CONCERNS OF LGBT PEOPLE IN SUB-SAHARAN AFRICA

As the first to respond to problems that face LGBT communities across the African continent, activists and leaders of LGBT community-based organizations (CBOs) witness firsthand the mental health challenges that ripple through these communities. These CBO leaders are also often the first to innovate programs delivering mental care, creating spaces for healing, or intervening in mainstream mental health services. At the root of widespread mental health challenges are the social environments in which LGBT people live. The social networks that for most provide support and nurturing, and channel resources across the community, often fail LGBT people, and in the most extreme cases endanger them. Many members of African LGBT communities have survived targeted violence not only from strangers but also from members of the communities and families in which they live. It is imperative to contextualize violence against LGBT persons across sub-Saharan Africa, particularly transgender women, taking into account the presence of neocolonialism even in contemporary African society. Violence against transgender women in sub-Saharan Africa, as in many parts of the world, has ties to neocolonialism throughout the region and has been institutionalized across social, political, and health care spheres. Homophobia/trans/queer phobia emerged from the religious fundamentalism that accompanied colonization, and these legacies have left African countries with harsh legal systems that criminalize queer identities (van der Merwe, 2017).

In this section, we present perspectives cumulated from consultations conducted by two activists and coauthors of this chapter from South Africa (van der Merwe and Makofane) with one activist from each of the following countries: Botswana, Kenya, Liberia, Tanzania, Zambia, and Zimbabwe. Interviews were conducted by phone, recorded and transcribed, and synthesized for themes. In these conversations we explore the observed need for mental health services in our diverse communities, the engagement of LGBT people with these services, and our vision for adequate mental health services. Specifically, we highlight feelings of isolation among LGBT people in sub-Saharan Africa, access to mental health services, stigma around mental health services and practices, community-delivered mental health services, and a vision for mental health delivery for LGBT people.

"There Is a Lot of Isolation": Social Isolation Among LGBT Populations

For some, coming out and disclosing sexual orientation, or being forced to come out, creates a sudden rupture in their social networks. Friends, family, and community members who would generally provide material and emotional support may reject LGBT people and withdraw their support, leaving them isolated. Isolation, in turn, has a negative impact on mental and physical health. As in private life, rejection and isolation can have dire consequences in public life. There are numerous accounts of LGBT people who were mistreated or discharged from work or even lost housing as a result of the homophobia and transphobia of employers and landlords (International Labour Organization, 2010). Some members of the LGBT community internalize the negative attitudes toward them and as a result have difficulty accepting their own sexual attraction or gender identity, which can lead to withdrawal from friends and family and reluctance to be associated with the LGBT community. This sense of shame is often heightened by religious prohibitions and the cultural expectations of the people around them.

LGBT people may feel isolated not only by close friends and family but also by other members of the LGBT community. As a Kenyan activist pointed out, insofar as they are excluded from social and sexual networks they might have been a part of when they were younger, older members "are no longer able to mingle with the [LGBT] world. . . . They are taken back to a certain closet." Transphobia within the LGBT community and a lack of understanding of transgender identity create divisions between transgender persons and sexual minorities. Isolation can be caused by transnormativity, such that many transgender women who identify as lesbian do not take up services for transgender women because of their sexual orientation (Johnson, 2016). Transgender lesbians also face discrimination from cisgender lesbians (McDonald, 2006). As one Zambian activist described to us,

> The fact that there are not many spaces like support groups where we can sit down and share stories and talk about experiences makes it so difficult even within the community of transgender women. There is a lot of isolation and the network is not very strong.

HIV-related stigma within the LGBT community makes it difficult for those who are living with HIV to be open about their status and to find sexual or romantic partners within the community. Many members of the LGBT community hold discriminatory views about people living with HIV, sometimes causing silence about HIV status and sometimes causing open hostility toward people living with HIV.

Finally, activists, who are usually members of the communities in which they work, also face isolation. Activists often carry the trauma of the people that they serve and "don't know where to drop it off." Over time this trauma can cause burnout. Furthermore, activists are often in conflict with authorities and the wider community. As one Tanzanian activist said, "You're fighting with the government, you're facing a lot of backlashes. . . . You feel alone and no one appreciates what you do."

"They Organize on Their Own": Accessing Mental Health Services Where They Are Lacking

Mental health services exist in a wider context of inadequate health service delivery for LGBT people. Despite low accessibility, some members of the LGBT community actively search for the mental health resources they need. Asked whether services are available for the mental health service needs of transgender women, a Kenyan activist responded, "Services are usually private—where they organize on their own to get the services they need." Because some people access services discreetly with private health care providers, it is difficult for CBOs to understand the quality or appropriateness of the services. In the best case, it might take little time for their providers to get acquainted with their needs and appropriate care, and in the worst, they might find themselves further traumatized by the providers they turned to for help. Due to the unique health needs of transgender people and widespread ignorance about those needs, some must cross national borders to access care themselves or to acquire hormones not available in their home countries. For example, many Tanzanian transgender women seek services in neighboring Kenya. In cases like this, it is even more difficult to access the mental health support or even medical expertise that might be needed when navigating gender transition.

There are instances where religious leaders and institutions are helpful. Although these are not to be confused with professional mental health services, they emerged in our conversations with activists as a place where members of the community seek help. A transgender woman activist from Zambia reported finding affirmation in a prominent Catholic leader in her country when she was coming out, saying, "[He spoke to me] in the perspective that trans is there [in our community]." In Kenya, there is an LGBT religious group that also manages a church. This church community mostly serves Ugandan LGBT refugees but includes a diverse group of LGBT people seeking mental health services and community.

"Ba re o Setsenwa": Stigmatizing Attitudes Toward Mental Health Services

Although some members of the LGBT community seek out professional mental health services, for many others, a lack of knowledge or negative perceptions about these services act as a barrier. As one Kenyan activist described, "You are treated like you are a crazy person, not that you have issues." An activist from Botswana further supported this idea by saying, "Ba re o setsenwa" meaning "They say you are a madman." The language, type of service, and service delivery settings for mental health care can moderate negative perceptions. For example, in Botswana accessing services at a mental health hospital is socially stigmatized, but accessing private psychological services is not. In Tanzania the term *mental* attracts stigma, so when naming services the LGBT community-based organization avoids using that word and instead use the term *psychological counseling*.

Although perceptions of mental health services held by LGBT community members seem to reflect wider perceptions about these services in their societies, they also differ in important ways. An activist from Zimbabwe reported feeling that LGBT people are more open to accessing these services than the general population. In this context, the provision of competent counseling services by an LGBT organization has increased demand for these services among LGBT community members. Conversely, a Zambian activist shared that among transgender people in her country there was such restricted access to mental health services and such little knowledge about these services that they were seen as "unnecessary because we don't know how well they can help us. . . . [It is] something that is marked as unimportant." A Tanzanian activist noted that the lack of integration of these services with other kinds of health service delivery was a contributing factor to the lack of knowledge about them and ultimately the limited engagement in them.

"Do You Want Us to Fix You?": Stigmatizing Mental Health Care Practices

Religious leaders and institutions are a double-edged sword; in some cases members of the LGBT community turn to them to find solace, and in others they are given a reception that is neither affirming nor supportive. A Kenyan activist described the case of a gay man who was sent to the church to be healed of homosexuality "and he was prayed over. When his mom asked whether the spirit of homosexuality had now left him, he said no. Ultimately he got support from friends." In some contexts, people believe that mental health issues are generally caused by problems of the spirit. For example, as a Zambian activist pointed out, when "someone is schizophrenic, people will believe that it can be healed with a prayer when that's not true."

Even among mental health professionals, there are misunderstandings about how to treat LGBT community members, based on the assumption that being a sexual or gender minority is a sickness. A Zimbabwean activist mentioned once hearing a psychologist argue on the radio that homosexuality is a mental issue. Younger psychologists, he finds, are more open-minded and more knowledgeable about same-sex sexuality. Although a transgender activist in Zambia pointed out that sustained advocacy is changing how mental health professionals think about transgender persons in her country, she also mentioned having been to a psychologist who asked if she wanted her gender identity changed to align with her biologic sex assigned at birth, asking "Do you want us to fix you?"

**"Addressing the Person as a Human":
Community-Delivered Mental Health Services**

In response to community needs, some LGBT community-based organizations have provided or facilitated access to affirming mental health services. This is in contrast to mental health services that, as a Tanzanian activist pointed out, seek to rescue LGBT people and help them to change rather than "addressing the [concerns they present with] and addressing the person as a human." Organizations in Zimbabwe and Kenya have provided one-on-one counseling, and others have created spaces either for group support specifically for HIV-related support or general support for LGBT people. Some continue to cultivate networks of mental health professionals or organizations to facilitate referrals. In one case, social workers and psychologists who are themselves part of the LGBT community offer their services on a volunteer basis and receive a stipend based on how many people they help. In other settings, MSM and transgender people are referred to larger HIV and AIDS service organizations for mental health services. When using these organizations as referral points, however, it is often the case that only those with HIV-related mental health issues are assisted. Even then, because mental health is a secondary organizational focus, there is no guarantee that everyone will be served. There is little to no funding of direct mental health services in the LGBT community outside of the context of HIV.

LGBT community organizations that have provided or facilitated access to one-on-one counseling see increasing demand for those services among their members. When these services are advertised through social media, they receive requests from members using online platforms. In Zimbabwe, one LGBT organization that previously provided on-site counseling but now provides referrals for mental health services noted that organization members not only request access to counseling but also strongly prefer to receive counseling from someone of the same sexual orientation as them.

**"Love Needs to Be There": A Vision of Mental Health
Service Delivery for LGBT People**

According to a Zambian transgender activist, the goal of a system of mental health services should be to offer patient- or client-focused services in a welcoming way.

> In the perfect world I see a health care system that is understanding and accepting and can help counsel in a positive way, where the patients decide for themselves what they want. For me a positive way is welcoming a transgender individual into health care institutions with open arms and being able to come to an understanding. . . . Love needs to be there when we seek mental care.

Activists whom we spoke to also offered concrete steps toward advancing mental health services in their settings. The integration of mental health services with other health care systems was a common suggestion, especially integration into the programs that LGBT community organizations implement. It is preferable that both peer support groups and individual counseling with trained professionals be offered. Engaging trained mental health professionals requires educating these professionals through on-the-job training, experiential learning, and preservice training. For on-the-job training and experiential learning, leaders and members of the LGBT community should play an important role in teaching non-LGBT professionals. In addition, other health care providers need to be equipped to detect mental health issues among the LGBT people they serve and refer them appropriately to sensitized and trained providers.

Religious and traditional healers also have a role to play. It is critical that local LGBT community organizations engage these religious and traditional leaders to ensure that they refer LGBT people to suitable services. Traditional healers can also serve an important role in reminding communities that sexual and gender minorities have existed through history. As one Zambian activist said,

> The role of traditional and alternative medicine would be to speak more to the issue of what is intersex and trans. . . . The culture of keeping things a secret has to die down and conversations need to be had regularly. They need to talk about the existence of trans and intersex.

RELEVANT CLINICAL ISSUES AND RECOMMENDATIONS FOR MENTAL HEALTH PRACTITIONERS

Minority stress theory asserts that experiences of stigma and discrimination related to sexual orientation and/or gender identity increase risk of mental health disorders among sexual and gender minorities (Semlyen, King, Varney, & Hagger-Johnson, 2016). Internalization of such discrimination and prejudice have a negative impact on the health of LGBT people and their health-seeking behaviors. In short, hostile social environments increase stress and lead to negative mental health outcomes (Meyer, 2003).

Health services including mental health counseling across the continent tend to be located within heteronormative and cisnormative health care systems (Rebe, De Swardt, Struthers, & McIntyre, 2013; Tucker et al., 2013). And although services have started emerging for gay men and other MSM often through HIV-related investments, there remains a significant gap in services for other LGBT communities. Sensitive health care services for transgender people are especially deficient, with a distinct lack of knowledge and clinical skills required to effectively serve this diverse population (Steele et al., 2017; Winter et al., 2016). Gender affirmative services are also important considerations for transgender people with an emerging understanding about the role of how body image and eating disorders also affect transgender populations (Murray, 2017).

People in the LGBT community across sub-Saharan Africa, similar to the rest of the world, are at increased risk for experiencing violence and discrimination, and this needs to be assessed when evaluating their mental health needs. And while trauma may affect an individual, there can also be community-level impact when violence affects one of its members. Survivors of trauma may be reluctant to engage in care or be open with a clinician about their needs, which may be especially true when trauma is consistently experienced. People with these types of experiences may present as angry, guarded, or withdrawn initially until they experience the clinician as someone who is clearly able to understand their needs and who feels safe to them. In these cases, it is important for the clinician to be able to form an alliance with the LGBT person and to assess their current safety and their risk of experiencing continued violence.

Availability of Services

Given the heteronormativity and cisnormativity of health services, specifically in countries that criminalize or stigmatize LGBT people, it is unsurprising that LGBT people struggle to access mental health care that is sensitive to their lived experiences. Certain countries across sub-Saharan Africa, including South Africa and Kenya, have started implementing large-scale training of health cadres to be sensitive and skilled in providing services to MSM and other key populations (Tucker et al., 2013). The need for integrated mental health services forms part of this training, which has been aimed primarily at the primary health care sector, staffed mainly by nurse clinicians. A large proportion of key populations continues to obtain care in nonspecialized services where the level of empathy and skill in working with them is likely to be variable. Some community-based organizations, such as Triangle Project in Cape Town, have filled the gap by engaging sessional psychologists to see members of LGBT communities on their premises, which are considered safe spaces by these communities. Triangle Project offers a range of one-to-one small-group and large-group services for LGBT and gender nonconforming people, facilitated by a social worker who is also trained as a sexologist.

In addition, it is worth articulating that targeted services for LGBT people who use drugs are virtually nonexistent. Despite the recommendation from WHO to provide harm reduction services inclusive of needles and syringe exchange and opioid substitution therapy, these services are seldom implemented. Lack of such services may increase the harms associated with drug use, such as the transmission of blood-borne infections including HIV and hepatitis C virus.

Advancing Clinical Services Across Sub-Saharan Africa

To effectively address the high burden of mental health disorders among LGBT people across sub-Saharan Africa, a difficult landscape needs to be navigated. Community activists and the health sector need to continue to advocate for improved LGBT services generally, as well as for increased mental health services. This is challenging given the need for this advocacy to avoid the impression that an LGBT identity is a mental disorder or that all LGBT people have mental health problems. It is important to note that guidelines for the management of LGBT people with mental health concerns do not differ substantially from that of the broader population, but such care needs to be delivered by sensitized and skilled providers who will not further stigmatize them. Clinical guidelines tools such as the WHO's (2011) Integrated Management of Key Populations and the Mental Health Gap Action Programme are examples of tools that can be used to ensure that evidence-based and human rights affirming care is provided.

CONCLUSION AND MOVING FORWARD

LGBT populations around the world experience stigma, discrimination, and violence that drive mental health disparities while reducing access to appropriate mental health services. As described in this chapter, these disparities are exacerbated in many countries in sub-Saharan Africa by antihomosexualilty legislation and prohibitions against "cross-dressing" as well as by limited availability of mental health services in general. A lack of LGBT-competent mental health services and a lack of mental health measures that are culturally appropriate and locally validated offer challenges to meeting the unique mental health needs of LGBT people in sub-Saharan Africa. The way forward will require a firm commitment to increasing the availability of mental health services for all people in sub-Saharan Africa and to ensuring that as many mental health providers as possible are trained in culturally appropriate and LGBT competent care. As efforts are made to scale-up research and training, we can move forward with the knowledge that expanding and supporting local communities to build social capital is an important part of addressing mental health among LGBT people in sub-Saharan Africa (Fay et al., 2011).

REFERENCES

Akyeampong, E. K., Hill, A., & Kleinman, A. (Eds.). (2015). *The culture of mental illness and psychiatric practice in Africa*. Bloomington: Indiana University Press.
Bayer, R. (1981). *Homosexuality and American psychiatry: The politics of diagnosis*. Princeton, NJ: Princeton University Press.
Benza, B. (2014, November 14). Botswana gay rights group wins legal recognition. *World News*. Retrieved from https://www.reuters.com/article/us-botswana-gay/botswana-gay-rights-group-wins-legal-recognition-idUSKCN0IY1KD20141114?feedType=RSSfeedName=worldNews
Bulhan, H. A. (1981). Psychological research in Africa: Genesis and function. *Race & Class, 23*, 25–41. http://dx.doi.org/10.1177/030639688102300102
Carroll, A., & Itaborahy, L. P. (2015, May). *State-sponsored homophobia. A world survey of laws: Criminalisation, protection and recognition of same-sex love* (10th ed.). Retrieved from https://ilga.org/downloads/ILGA_State_Sponsored_Homophobia_2015.pdf
Chatora, R. (2003). An overview of the traditional medicine situation in the African region. *African Health Monitor, 4*, 4–7.

Drescher, J., & Merlino, J. P. (2007). *American psychiatry and homosexuality: An oral history.* New York, NY: Harrington Park Press.

Epprecht, M. (2008). *Unspoken facts: A history of homosexualities in Africa.* Harare, Zimbabwe: Gays and Lesbians of Zimbabwe.

Epprecht, M. (2012). Sexual minorities, human rights and public health strategies in Africa. *African Affairs, 111,* 223–243. http://dx.doi.org/10.1093/afraf/ads019

Fay, H., Baral, S. D., Trapence, G., Motimedi, F., Umar, E., Iipinge, S., . . . Beyrer, C. (2011). Stigma, health care access, and HIV knowledge among men who have sex with men in Malawi, Namibia, and Botswana. *AIDS and Behavior, 15,* 1088–1097. http://dx.doi.org/10.1007/s10461-010-9861-2

Human Rights Watch. (2015, April 28). Kenya: High court orders LGBT group registration. Retrieved from https://www.hrw.org/news/2015/04/28/kenya-high-court-orders-lgbt-group-registration

International Labour Organization. (2010). Christine Ehlers v. Bohler Uddeholm Africa (PTY) Ltd. Retrieved from http://www.ilo.org/aids/legislation/WCMS_329495/lang—en/index.htm

Johnson, A. H. (2016). Transnormativity: A new concept and its validation through documentary film about transgender men. *Sociological Inquiry, 86,* 465–491. http://dx.doi.org/10.1111/soin.12127

Lane, T., Mogale, T., Struthers, H., McIntyre, J., & Kegeles, S. M. (2008). "They see you as a different thing": The experiences of men who have sex with men with healthcare workers in South African township communities. *Sexually Transmitted Infections, 84,* 430–433. http://dx.doi.org/10.1136/sti.2008.031567

McDonald, M. (2006). An other space: Between and beyond lesbian-normativity and trans-normativity. *Journal of Lesbian Studies, 10,* 201–214. http://dx.doi.org/10.1300/J155v10n01_10

Meyer, I. H. (2003). Prejudice, social stress, and mental health in lesbian, gay, and bisexual populations: Conceptual issues and research evidence. *Psychological Bulletin, 129,* 674–697. http://dx.doi.org/10.1037/0033-2909.129.5.674

Murray, S. B. (2017). Gender identity and eating disorders: The need to delineate novel pathways for eating disorder symptomatology. *Journal of Adolescent Health, 60,* 1–2. http://dx.doi.org/10.1016/j.jadohealth.2016.10.004

Rebe, K., De Swardt, G., Struthers, H., & McIntyre, J. A. (2013). Towards "men who have sex with men-appropriate" health services in South Africa. *Southern African Journal of HIV Medicine, 14,* 52–57. http://dx.doi.org/10.4102/sajhivmed.v14i2.78

Semlyen, J., King, M., Varney, J., & Hagger-Johnson, G. (2016). Sexual orientation and symptoms of common mental disorder or low wellbeing: Combined meta-analysis of 12 UK population health surveys. *BMC Psychiatry, 16,* 67. http://dx.doi.org/10.1186/s12888-016-0767-z

Southern Africa Litigation Centre. (2017, September 29). *Botswana High Court rules in landmark gender identity case* [News release]. Retrieved from https://www.southernafricalitigationcentre.org/2017/09/29/press-release-botswana-high-court-rules-in-landmark-gender-identity-case/

Steele, L. S., Daley, A., Curling, D., Gibson, M. F., Green, D. C., Williams, C. C., & Ross, L. E. (2017). LGBT identity, untreated depression, and unmet need for mental health services by sexual minority women and trans-identified people. *Journal of Women's Health, 26,* 116–127. http://dx.doi.org/10.1089/jwh.2015.5677

Thoreson, R. R. (2014). Troubling the waters of a "wave of homophobia": Political economies of anti-queer animus in sub-Saharan Africa. *Sexualities, 17*(1–2), 23–42. http://dx.doi.org/10.1177/1363460713511098

Tucker, A., Liht, J., de Swardt, G., Jobson, G., Rebe, K., McIntyre, J., & Struthers, H. (2013). An exploration into the role of depression and self-efficacy on township men who have sex with men's ability to engage in safer sexual practices. *AIDS Care, 25,* 1227–1235. http://dx.doi.org/10.1080/09540121.2013.764383

van der Merwe, L. L. A. (2017). Transfeminism(s) from the Global South: Experiences from South Africa. *Development, 60,* 90–95.

Wilson, D., Marais, A., de Villiers, A., Addinall, R., & Campbell, M. M. (2014). Transgender issues in South Africa, with particular reference to the Groote Schuur Hospital Transgender Unit. *South African Medical Journal, 104,* 449. http://dx.doi.org/10.7196/SAMJ.8392

Winter, S., Diamond, M., Green, J., Karasic, D., Reed, T., Whittle, S., & Wylie, K. (2016). Transgender people: Health at the margins of society. *The Lancet, 388,* 390–400. http://dx.doi.org/10.1016/S0140-6736(16)00683-8

World Health Organization. (2011). *mhGAP Intervention Guide for mental, neurological and substance use disorders in non-specialized health settings.* Retrieved from http://apps.who.int/iris/bitstream/10665/44406/1/9789241548069_eng.pdf

World Health Organization. (2017). *Traditional medicine.* Retrieved from http://www.afro.who.int/health-topics/traditional-medicine

Conclusion

Nadine Nakamura and Carmen H. Logie

This book aims to expand the standard Western narrative on what it means to be lesbian, gay, bisexual, transgender, and/or queer (LGBTQ) by providing a variety of international perspectives. We attempt to disrupt the dominant narrative that there are normative LGBTQ experiences mirrored off of the experiences in North America, and instead we provide the opportunity to consider the unique challenges and strengths faced by LGBTQ communities around the world. The authors address how being LGBTQ impacts mental health in different international contexts, and they highlight challenges faced by LGBTQ populations across social ecological domains, from legal and policy, to religious and cultural beliefs, and among family and friends. As much as possible, authors with firsthand knowledge of these countries were solicited to provide an insider perspective with appropriate cultural understandings. Although this book is, of course, unable to cover every country around the globe and every experience within each country, we believe that it does help to deepen our collective understanding of what it means to be LGBTQ outside of the customary Western paradigm. Several important themes emerged from the chapters, and a brief overview of some of those themes is given next.

http://dx.doi.org/10.1037/0000159-012
LGBTQ Mental Health: International Perspectives and Experiences, N. Nakamura and C. H. Logie (Editors)

OVERARCHING THEMES

Several chapters discuss the fact that LGBTQ people have existed well before modern conceptualizations of these identities did. For example, Chapter 9 on Thailand by Ojanen, Newman, Ratanashevorn, de Lind van Wijngaarden, and Tepjan includes information on Thai historical documents that describe same-sex behaviors. Chapter 6 on Mongolia by Koch, Knutson, and Nyamdorj includes acknowledgment of a traditional Mongolian society that accepted queer people. India has had a rich history of sexual and gender diversity for centuries, evidenced in scripts such as the Kama Sutra, ancient temple sculptures, and mythologies (see Chakrapani, Newman, and Shunmugam in Chapter 7).

Several chapters raise the issue of hegemonic gender norms. Many cultures have strongly defined rules about how men and women should behave for society to run smoothly. When LGBTQ people step outside of these norms, for example, in moving away from heterosexual marriage, this can be perceived as disruptive within families and in religious and larger community settings. Chapter 4 on lesbian and bisexual women in Jamaica by Marcus, Logie, Jones, Bryan, and Levermore addresses the expectation of how women are supposed to look and behave. Gender expression outside of socially sanctioned scripts can elicit discrimination from both outside and inside the lesbian community, with particularly harmful effects for bisexual women. Gender norms in Peru resulted in challenges for transgender men in negotiating daily life, familial relationships, and public spaces (see Chapter 1 by Perez-Brumer, Silva-Santisteban, Salazar, Vilela, & Reisner). In Peru, transgender men's inability to change gender markers on their national identity document presents a barrier to access employment and health care, among other resources. This is part of the benefit of applying an intersectional framework to this book: We can begin to explore the complexities of lived experiences within and between LGBTQ persons.

The concept of coming out is challenged in some chapters. Many of the countries included in this book are collectivistic, rendering the idea of asserting one's individual identity culturally incongruent. For example, in Chapter 9, Ojanen and colleagues explain the importance of familial harmony and that family was not seen as a context in which one should assert one's identity. Chapter 8 on Malaysia by Singaravelu and Cheah also notes that many gay and lesbian Malaysians do not formally come out to their parents. In Mongolia, where more than 85% of LGBTQ people surveyed said they are not formally out to their families, it is common for LGBTQ people to enter into heterosexual marriages and have same-sex relationships conjointly (see Chapter 6 by Koch et al.). Chapter 3 on Ecuador by Di Marco, Arenas, Hoel, and Munduate specifically addresses the stigma that challenges being out in the workplace. These chapters provide important information that our concept of what normative, healthy behavior looks like for LGBTQ people is culturally specific. They also challenge the idea that there is a linear pathway toward "outness" and query if outness necessarily leads to well-being. Instead, well-being may be negotiated carefully within collectivist contexts.

Several chapters address the impact of colonization on culture and laws. In many cases, the precolonial culture did not condemn LGBTQ people. Rather, it was the influence of the colonizers that brought stigma and oppression to LGBTQ people, which remains even postcolonization. For example, in Chapter 4, Marcus et al. address the influence of British colonialism, slavery, Christianity, and Victorian values on the current anti-LGBTQ climate in Jamaica. Chapter 8 examines the influence of British colonization in terms of anti-homosexuality laws, which coexist with Shariah Law to create a climate in which there are no legal protections for LGBTQ people (Singaravelu & Cheah). In Chapter 3, Di Marco et al. note the arrival of Spanish colonization and Catholicism in Ecuador, which lead to repression of same-sex sexuality. In Chapter 6, Koch et al. acknowledge the effects of Mongolia's status as satellite state of the Soviet Union for more than 50 years. We had asked authors to search for data on Indigenous and precolonization experiences of sexual and gender diversity in each context; it is likely due to the effects of colonization on destroying this information across settings in this book that most authors could not locate such data. Although many now see the West as progressive and a beacon of LGBTQ acceptance (and many also see LGBTQ identities as a Western "influence" on "traditional" culture), it was in fact the influence of Western colonization that introduced and, in some cases, continues to spread many homophobic laws and attitudes in formerly colonized countries. This has been described as "the irony of homophobia in Africa" (Semugoma, Nemande, & Baral, 2012). Understanding the role of colonization in spreading homophobia is important to counter the notion that LGBTQ identities are an affront to tradition and culture.

Just as outside governments have influenced many of the countries written about in this book, beliefs about homosexuality as a mental illness have also had an influence in the United States. In many cases, lesbian, bisexual, gay, and other sexually diverse identities continue to be pathologized even though the *Diagnostic and Statistical Manual of Mental Disorders* removed homosexuality as a mental disorder in 1973 (see Drescher, 2015). Chapter 10 regarding sub-Saharan Africa addresses this issue (Brown et al.), as does Chapter 5 on Russia (Horne & White). Chapter 7 on India also begins with a case study in which a patient is asking the doctor to cure him of his same-sex attraction, reflecting the persistence of beliefs of sexual diversity as an illness (Chakrapani et al.).

Stigma plays an important role in perpetuating mental health challenges for LGBTQ people around the globe. For example, Chapter 9 links Thai family rejection, isolation, and homophobic or transphobic bullying with depression and suicidality (Ojanen et al.). Similarly, stigma targeting transgender men in Peru compromises mental health and well-being and contributes to depression, anxiety, self-harm, and suicidality (Perez-Brumer et al.). Chapter 5 on Russia includes information on the relationship between stigma related to sexual orientation and depression (Horne & White). Chapter 4 on Jamaica outlines various forms of violence from several sources, including family, work, and school, and the church that lesbian, bisexual, and queer women encounter because of stigma (Marcus et al.). This stigma impacts some women in terms of avoiding support structures, and in turn stigma and lack of support can lead to depression and substance use. Chapter 2 on Colombia by Nieves-Lugo, Barnett, Pinho, Rueda Sáenz, and Zea also addresses the roles that homophobia plays in shaping negative mental health outcomes. In this way, we can see that homophobia and stigma harms LGBTQ persons around the world with deleterious mental health effects.

Another issue that emerges in several chapters is cultural conceptualizations of mental health and mental health treatment. These vary among countries, but seeking mental health services is often stigmatized. In many cultures, there is more of a focus on the whole person with an appreciation for the mind and body connection. In some cases, mental health care looks quite different than it does in Western countries. This is addressed in Chapter 9, in which the authors describe both traditional indigenous practices, such as fortune-tellers, mediums, and shamans, as well as modern medical options, such as psychiatry, for addressing mental health issues. In Chapter 10 on sub-Saharan Africa, the results from qualitative interviews highlight stigma associated with accessing mental health services (Brown et al.).

Lack of training around providing competent services for LGBTQ populations seems to be a common issue in many countries. For example, Chapter 5 on Russia notes that mental health providers do not receive training on working with LGBTQ clients and that myths about LGBTQ people are commonplace (Horne & White). Underresourced mental health systems are in part responsible for this lack of training, and insufficient resources and services present additional barriers for LGBTQ people to receive adequate mental health care. For example, Chapter 10 on sub-Saharan Africa includes information on the scarcity of medical doctors in the region compared with the high number of traditional healers (Brown et al.). Chapter 2 on Colombia addressed the need for LGBTQ-affirmative training for mental health providers and reported that workshops on LGBTQ cultural competence were helpful (Nieves-Lugo et al.). There is much work needed in terms of translating resources on affirmative LGBTQ mental health care, not just linguistically but also culturally.

Another consequence of LGBTQ stigma is negative health outcomes, including victimization, sexual practices, and substance use that both increase HIV exposure and reduce access to HIV care. Chapter 2 on Colombia addressed how marginalization can lead to survival sex work. Experiences of discrimination in health care settings is also an issue, as is lack of health insurance due to unemployment, which is often related to discrimination (Nieves-Lugo et al.). Chapter 10 on sub-Saharan Africa highlights HIV-related stigma within LGBTQ communities that can present challenges for both HIV prevention engagement as well as LGBTQ persons living with HIV to achieve optimal social, mental, and physical health. Similarly, Chapter 7 on India reports that HIV-related stigma presents a barrier for men who have sex with men and trans women living with HIV to access HIV care (Chakrapani et al.).

Despite the lack of resources for many LGBTQ populations, chapters address the resiliency of LGBTQ people. Some seek out and organize the services that they need for themselves. In Zimbabwe, there is an LGBTQ organization that provides mental health counseling and advertises through social media. In some cases in sub-Saharan Africa, transgender people cross international borders to access the health care that they need to affirm their gender identities (Brown et al.). Others resist oppression through self-acceptance and building community support as described in Chapter 4. Resilience is also demonstrated through successful social movements—for example, an LGBTQ community in Colombia helped to change the country's constitution (Nieves-Lugo et al.). In Peru, transgender persons engage in self-love and resiliency practices, including finding support through online social media platforms (Perez-Brumer et al.).

Another way that LGBTQ people may choose to cope with discrimination is to migrate from more rural areas and small towns to bigger cities, where they can find more diversity and anonymity. For example, Chapter 2 opens with an example of a man who faces persecution in his hometown and decides to migrate to Colombia's capital. Chapter 6 addresses the differences in resources for LGBTQ people between rural and urban areas in Mongolia, demonstrating how this may contribute to migration. Chapter 9 includes a vignette about a gay Thai man whose family tried to change his sexual orientation, which led to him experience depression until he went to the United States to study, where he was able to gain self-confidence as a gay man. Chapter 2 also addresses the topic of international migration whereby LGBTQ Colombians may migrate to other countries, where they hope to live a more "out" life without persecution. Chapter 5 includes information on the increased number of asylum applications by Russians to the United States and ethnic Chechens to Germany. Although this book does not specifically focus on international migration, we can see how persecution can lead LGBTQ people to seek opportunities to move abroad or even to flee their home countries if they feel their lives are in jeopardy. The social, economic, and cultural implications of LGBTQ migration on home countries requires further exploration.

Another issue that several chapters raise is that although countries may have LGBTQ affirming laws, in practice LGBTQ people still face hostility and violence. This demonstrates the disjuncture between rights and laws in national constitutions and the lived realities on the ground for LGBTQ persons who continue to experience human rights violations. For example, Chapter 2 on Colombia describes a number of pro-LGBT laws including the right for same-sex couples to marry and the right for transgender people to change their legal names and gender markers on government identification cards. At the same time, the authors describe the murders of LGBT Colombians by armed forces. The disconnection between the laws on the books and experiences of violence highlights the complication that can arise for LGBTQ asylum seekers and may have difficult convincing a judge that they should be granted asylum.

Of course, each country represented in this book has a great deal of diversity and would require its own book focused on each LGBTQ population to be able to begin to adequately address the nuance and complexities of LGBTQ experiences thoroughly. For example, Chapter 7 on India, which focuses on gay men and transgender women, reflects the authors' areas of expertise but does not explore the experiences of lesbians. Chapter 8 addresses the experiences of gay and lesbian Malaysians of Chinese and Indian descent but does not cover the experiences of the Muslim majority in Malaysia or the experiences of bisexual or transgender people in Malaysia. Chapter 1 on Peru focuses on experiences of transgender men. Given the page limits imposed on the authors, they were unable to cover every group and often chose to focus on their own areas of research. This means that there is still a great need for more to be written about the experiences of LGBTQ people in the countries included in this book and, of course, in those countries that were not included. We hope this book serves as a launching pad to inspire more research with LGBTQ persons across the globe.

RECOMMENDATIONS

Drawing from the findings discussed in this book, we offer several broad recommendations to mental health providers. The most obvious recommendation is to consider the specific cultural, historical, and political contexts of LGBTQ individuals to provide them with culturally responsive care. For example, it is normative in many countries to conceal one's sexual orientation, especially from family members. Understanding the worldview of the client will allow the therapist to provide support and treatment that affirms both the client's LGBTQ identity and their cultural identity. These do not necessarily need to be at odds with each other and can expand our understanding of what "healthy" disclosure processes might look like across contexts and cultures.

Globalization and migration demand that we have a broader understanding of the experiences of people in other parts of the world. Mobility underscores the need to understand geographic variability in lived experiences and appropriate intervention strategies. This knowledge is imperative for clinicians who are likely to have clients who are influenced by their own experiences or their families in other parts of the world. An LGBTQ person in Jamaica or India will have a very different experience than an LGBTQ person in the United States or Canada, and this is critical to keep in mind when working with diverse clients. Without a contextual understanding of LGBTQ experiences outside of the West, we run the risk of further marginalizing our clients.

Researchers and scholars whose work focuses on LGBTQ populations can benefit from having a deeper understanding of lived experiences outside of the dominant narrative. Comparative work can identify population and context-specific insights to develop generalizable theoretical and intervention models. For instance, it does seem that the minority stress model (Meyer, 1995, 2003) that outlines the ways by which stigma can harm mental health, and how coping strategies and social support can moderate the impact of stigma on mental health, can apply across various international contexts. Intersectionality (Crenshaw, 1991) is another theoretical framework that may have cross-cultural utility for illuminating the ways in which experiences are shaped by multiple identities, particularly gender, race and ethnicity, age, sexuality, poverty, education, and religion. Hegemonic inequitable gender norms underpin much of the social exclusion experienced by LGBTQ people globally. Thus, although there are undoubtedly important culturally specific theoretical frameworks for understanding and addressing LGBTQ persons' mental health across the globe, some theories may be germane across contexts. Researchers can also examine culturally specific ways to transform hegemonic gender norms, and when and how strategies might work across various contexts. For instance, how are the social media platforms discussed in Peru taken up in other contexts to reduce social isolation and build solidarity among LGBTQ persons? What might appropriate and feasible interventions to support mental health among LGBTQ persons look like in the Global South, particularly in low- and middle-income countries with limited finances, poor infrastructure, and insufficient resources and training to formally address mental health? What role can communities play in reducing stigma and providing psychosocial support? Researchers and practitioners can develop and evaluate multipronged approaches that address the social determinants of health, legal barriers to well-being, and health care and educator training on LGBTQ persons in diverse international contexts to contribute to the evidence base. Further studies can also document not only the heterogeneity within and between LGBTQ persons in diverse international contexts but also mental health priorities, coping, and resilience strategies to inform policy and practice. We hope that this book has highlighted the urgent need to understand LGBTQ persons' mental health across the globe and inspired reflection on the complexity of LGBTQ people that can inform the ways in which we provide mental health care.

REFERENCES

Crenshaw, K. (1991). Mapping the margins: Identity politics, intersectionality, and violence against women. *Stanford Law Review, 43*, 1241–1299. http://dx.doi.org/10.2307/1229039

Drescher, J. (2015). Out of *DSM*: Depathologizing homosexuality. *Behavioral Sciences, 5*, 565–575. http://dx.doi.org/10.3390/bs5040565

Meyer, I. H. (1995). Minority stress and mental health in gay men. *Journal of Health and Social Behavior, 36*, 38–56.

Meyer, I. H. (2003). Prejudice, social stress, and mental health in lesbian, gay, and bisexual populations: Conceptual issues and research evidence. *Psychological Bulletin, 129*, 674–697.

Semugoma, P., Nemande, S., & Baral, S. D. (2012). The irony of homophobia in Africa. *The Lancet, 380*, 312–314. http://dx.doi.org/10.1016/S0140-6736(12)60901-5

INDEX

ABOUT THE EDITORS

Nadine Nakamura, PhD, is an associate professor in the Department of Psychology at the University of La Verne. Dr. Nakamura was born in Stockholm, Sweden, and grew up in Los Angeles, California. She earned her BA in psychology with a specialization in Asian American studies from the University of California, Los Angeles. She earned her doctorate in clinical psychology from The George Washington University. She was then a postdoctoral research fellow at the University of California, San Diego. She has received research funding from the National Institute of Mental Health, National Institute on Drug Abuse, the Canadian Institute of Health Research, and the Society for the Study of Social Issues. Dr. Nakamura's research focuses broadly on multiculturalism and intersectionality, with an emphasis on understanding the unique experiences of lesbian, gay, bisexual, transgender, and queer (LGBTQ) people of color; LGBTQ immigrants and asylum seekers; and LGBTQ international issues. She was awarded the American Psychological Association (APA) Minority Fellowship Program (MFP) Early Career Achievement Award in 2014 and the National Multicultural Conference and Summit's Rising Star Award in 2017. She served on the APA Presidential Task Force on Immigration and is currently cochair of the APA Task Force for Revising the Professional Practice Guidelines for Working with Sexual Minority Clients. She is a member of the APA Committee on Sexual Orientation and Gender Diversity and of APA's MFP Training Advisory Committee. She is also active in the Asian American Psychological Association (AAPA), where she is serving as cochair of the AAPA Leadership Fellows Program. Dr. Nakamura is a licensed psychologist in the state of California. She resides in Southern California with her wife and twins.

Carmen H. Logie, PhD, is an associate professor in the Factor-Inwentash Faculty of Social Work at the University of Toronto, Canada Research Chair in Global Health Equity and Social Justice with Marginalized Populations (2018–2023), and an Ontario Ministry of Research & Innovation Early Researcher (2016–2021). She is also an adjunct scientist at Women's College Hospital. She received her BA in sociology and PhD in social work from the University of Toronto and her MSW from Eastern Michigan University. Dr. Logie has been awarded funding from the Canadian Institutes of Health Research, Social Sciences & Humanities Research Council of Canada, Grand Challenges Canada, and Canada Foundation for Innovation, to lead global research focused on sexual health and rights. She is particularly interested in understanding and addressing stigma associated with the intersection of multiple marginalized identities, including race and ethnicity, sexuality, gender and gender identity, HIV, poverty, sex work, and substance use. She is currently conducting mixed methods and intervention sexual and reproductive health and rights research with Indigenous and Northern adolescents in Northern Canada, sexual rights movements (HIV-related, LGBTQ, sex worker, abortion rights) in Brazil, and urban refugee and displaced adolescents in Uganda. Her research is internationally recognized and influences global policy, as demonstrated in her consultations with the World Health Organization, United Nations University, U.S. National Institute of Health, U.S. National Institute of Mental Health, White House, U.S. President's Emergency Plan for AIDS Relief, and Canadian Institutes of Health Research Institute of Gender & Health as a Sex & Gender Champion. She lives in Toronto, Canada, with her wife, senior dog, and three motorcycles.